SPIDER-MAN 2™

THE OFFICIAL COMIC

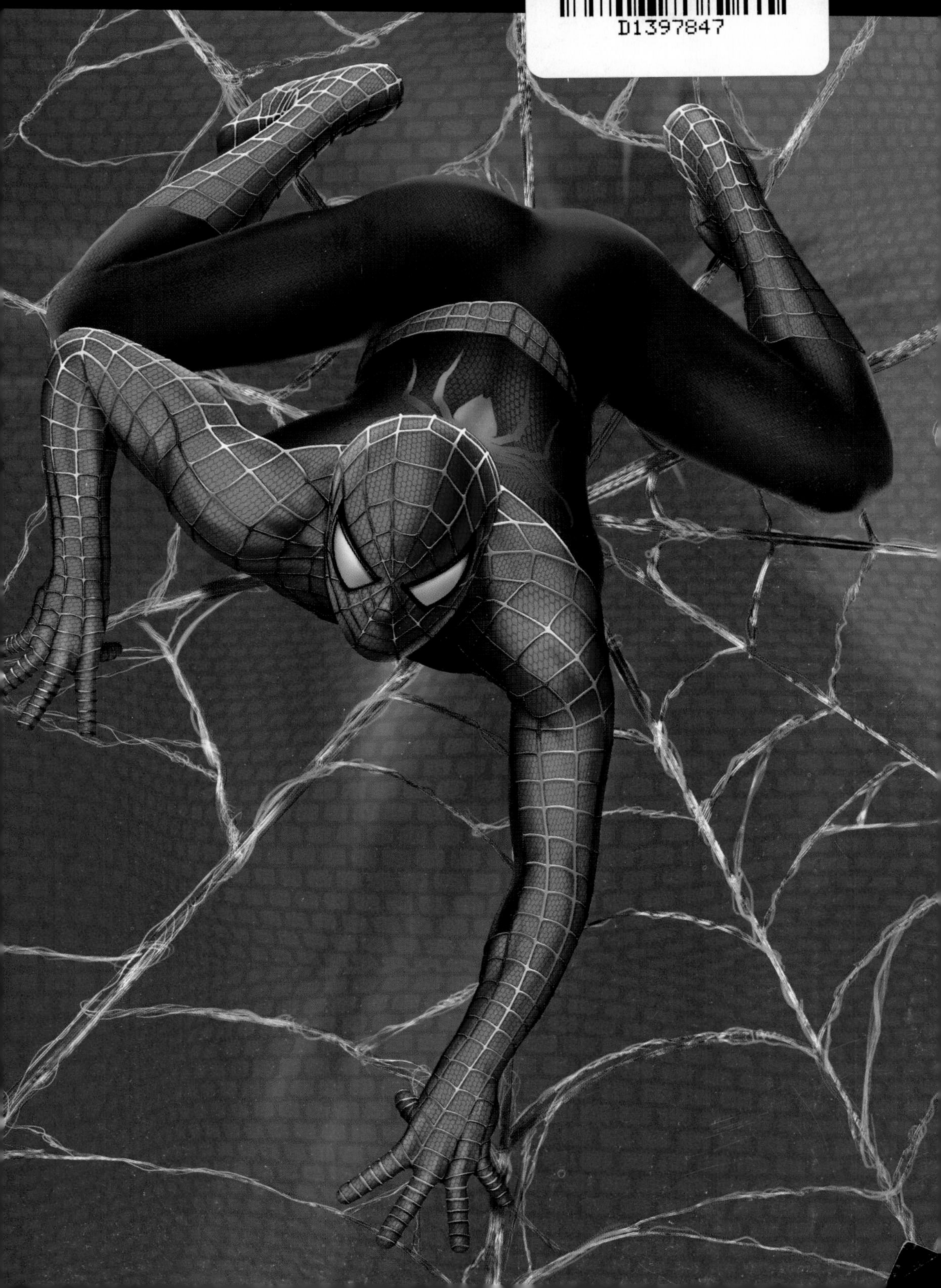

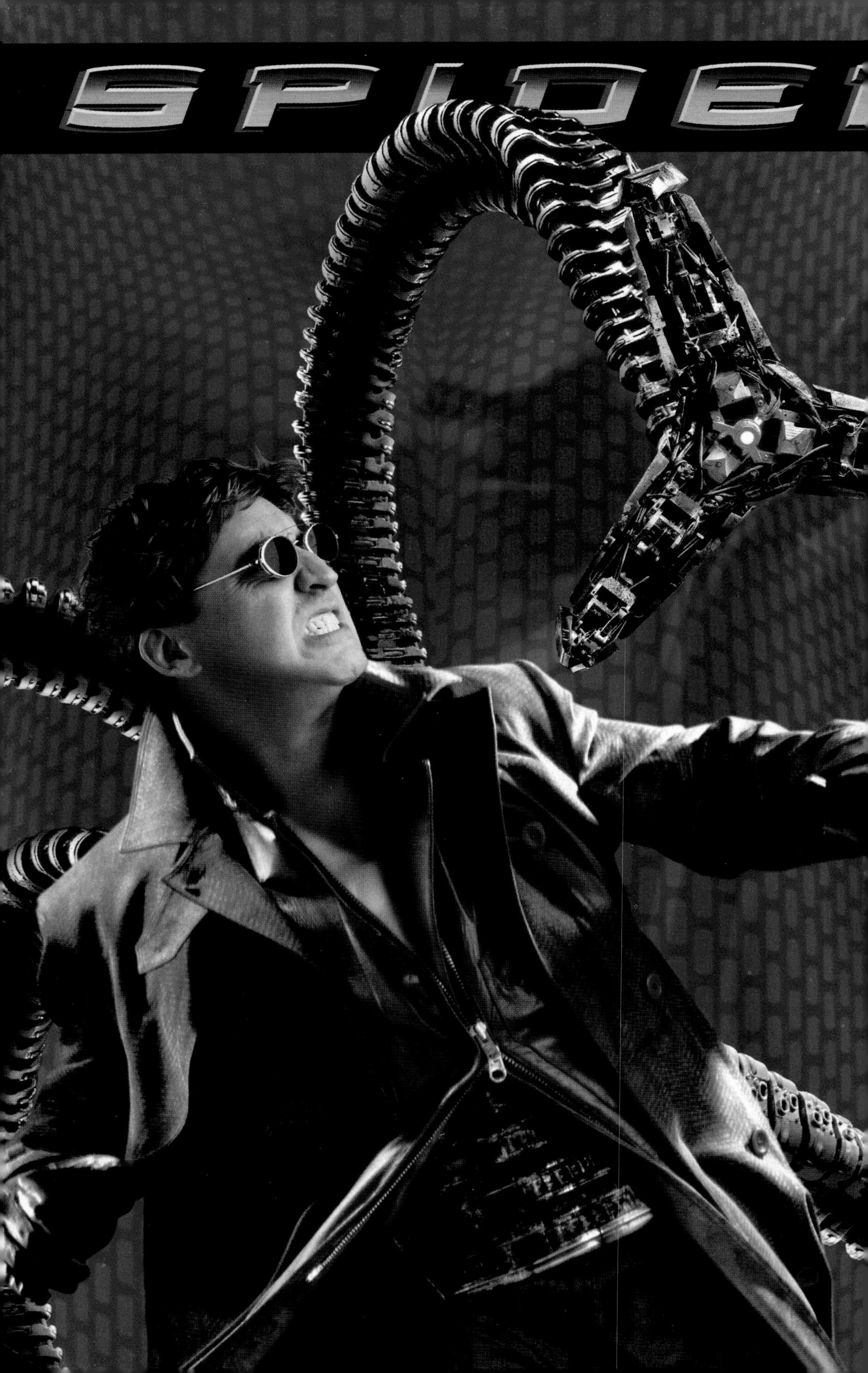
SPIDE

THE OFFICIAL COMIC ADAPTATION

WRITER *Roberto Aguirre Sacasa*
BASED ON THE MOTION PICTURE
SCREENPLAY BY *Alvin Sargent*
SCREEN STORY BY *Alfred Gough & Miles Millar and Michael Chabon*
BASED ON THE MARVEL COMIC BOOK BY *Stan Lee and Steve Ditko*

PENCILS *Staz Johnson, Ron Lim & Pat Olliffe*
INKS *Scott Koblish & Rodney Ramos*
COLORS *Chris Sotomayor*
ASSISTANT EDITOR *Nick Lowe*
ASSOCIATE EDITOR *CB Cebulski*
EDITOR *Ralph Macchio*

AMAZING SPIDER-MAN #50

WRITER *Stan Lee*
PENCILS *John Romita*
INKS *Mike Esposito*
LETTERS *Sam Rosen*

ULTIMATE SPIDER-MAN #14-15

WRITER *Brian Michael Bendis*
PENCILS *Mark Bagley*
INKS *Art Thibert*
COLORS *Transparency Digital*
LETTERS *Dave Sharpe*
ASSOCIATE EDITOR *Brian Smith*
EDITOR *Ralph Macchio*

COLLECTIONS EDITOR *Jeff Youngquist*
ASSISTANT EDITOR *Jennifer Grünwald*
BOOK DESIGNER *Patrick McGrath*

EDITOR IN CHIEF *Joe Quesada*
PUBLISHER *Dan Buckley*
VERY SPECIAL THANKS TO *Teresa Focarile*

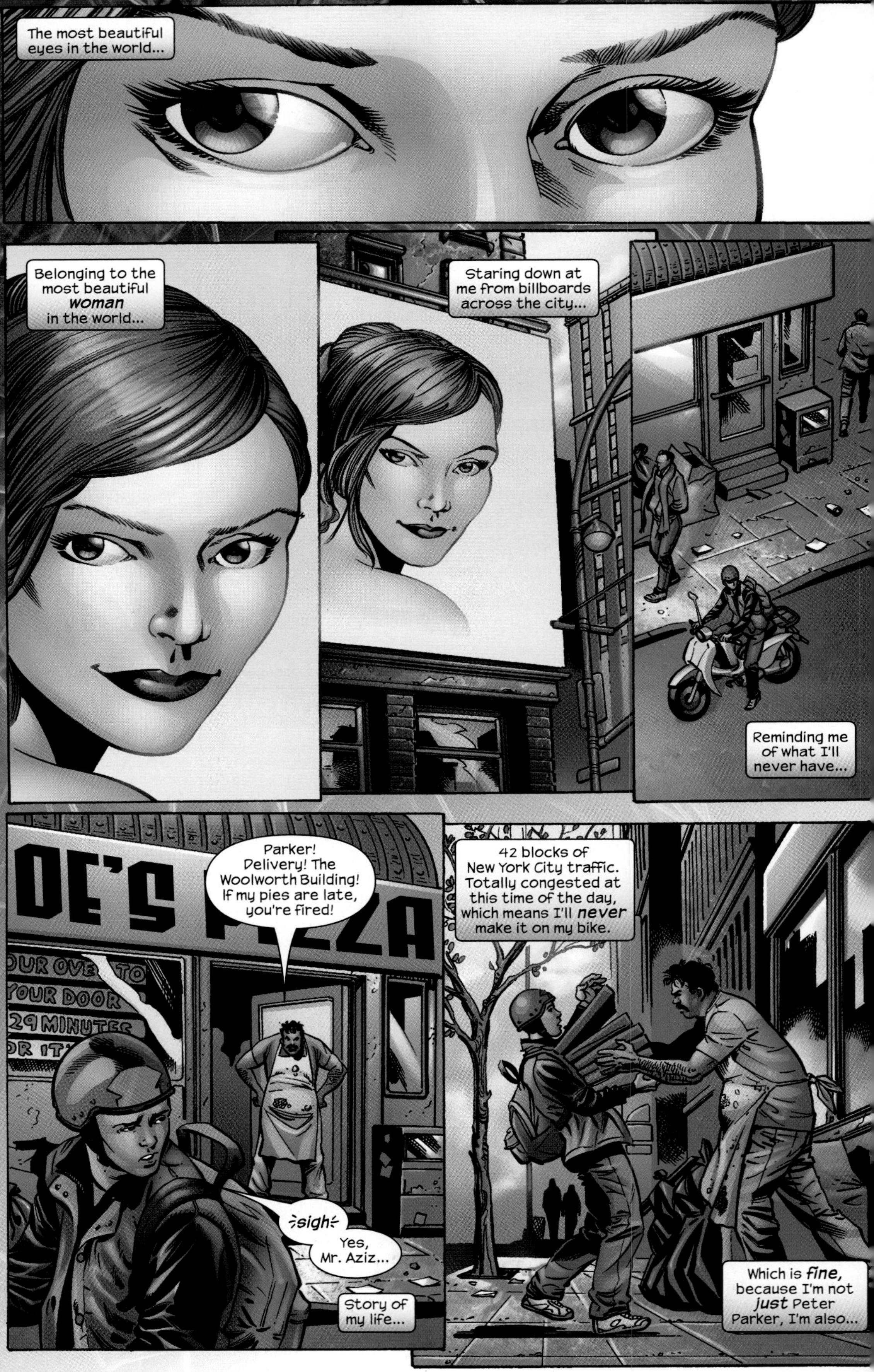

The most beautiful eyes in the world...
Belonging to the most beautiful woman in the world...
Staring down at me from billboards across the city...
Reminding me of what I'll never have...
OE'S PIZZA
OUR OVEN TO YOUR DOOR 29 MINUTES OR IT'
Parker! Delivery! The Woolworth Building! If my pies are late, you're fired!
sigh
Yes, Mr. Aziz...
Story of my life...
42 blocks of New York City traffic. Totally congested at this time of the day, which means I'll never make it on my bike.
Which is fine, because I'm not just Peter Parker, I'm also...

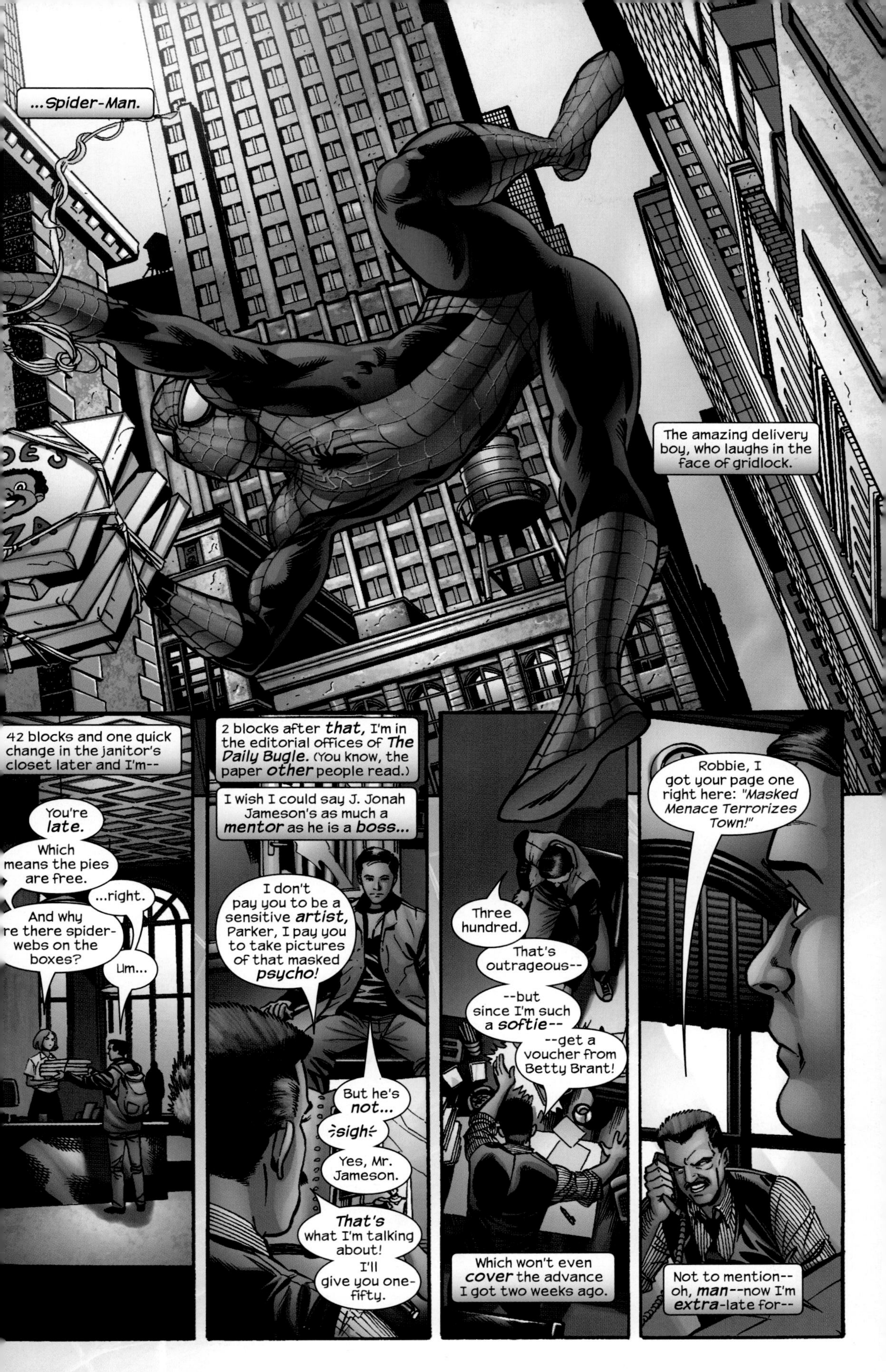
...Spider-Man.
The amazing delivery boy, who laughs in the face of gridlock.
42 blocks and one quick change in the janitor's closet later and I'm--
You're late.
Which means the pies are free.
...right.
And why are there spider-webs on the boxes?
Um...
2 blocks after that, I'm in the editorial offices of The Daily Bugle. (You know, the paper other people read.)
I wish I could say J. Jonah Jameson's as much a mentor as he is a boss...
I don't pay you to be a sensitive artist, Parker, I pay you to take pictures of that masked psycho!
But he's not...
sigh
Yes, Mr. Jameson.
That's what I'm talking about!
I'll give you one-fifty.
Three hundred.
That's outrageous--
--but since I'm such a softie--
--get a voucher from Betty Brant!
Which won't even cover the advance I got two weeks ago.
Robbie, I got your page one right here: "Masked Menace Terrorizes Town!"
Not to mention-- oh, man--now I'm extra-late for--

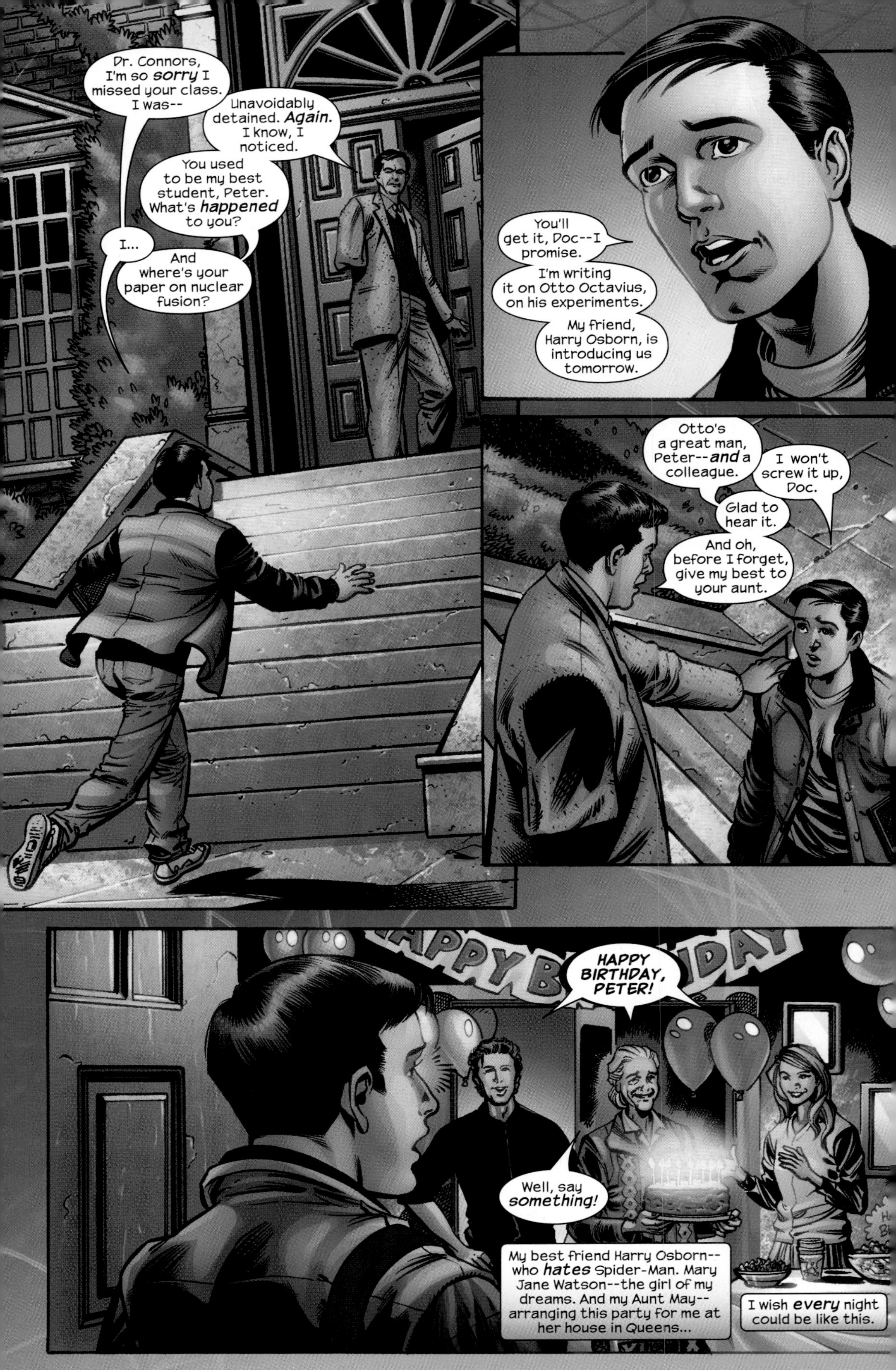
Dr. Connors, I'm so *sorry* I missed your class. I was--
Unavoidably detained. *Again.* I know, I noticed.
You used to be my best student, Peter. What's *happened* to you?
I...
And where's your paper on nuclear fusion?
You'll get it, Doc--I promise.
I'm writing it on Otto Octavius, on his experiments.
My friend, Harry Osborn, is introducing us tomorrow.
Otto's a great man, Peter--*and* a colleague.
I won't screw it up, Doc.
Glad to hear it.
And oh, before I forget, give my best to your aunt.
HAPPY BIRTHDAY, PETER!
Well, say *something!*
My best friend Harry Osborn--who *hates* Spider-Man. Mary Jane Watson--the girl of my dreams. And my Aunt May--arranging this party for me at her house in Queens...
I wish *every* night could be like this.

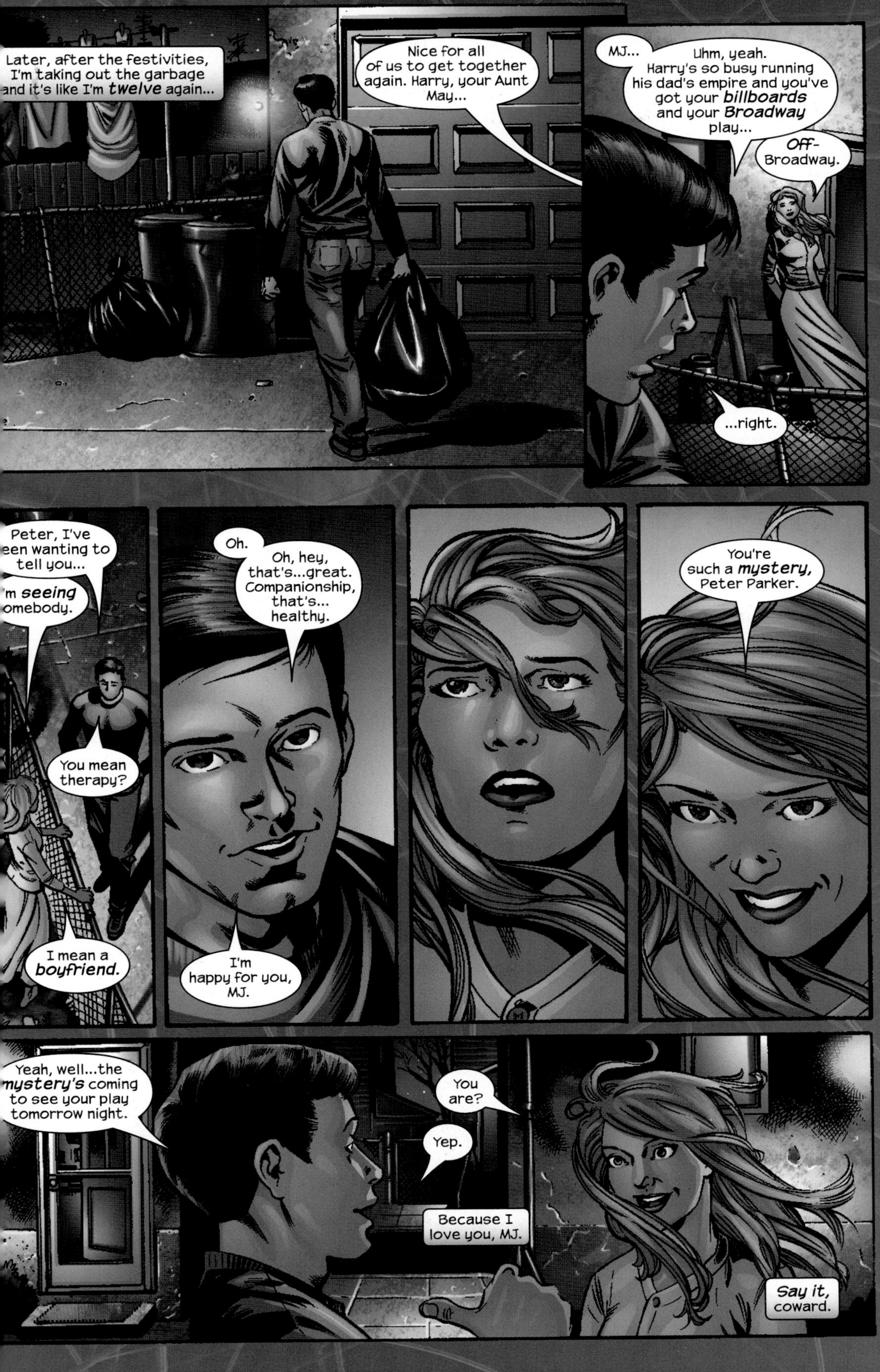

Later, after the festivities, I'm taking out the garbage and it's like I'm *twelve* again...
Nice for all of us to get together again. Harry, your Aunt May...
MJ...
Uhm, yeah. Harry's so busy running his dad's empire and you've got your *billboards* and your *Broadway* play...
Off-Broadway.
...right.
Peter, I've een wanting to tell you...
'm *seeing* omebody.
You mean therapy?
I mean a *boyfriend.*
Oh.
Oh, hey, that's...great. Companionship, that's... healthy.
I'm happy for you, MJ.
You're such a *mystery,* Peter Parker.
Yeah, well...the *mystery's* coming to see your play tomorrow night.
You are?
Yep.
Because I love you, MJ.
Say it, coward.

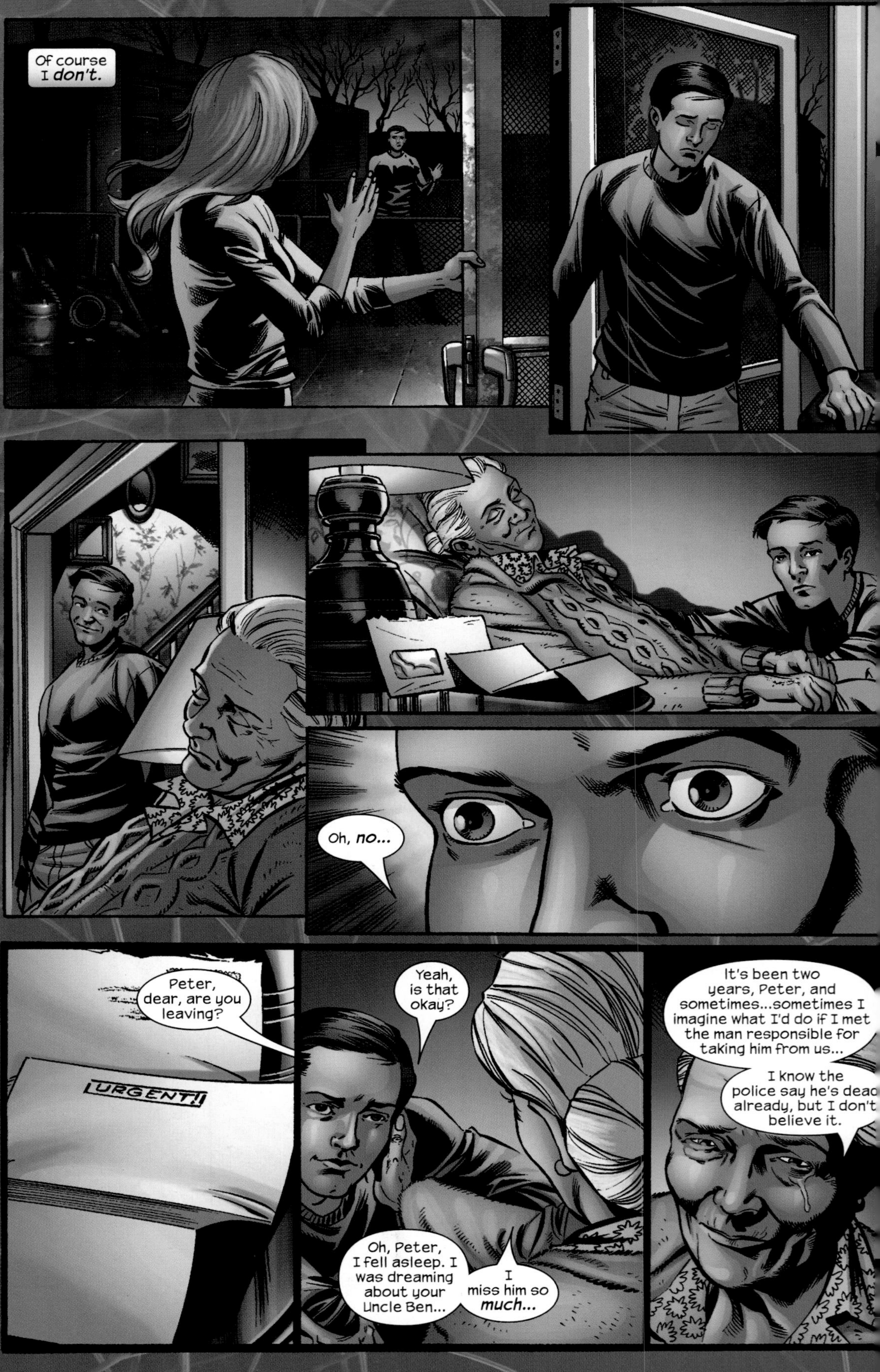
Of course I *don't.*
Oh, *no...*
URGENT!!
Peter, dear, are you leaving?
Yeah, is that okay?
Oh, Peter, I fell asleep. I was dreaming about your Uncle Ben...
I miss him so *much...*
It's been two years, Peter, and sometimes...sometimes I imagine what I'd do if I met the man responsible for taking him from us...
I know the police say he's dead already, but I don't believe it.

Aunt May...

Yes, Peter?

Oh, pish-*tush.* I'm a little behind, that's all.

I'll get you some cake and then you run along home...

I'm *worried* about you, living here alone...

And money's *tight,* I know.

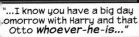

"...I know you have a big day tomorrow with Harry and that Otto *whoever-he-is...*"

Nice to see you take an interest in someone *other* than Spider-Man for a change.

Lay off, Harry.

You or Spider-Man?

Both of us.

He killed my *father,* Peter.

You don't know that.

You weren't there! He was standing over his dead body!

I *was* there-- as Spider-Man.

But I *didn't* kill Norman Osborn, though I understand Harry's confusion and rage...

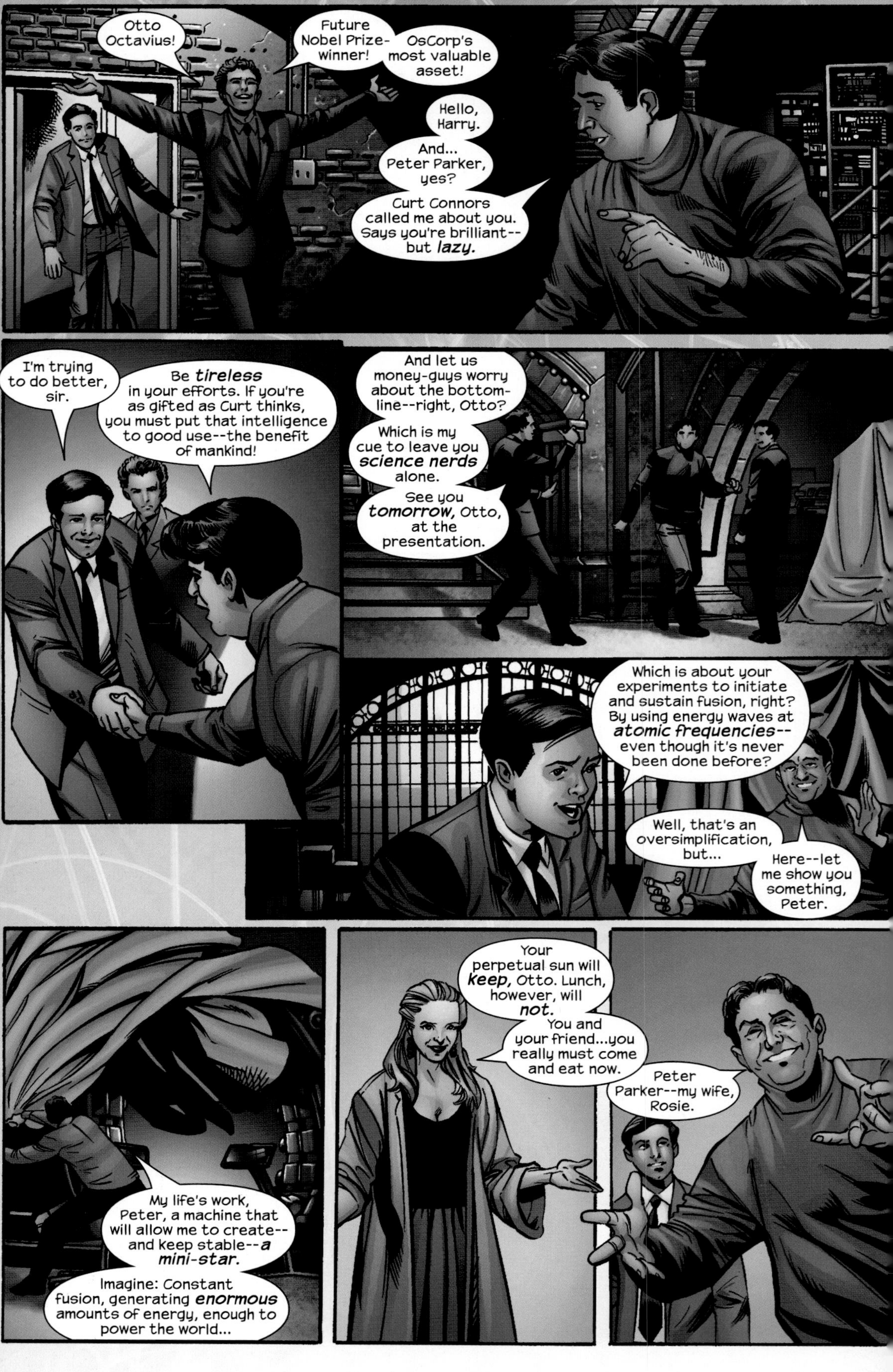
Otto Octavius!
Future Nobel Prize-winner!
OsCorp's most valuable asset!
Hello, Harry.
And... Peter Parker, yes?
Curt Connors called me about you. Says you're brilliant--but lazy.
I'm trying to do better, sir.
Be tireless in your efforts. If you're as gifted as Curt thinks, you must put that intelligence to good use--the benefit of mankind!
And let us money-guys worry about the bottom-line--right, Otto?
Which is my cue to leave you science nerds alone.
See you tomorrow, Otto, at the presentation.
Which is about your experiments to initiate and sustain fusion, right? By using energy waves at atomic frequencies--even though it's never been done before?
Well, that's an oversimplification, but...
Here--let me show you something, Peter.
My life's work, Peter, a machine that will allow me to create--and keep stable--a mini-star.
Imagine: Constant fusion, generating enormous amounts of energy, enough to power the world...
Your perpetual sun will keep, Otto. Lunch, however, will not.
You and your friend...you really must come and eat now.
Peter Parker--my wife, Rosie.

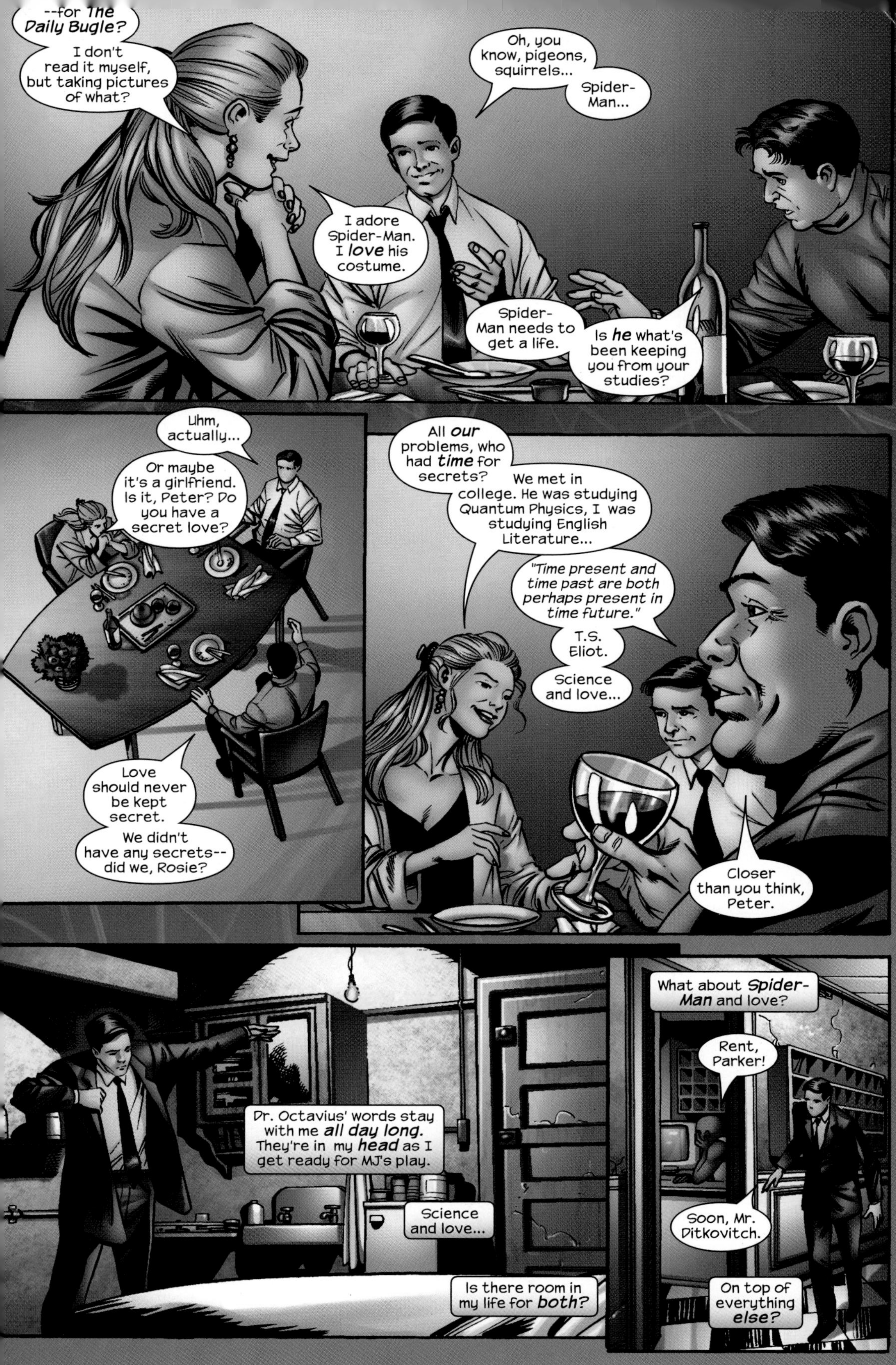
--for The Daily Bugle?
I don't read it myself, but taking pictures of what?
Oh, you know, pigeons, squirrels...
Spider-Man...
I adore Spider-Man. I *love* his costume.
Spider-Man needs to get a life.
Is *he* what's been keeping you from your studies?
Uhm, actually...
Or maybe it's a girlfriend. Is it, Peter? Do you have a secret love?
Love should never be kept secret.
We didn't have any secrets--did we, Rosie?
All *our* problems, who had *time* for secrets?
We met in college. He was studying Quantum Physics, I was studying English Literature...
"Time present and time past are both perhaps present in time future."
T.S. Eliot.
Science and love...
Closer than you think, Peter.
Dr. Octavius' words stay with me *all day long.* They're in my *head* as I get ready for MJ's play.
Science and love...
Is there room in my life for *both?*
What about *Spider-Man* and love?
Rent, Parker!
Soon, Mr. Ditkovitch.
On top of everything *else?*

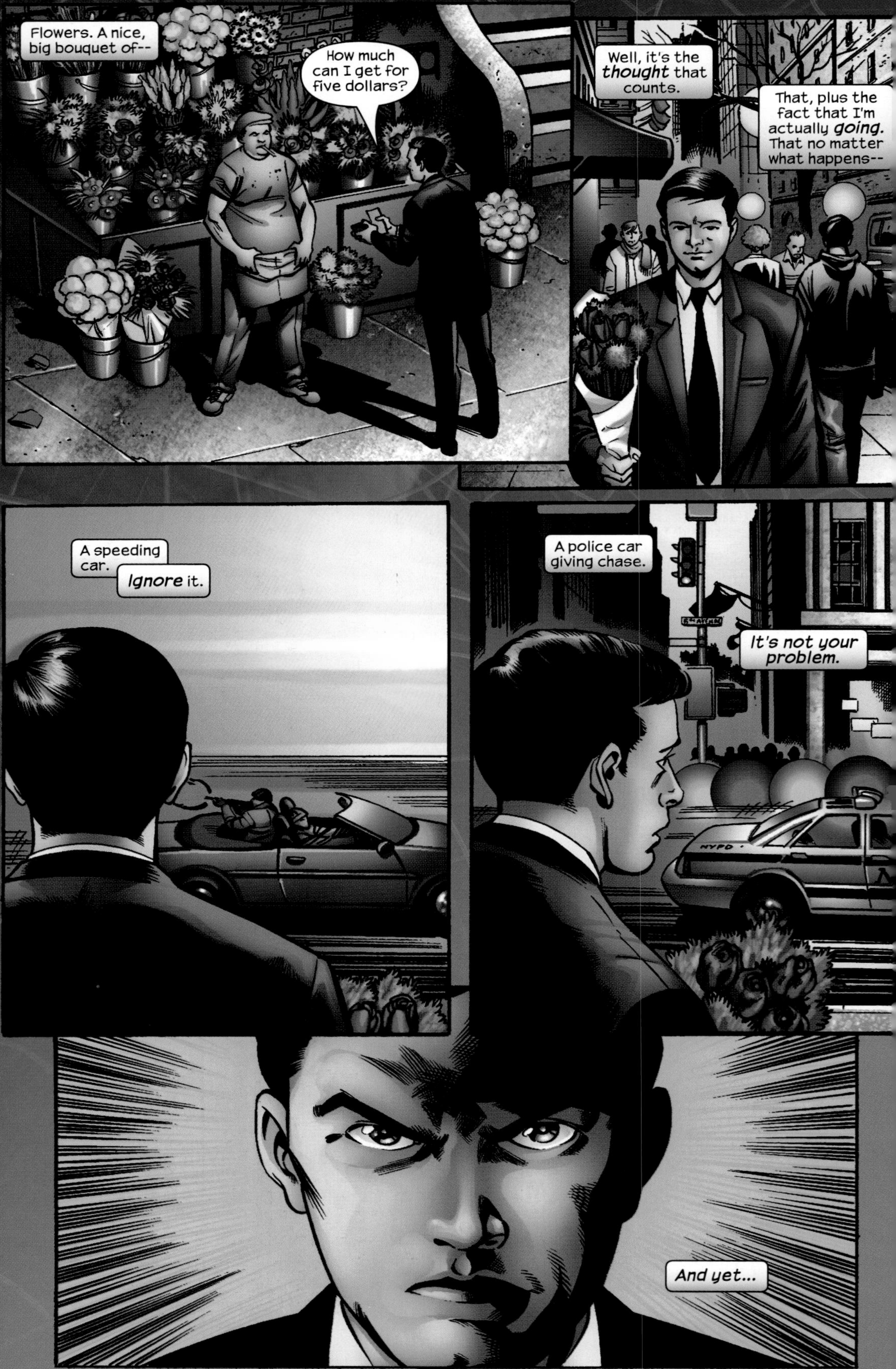

Flowers. A nice, big bouquet of--
How much can I get for five dollars?
Well, it's the *thought* that counts.
That, plus the fact that I'm actually *going.* That no matter what happens--
A speeding car.
Ignore it.
A police car giving chase.
It's not your problem.
And yet...

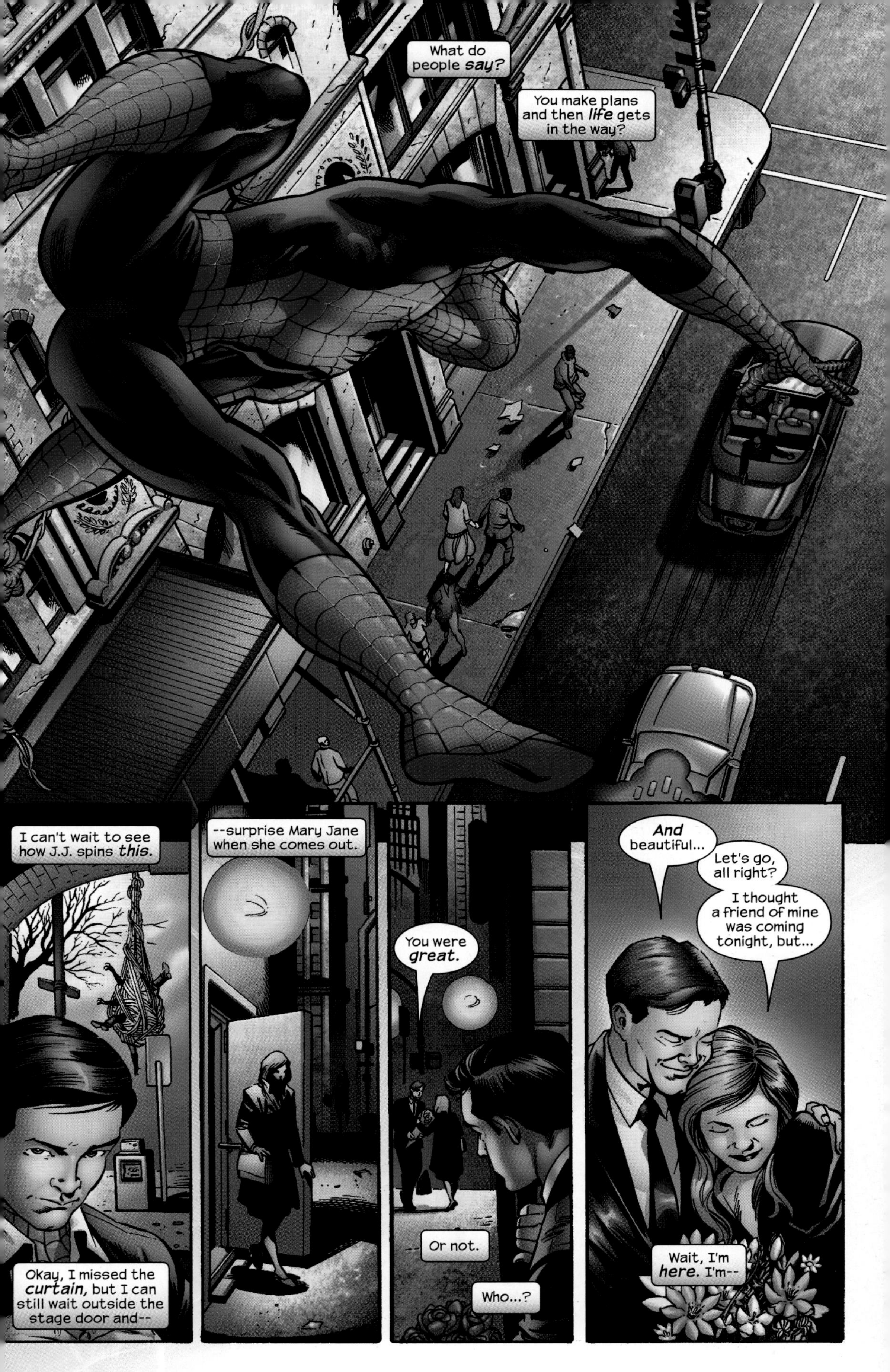

What do people *say?*
You make plans and then *life* gets in the way?
I can't wait to see how J.J. spins *this.*
Okay, I missed the *curtain,* but I can still wait outside the stage door and--
--surprise Mary Jane when she comes out.
You were *great.*
Or not.
Who...?
And beautiful...
Let's go, all right?
I thought a friend of mine was coming tonight, but...
Wait, I'm *here.* I'm--

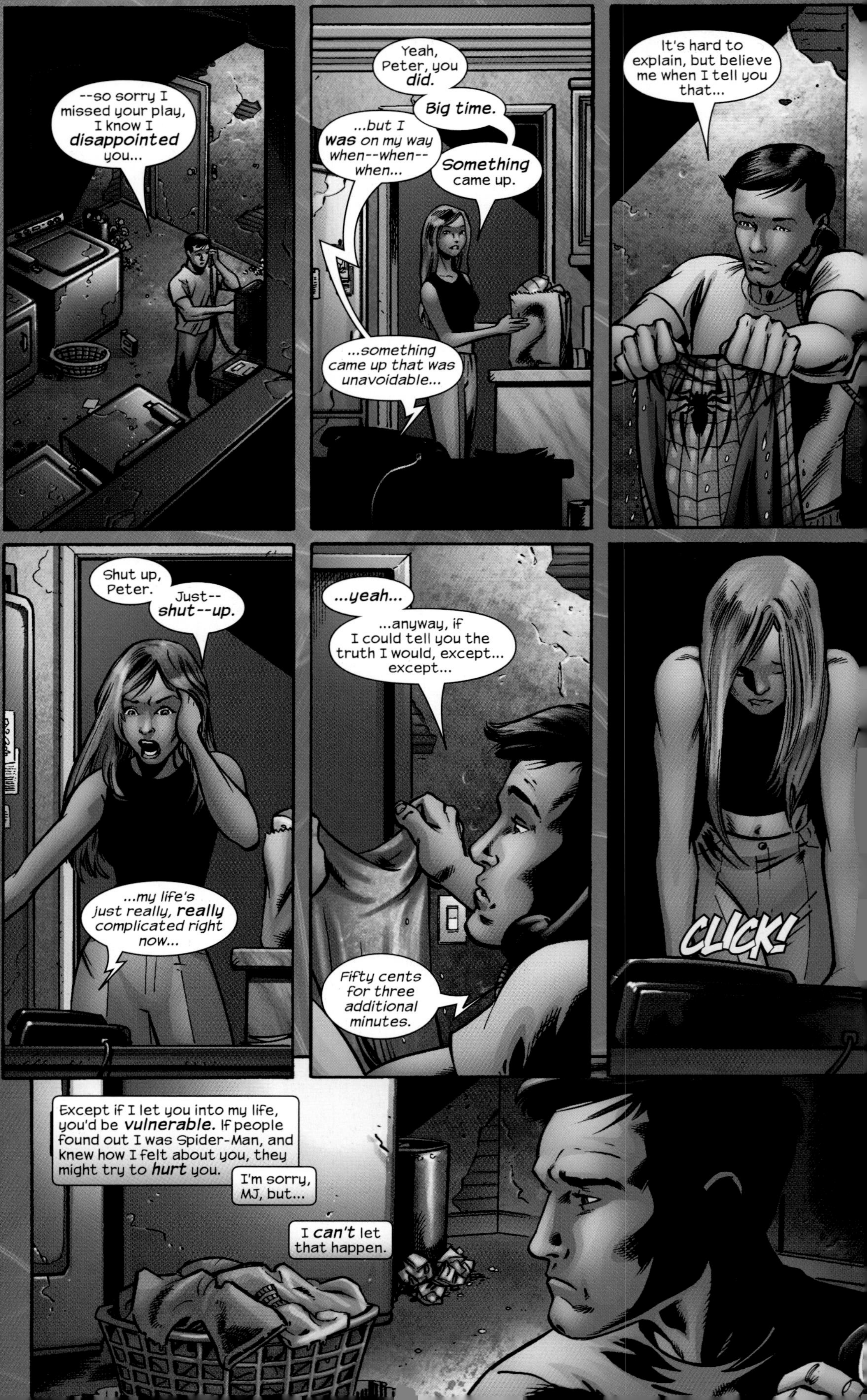
--so sorry I missed your play, I know I disappointed you...
Yeah, Peter, you did.
Big time.
...but I was on my way when--when--when...
Something came up.
...something came up that was unavoidable...
It's hard to explain, but believe me when I tell you that...
Shut up, Peter.
Just--shut--up.
...my life's just really, really complicated right now...
...yeah...
...anyway, if I could tell you the truth I would, except... except...
Fifty cents for three additional minutes.
CLICK!
Except if I let you into my life, you'd be vulnerable. If people found out I was Spider-Man, and knew how I felt about you, they might try to hurt you.
I'm sorry, MJ, but...
I can't let that happen.

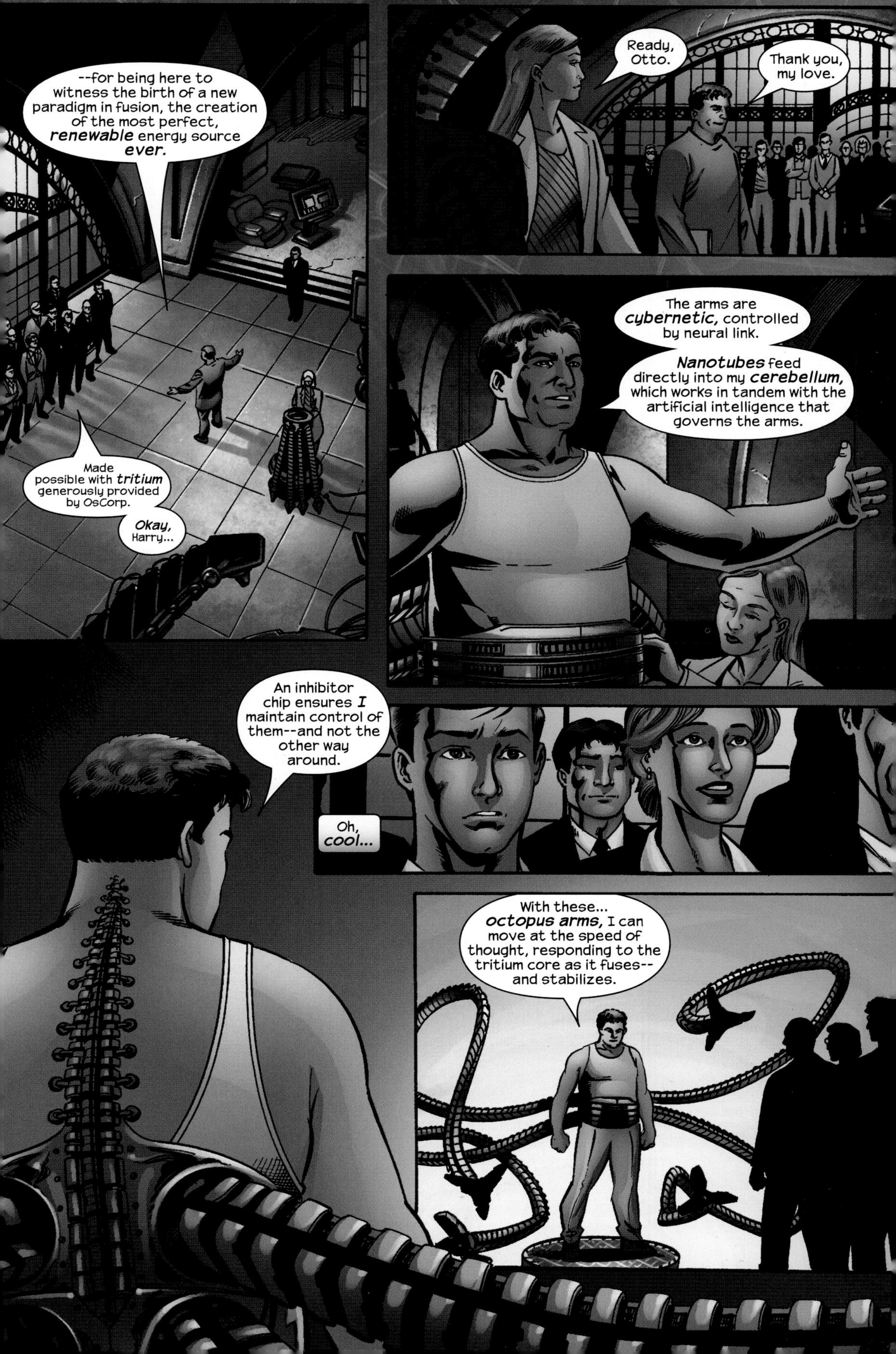
--for being here to witness the birth of a new paradigm in fusion, the creation of the most perfect, renewable energy source ever.
Made possible with tritium generously provided by OsCorp.
Okay, Harry...
Ready, Otto.
Thank you, my love.
The arms are cybernetic, controlled by neural link.
Nanotubes feed directly into my cerebellum, which works in tandem with the artificial intelligence that governs the arms.
An inhibitor chip ensures I maintain control of them--and not the other way around.
Oh, cool...
With these... octopus arms, I can move at the speed of thought, responding to the tritium core as it fuses--and stabilizes.

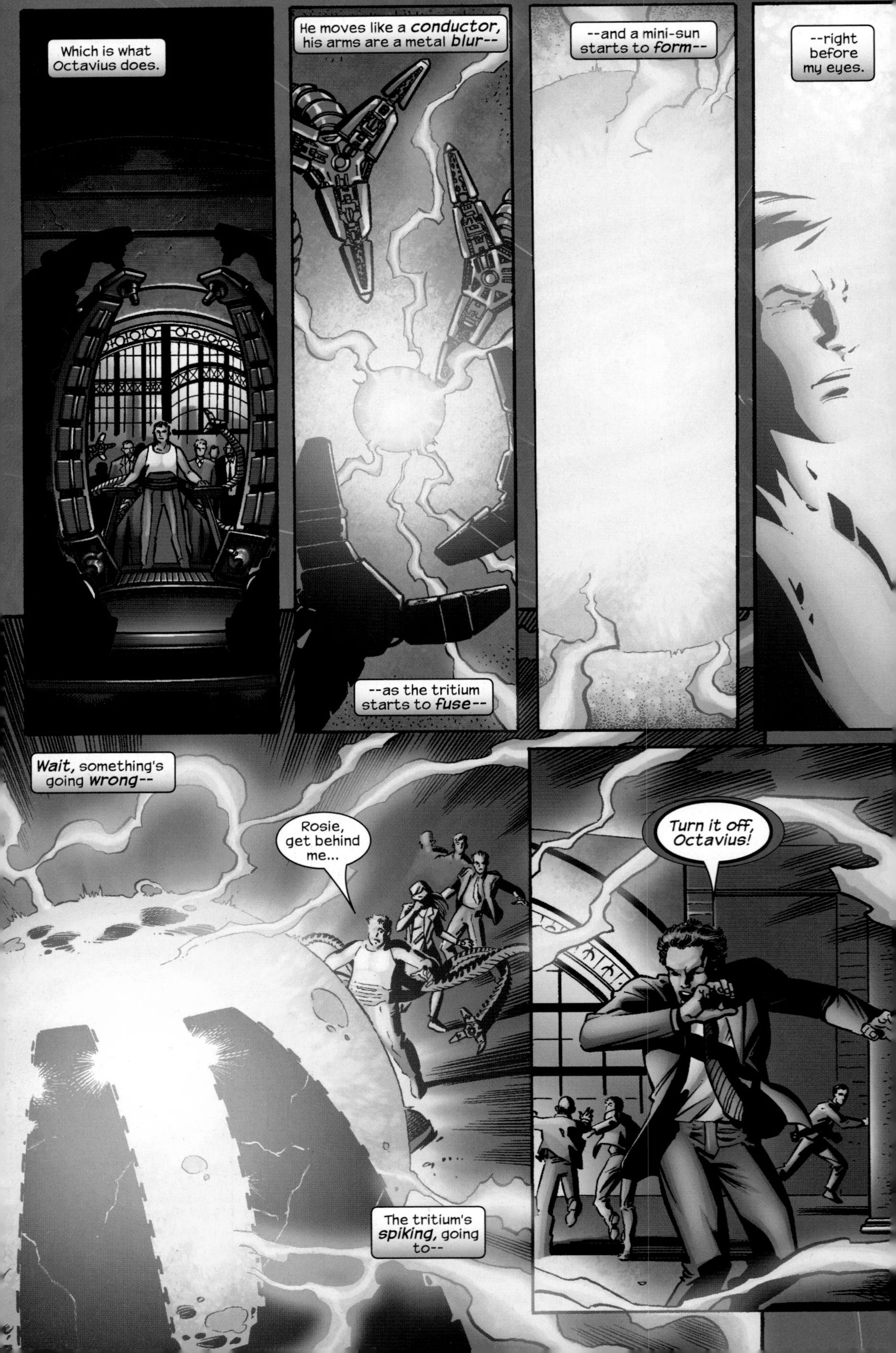
Which is what Octavius does.
He moves like a conductor, his arms are a metal blur--
--as the tritium starts to fuse--
--and a mini-sun starts to form--
--right before my eyes.
Wait, something's going wrong--
Rosie, get behind me...
The tritium's spiking, going to--
Turn it off, Octavius!

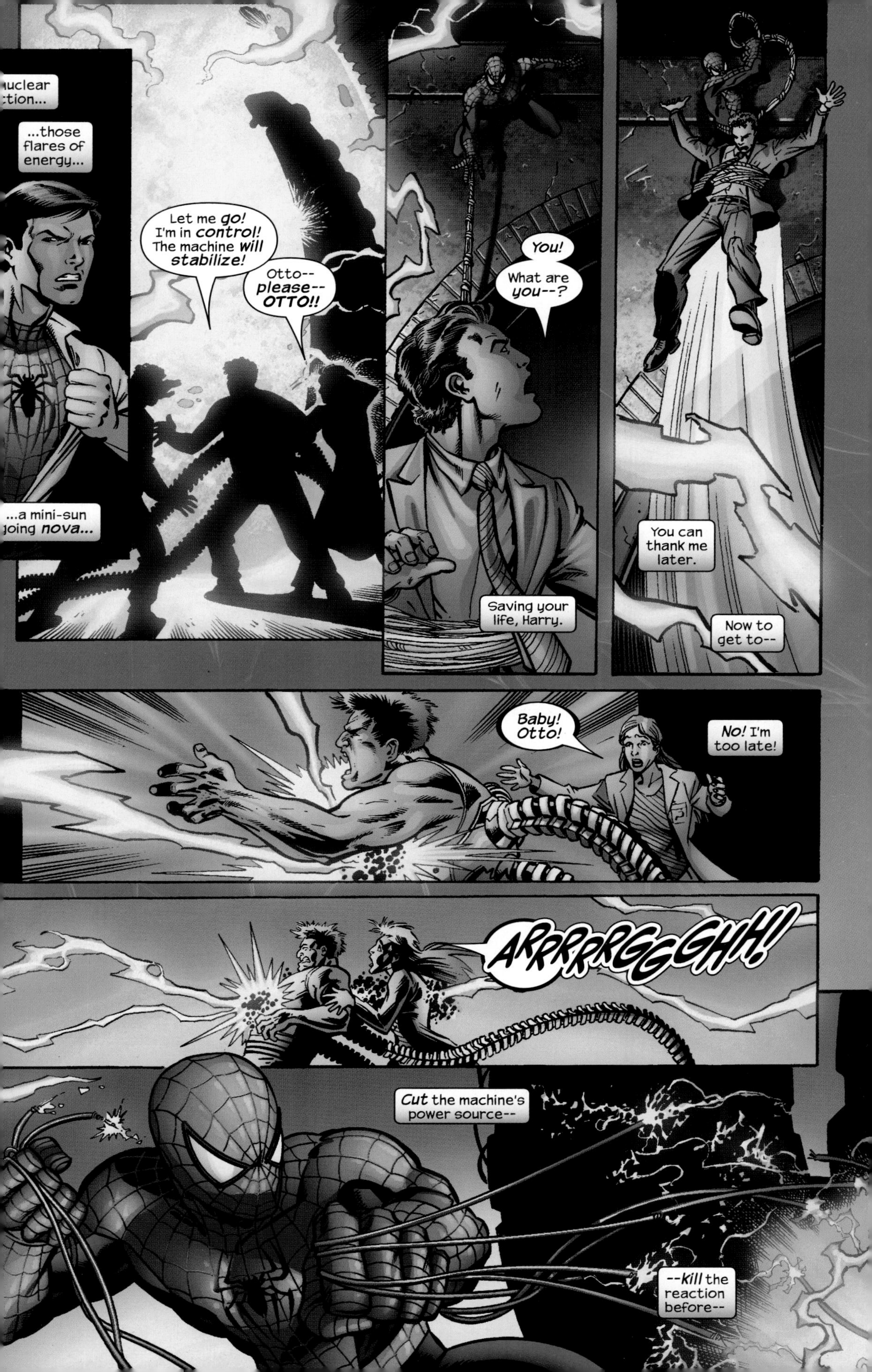

uclear
ction...
...those flares of energy...
Let me go! I'm in control! The machine will stabilize!
Otto-- please-- OTTO!!
...a mini-sun
oing nova...
You! What are you--?
Saving your life, Harry.
You can thank me later.
Now to get to--
Baby! Otto!
No! I'm too late!
ARRRRRGGGGH!
Cut the machine's power source--
--kill the reaction before--

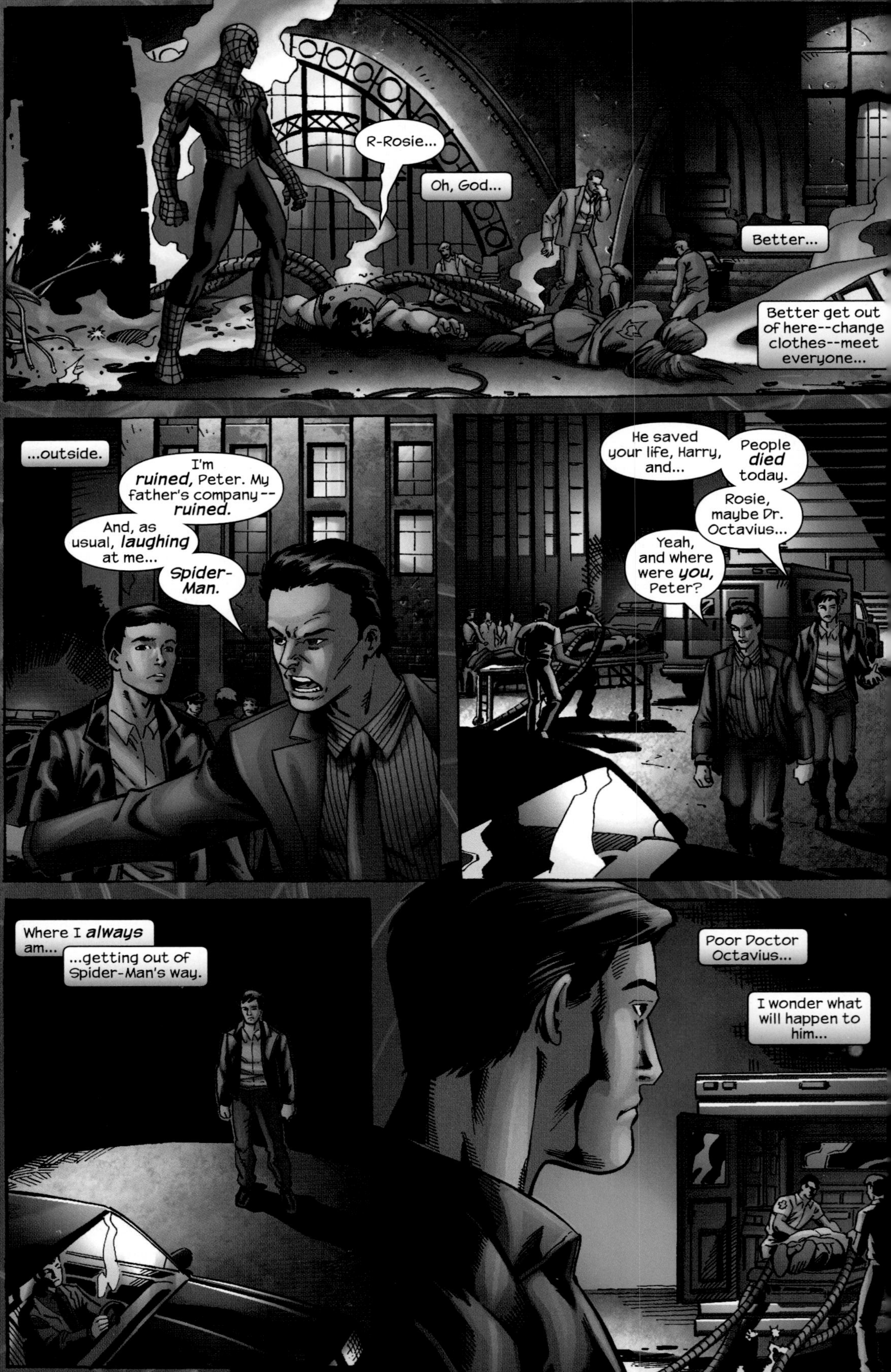
R-Rosie...
Oh, God...
Better...
Better get out of here--change clothes--meet everyone...
...outside.
I'm ruined, Peter. My father's company--ruined.
And, as usual, laughing at me...
Spider-Man.
He saved your life, Harry, and...
People died today.
Rosie, maybe Dr. Octavius...
Yeah, and where were you, Peter?
Where I always am...
...getting out of Spider-Man's way.
Poor Doctor Octavius...
I wonder what will happen to him...

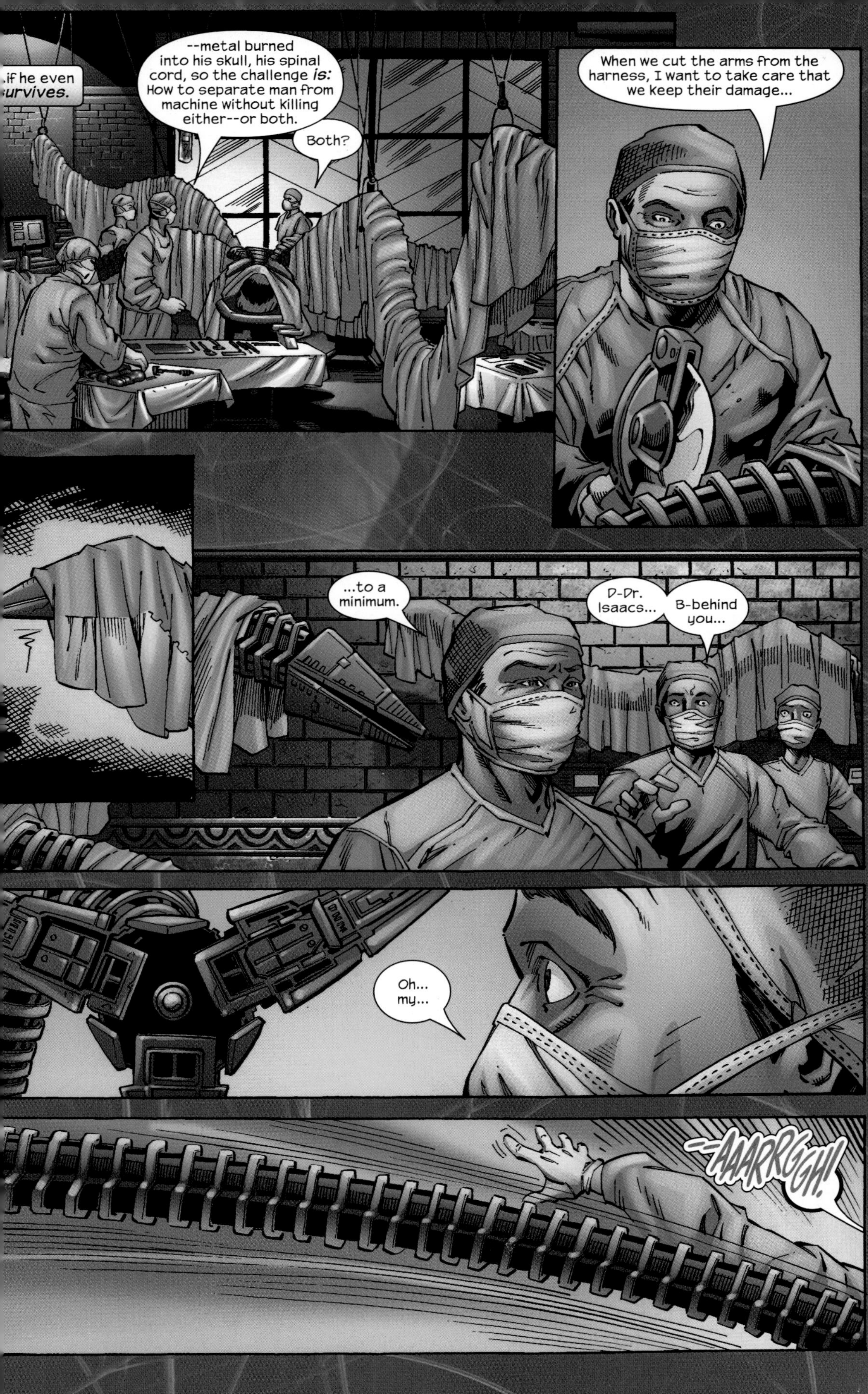
...if he even survives.
--metal burned into his skull, his spinal cord, so the challenge *is:* How to separate man from machine without killing either--or both.
Both?
When we cut the arms from the harness, I want to take care that we keep their damage...
...to a minimum.
D-Dr. Isaacs...
B-behind you...
Oh... my...
--AAARRGGH!

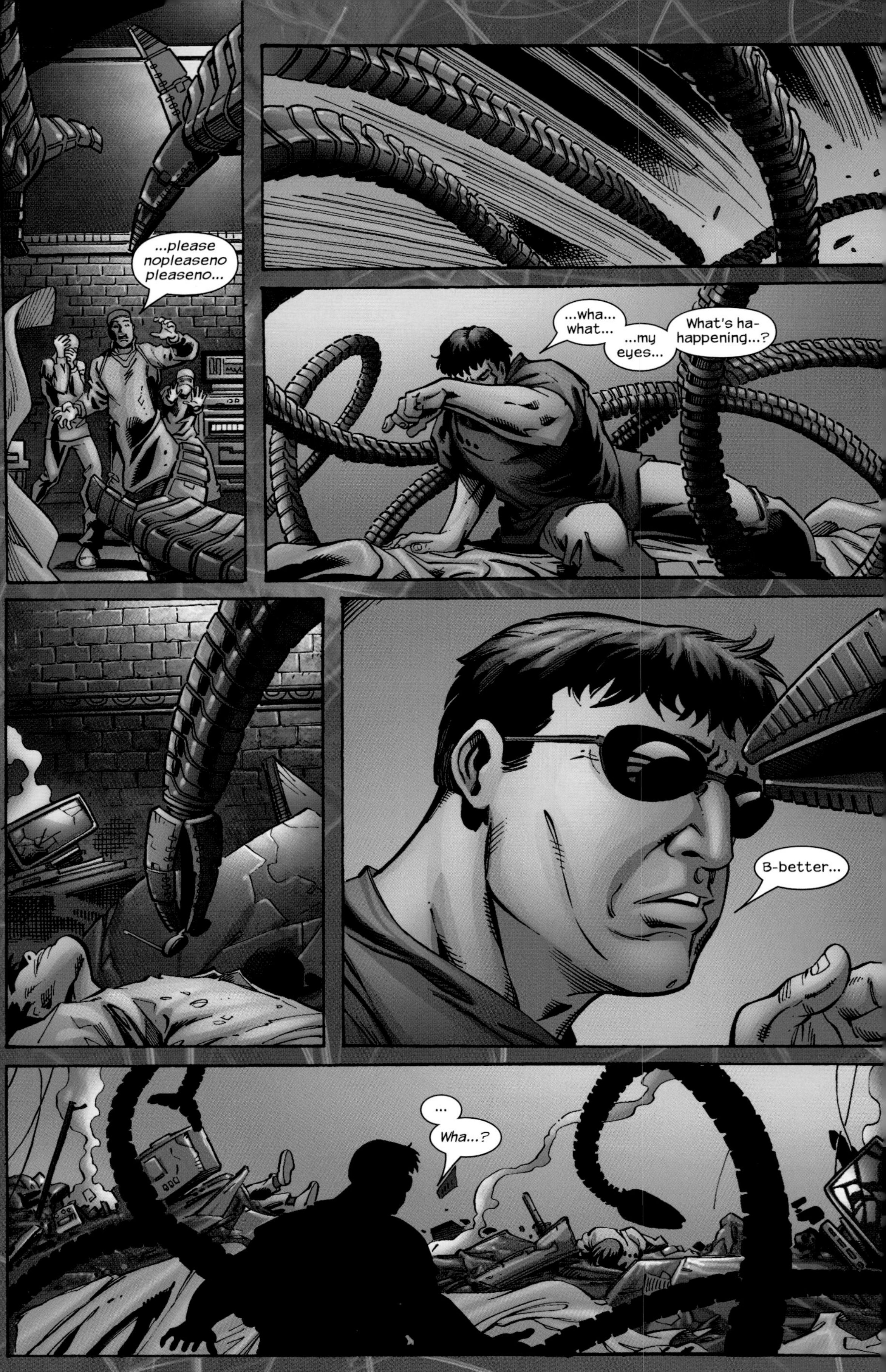
...please nopleaseno pleaseno...
...wha... what...
...my eyes...
What's ha-happening...?
B-better...
...
Wha...?

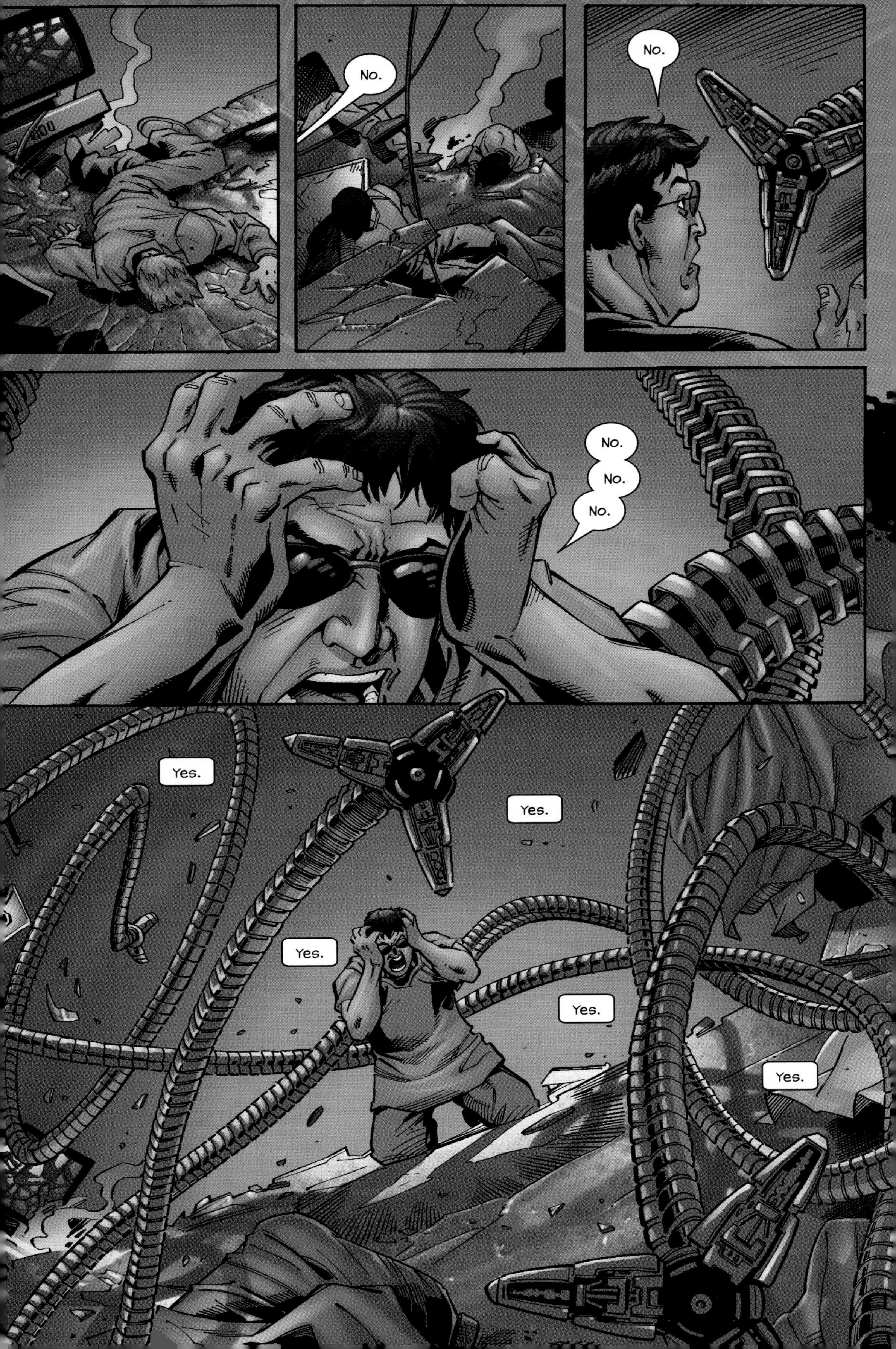
No.
No.
No.
No.
No.
Yes.
Yes.
Yes.
Yes.
Yes.

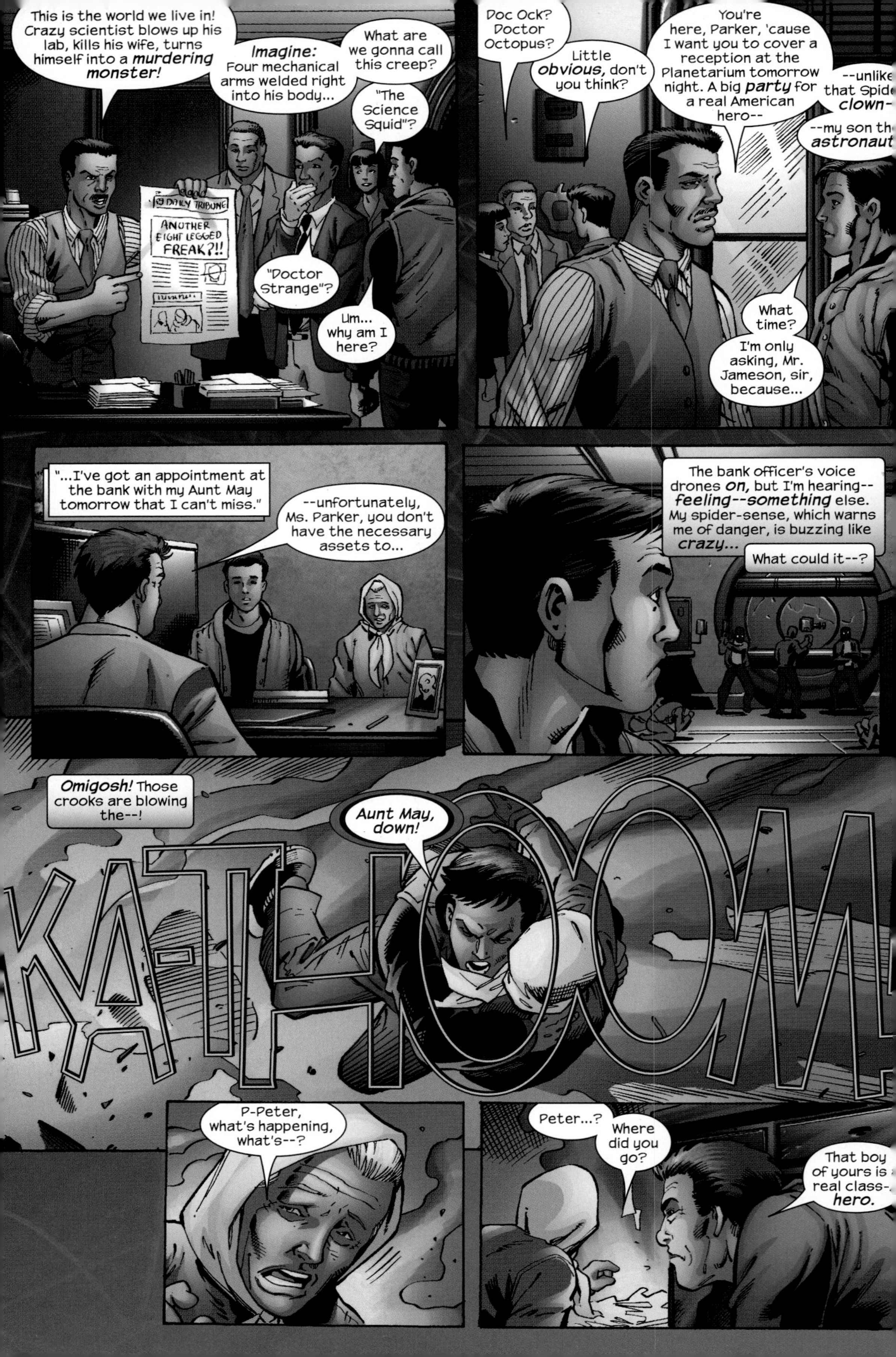
This is the world we live in! Crazy scientist blows up his lab, kills his wife, turns himself into a murdering monster!
Imagine: Four mechanical arms welded right into his body...
What are we gonna call this creep?
"The Science Squid"?
DAILY TRIBUNE
ANOTHER EIGHT LEGGED FREAK?!!
"Doctor Strange"?
Um... why am I here?
Doc Ock? Doctor Octopus?
Little obvious, don't you think?
You're here, Parker, 'cause I want you to cover a reception at the Planetarium tomorrow night. A big party for a real American hero--
--unlike that Spide clown-
--my son th astronaut
What time?
I'm only asking, Mr. Jameson, sir, because...
"...I've got an appointment at the bank with my Aunt May tomorrow that I can't miss."
--unfortunately, Ms. Parker, you don't have the necessary assets to...
The bank officer's voice drones on, but I'm hearing-- feeling--something else. My spider-sense, which warns me of danger, is buzzing like crazy...
What could it--?
Omigosh! Those crooks are blowing the--!
Aunt May, down!
KA-THOOM
P-Peter, what's happening, what's--?
Peter...?
Where did you go?
That boy of yours is real class- hero.

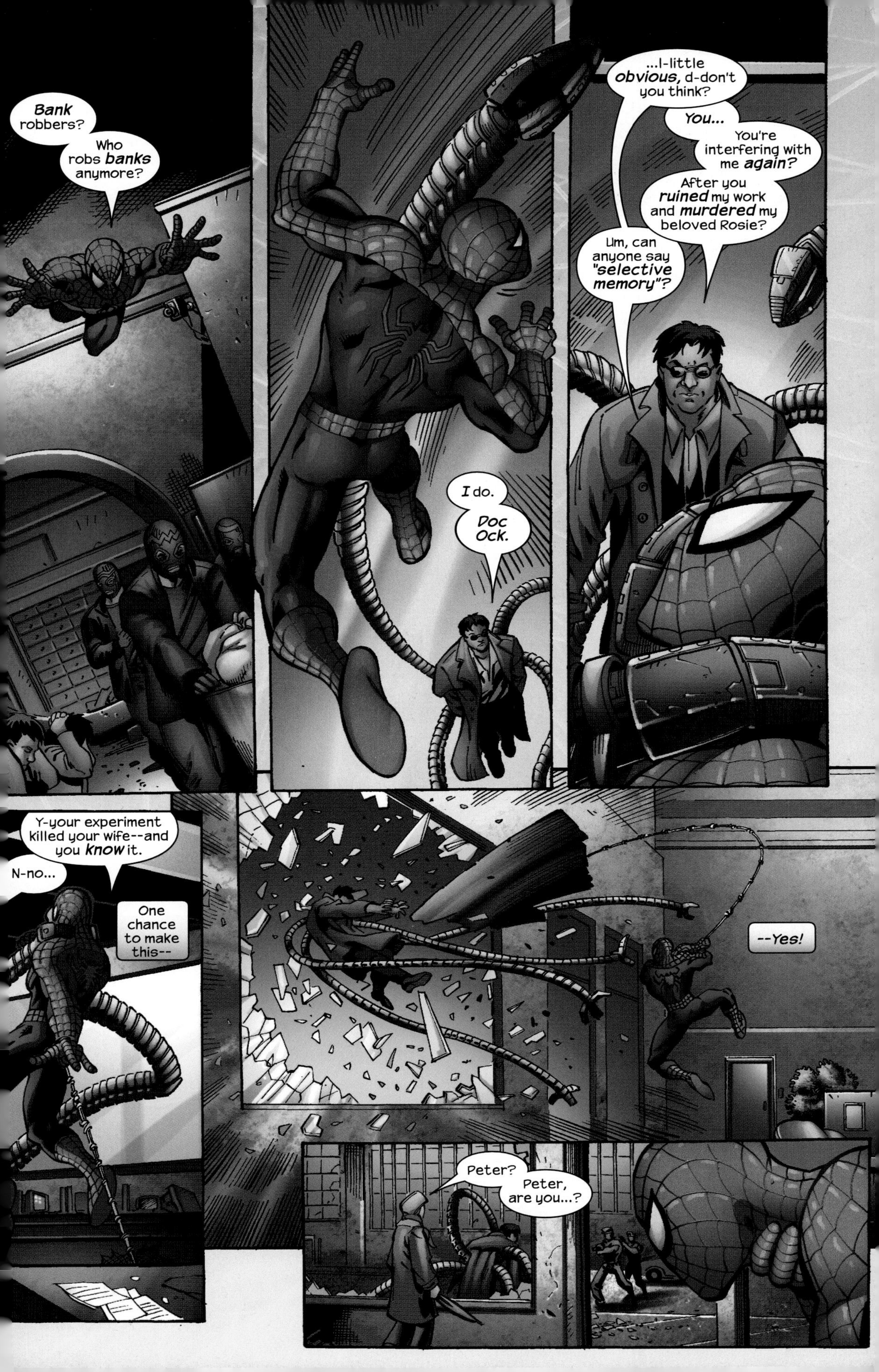
Bank robbers?
Who robs banks anymore?
I do.
Doc Ock.
...l-little obvious, d-don't you think?
You...
You're interfering with me again?
After you ruined my work and murdered my beloved Rosie?
Um, can anyone say "selective memory"?
Y-your experiment killed your wife--and you know it.
N-no...
One chance to make this--
--Yes!
Peter?
Peter, are you...?

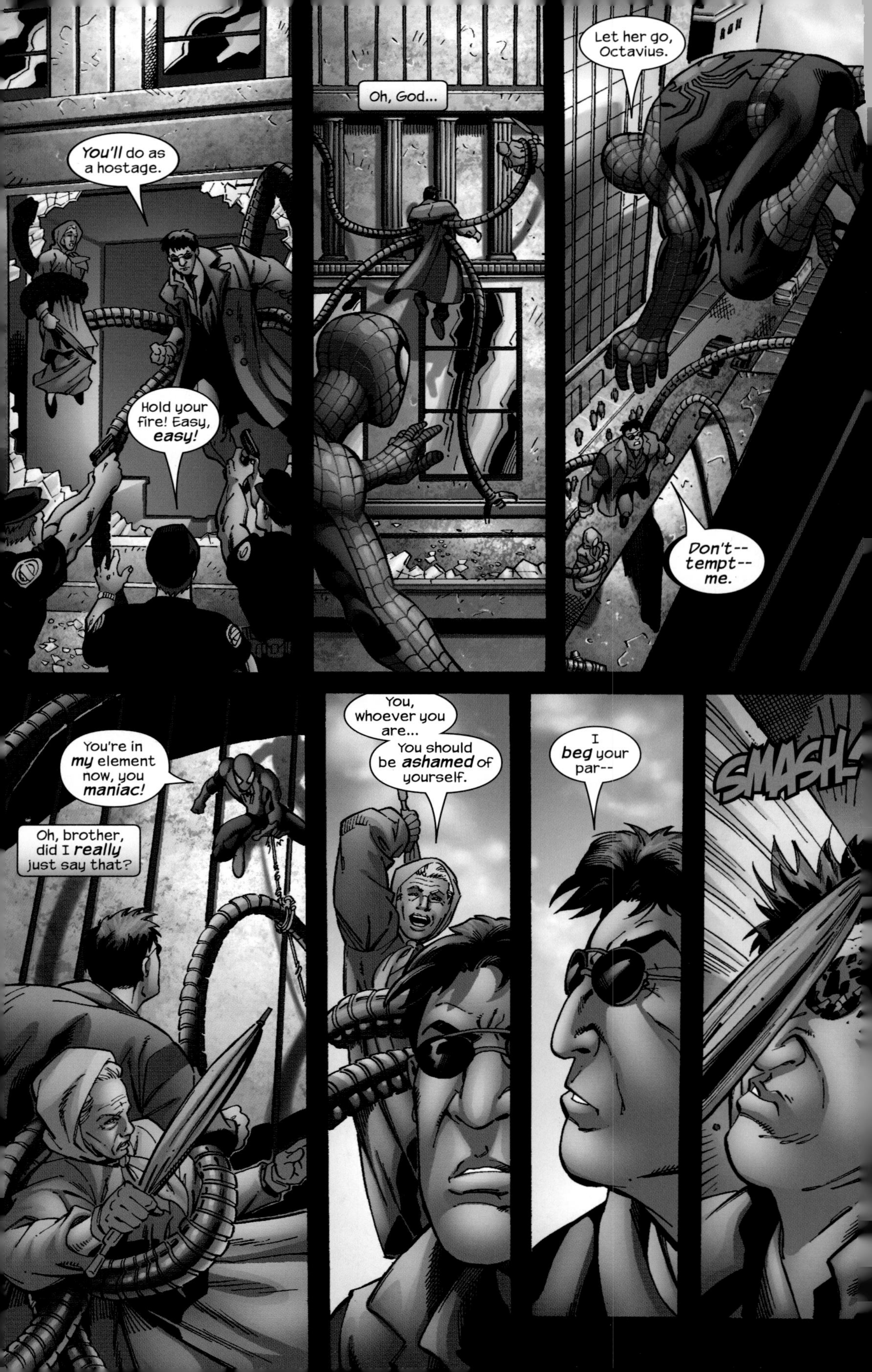
You'll do as a hostage.
Hold your fire! Easy, easy!
Oh, God...
Let her go, Octavius.
Don't--tempt--me.
You're in my element now, you maniac!
Oh, brother, did I really just say that?
You, whoever you are...
You should be ashamed of yourself.
I beg your par--
SMASH!

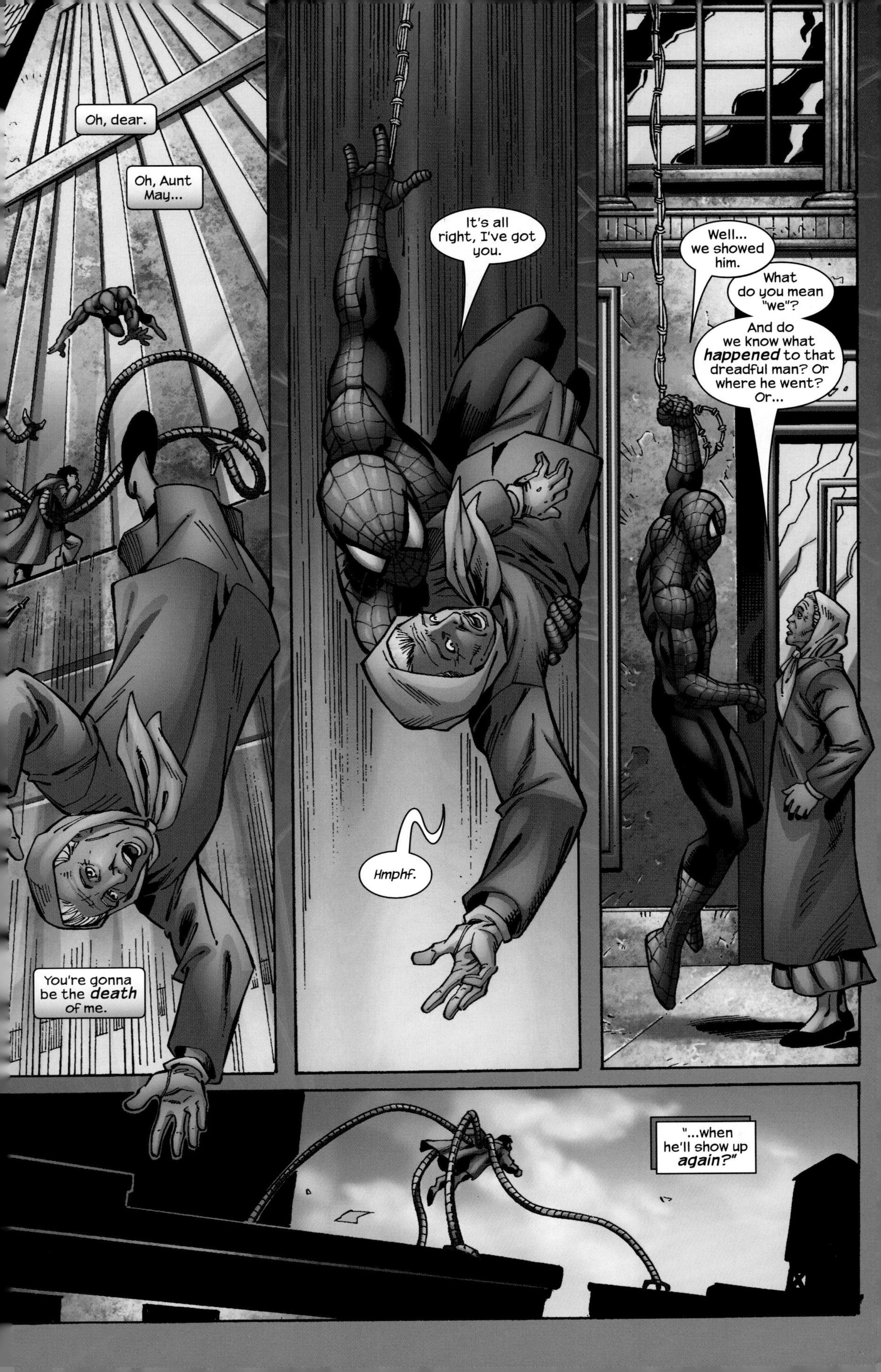
Oh, dear.
Oh, Aunt May...
You're gonna be the death of me.
It's all right, I've got you.
Hmphf.
Well... we showed him.
What do you mean "we"?
And do we know what happened to that dreadful man? Or where he went? Or...
"...when he'll show up again?"

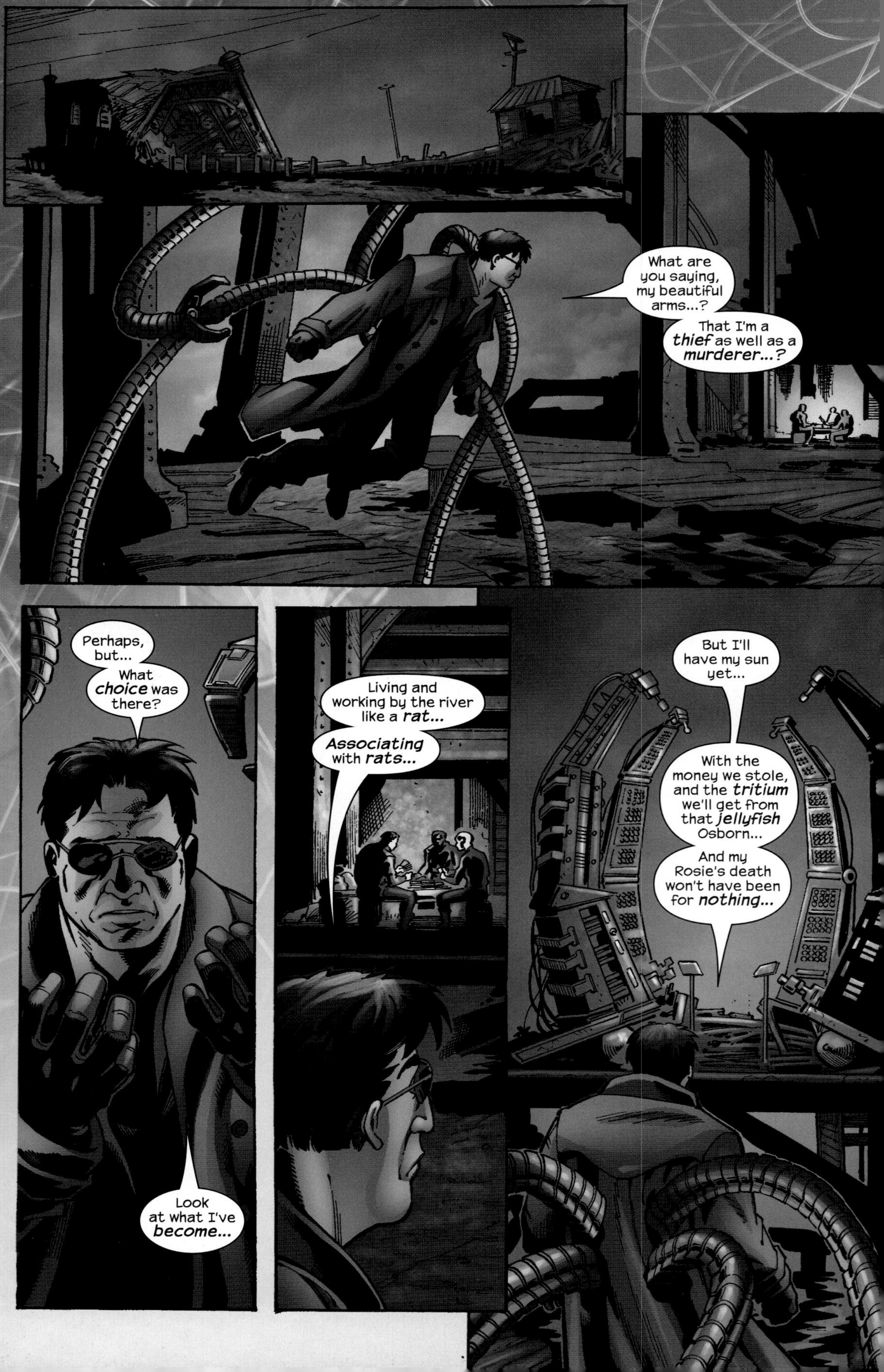
What are you saying, my beautiful arms...?
That I'm a *thief* as well as a *murderer...?*
Perhaps, but...
What *choice* was there?
Look at what I've *become...*
Living and working by the river like a *rat...*
Associating with *rats...*
But I'll have my sun yet...
With the money we stole, and the *tritium* we'll get from that *jellyfish* Osborn...
And my Rosie's death won't have been for *nothing...*

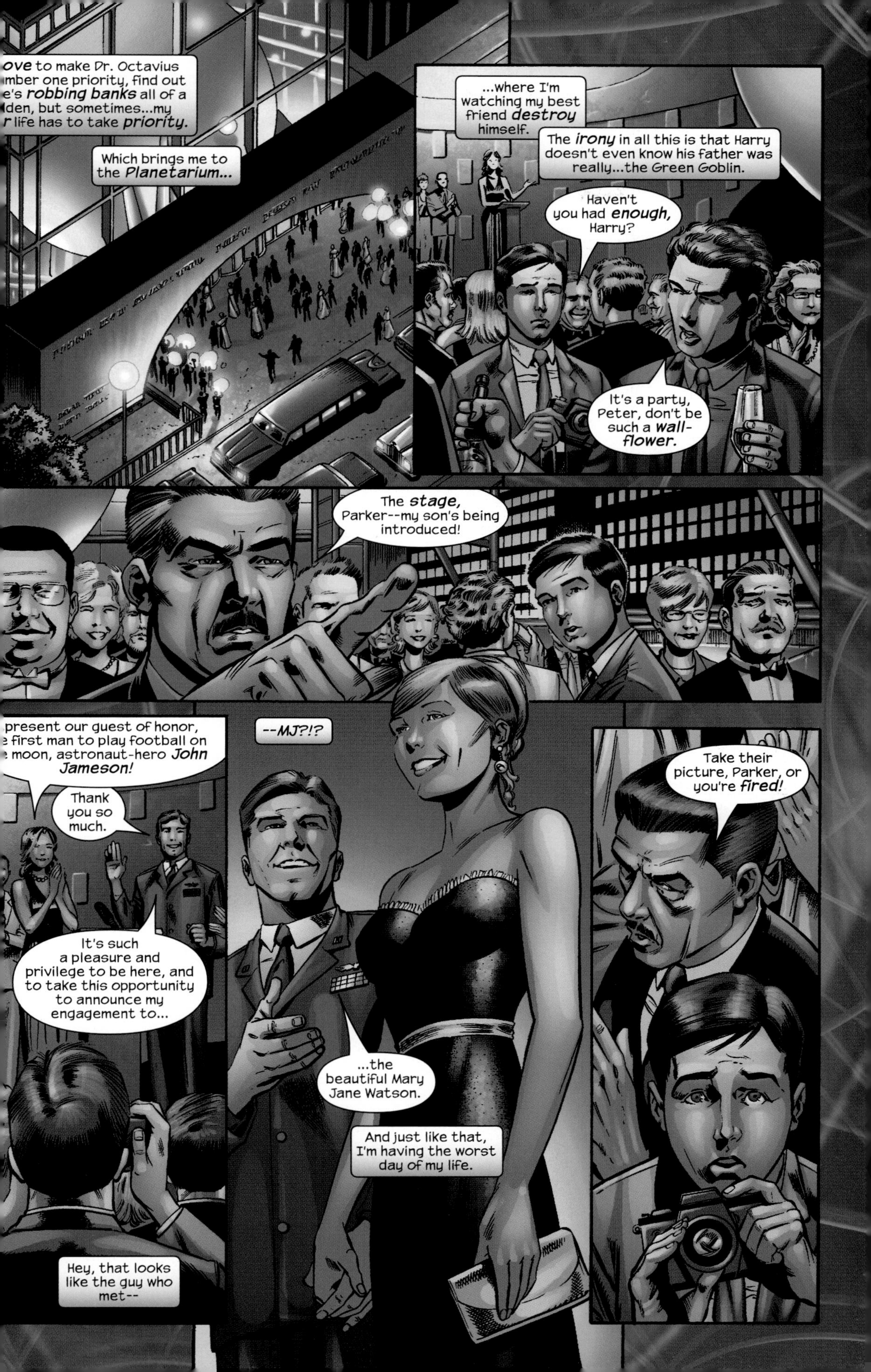

ove to make Dr. Octavius
mber one priority, find out
e's robbing banks all of a
den, but sometimes...my
r life has to take priority.
Which brings me to the Planetarium...
...where I'm watching my best friend destroy himself.
The irony in all this is that Harry doesn't even know his father was really...the Green Goblin.
Haven't you had enough, Harry?
It's a party, Peter, don't be such a wall-flower.
The stage, Parker--my son's being introduced!
present our guest of honor,
e first man to play football on
e moon, astronaut-hero John
Jameson!
Thank you so much.
It's such a pleasure and privilege to be here, and to take this opportunity to announce my engagement to...
Hey, that looks like the guy who met--
--MJ?!?
...the beautiful Mary Jane Watson.
And just like that, I'm having the worst day of my life.
Take their picture, Parker, or you're fired!

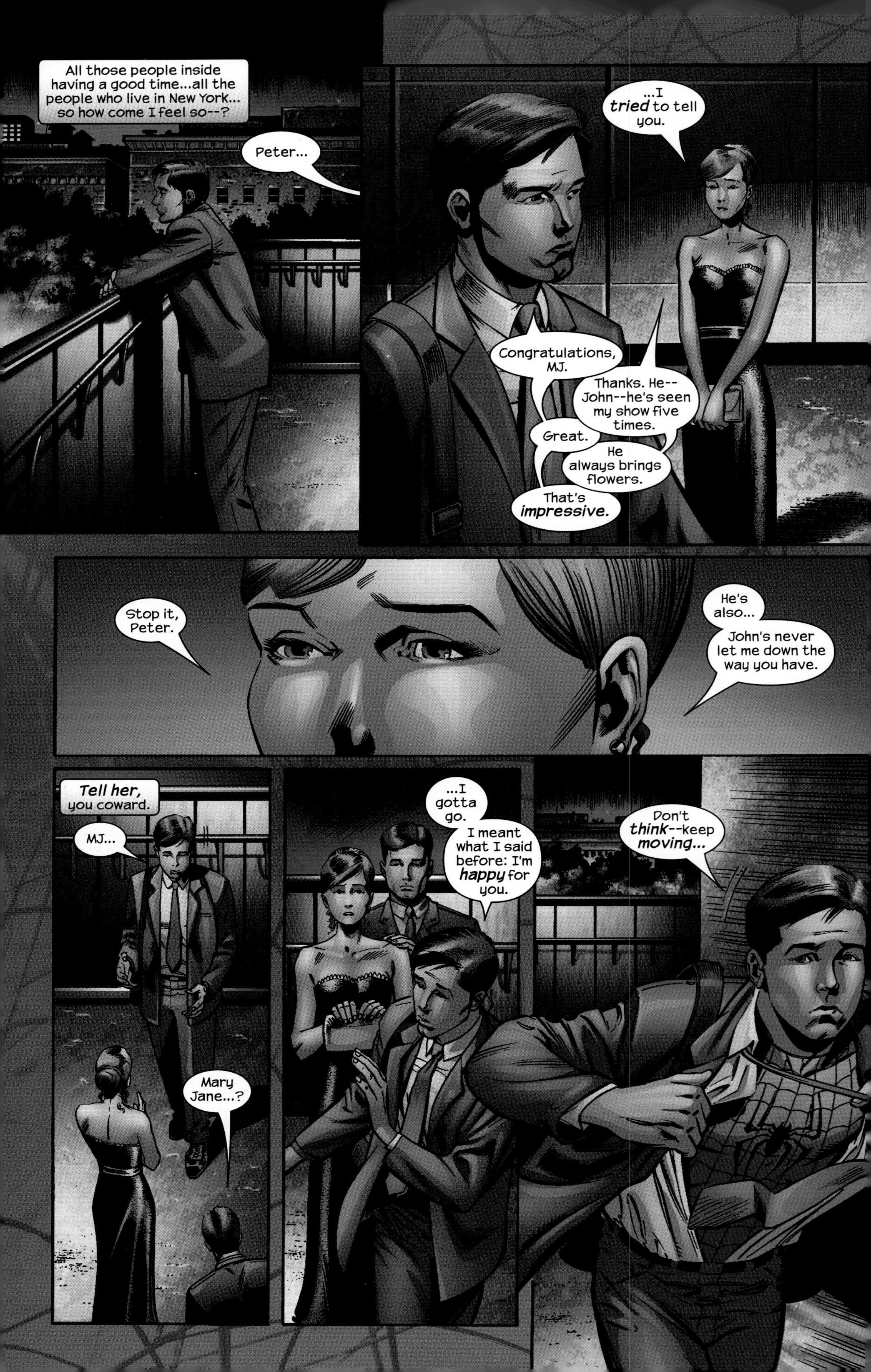
All those people inside having a good time...all the people who live in New York... so how come I feel so--?
Peter...
...I *tried* to tell you.
Congratulations, MJ.
Thanks. He-- John--he's seen my show five times.
Great.
He always brings flowers.
That's *impressive.*
Stop it, Peter.
He's also...
John's never let me down the way you have.
Tell her, you coward.
MJ...
Mary Jane...?
...I gotta go.
I meant what I said before: I'm *happy* for you.
Don't *think*--keep *moving...*

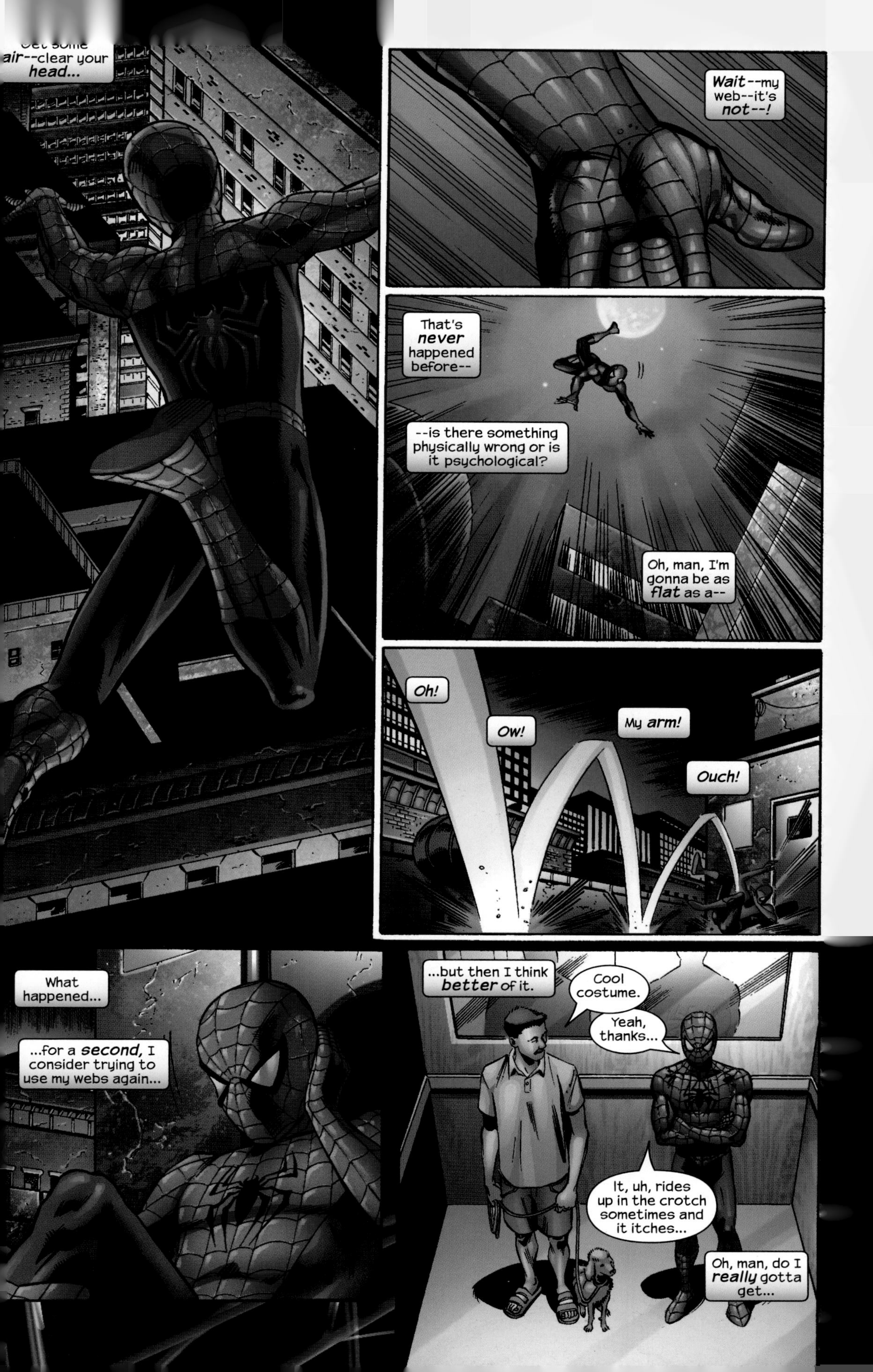
air--clear your head...
Wait--my web--it's not--!
That's never happened before--
--is there something physically wrong or is it psychological?
Oh, man, I'm gonna be as flat as a--
Oh!
Ow!
My arm!
Ouch!
What happened...
...for a second, I consider trying to use my webs again...
...but then I think better of it.
Cool costume.
Yeah, thanks...
It, uh, rides up in the crotch sometimes and it itches...
Oh, man, do I really gotta get...

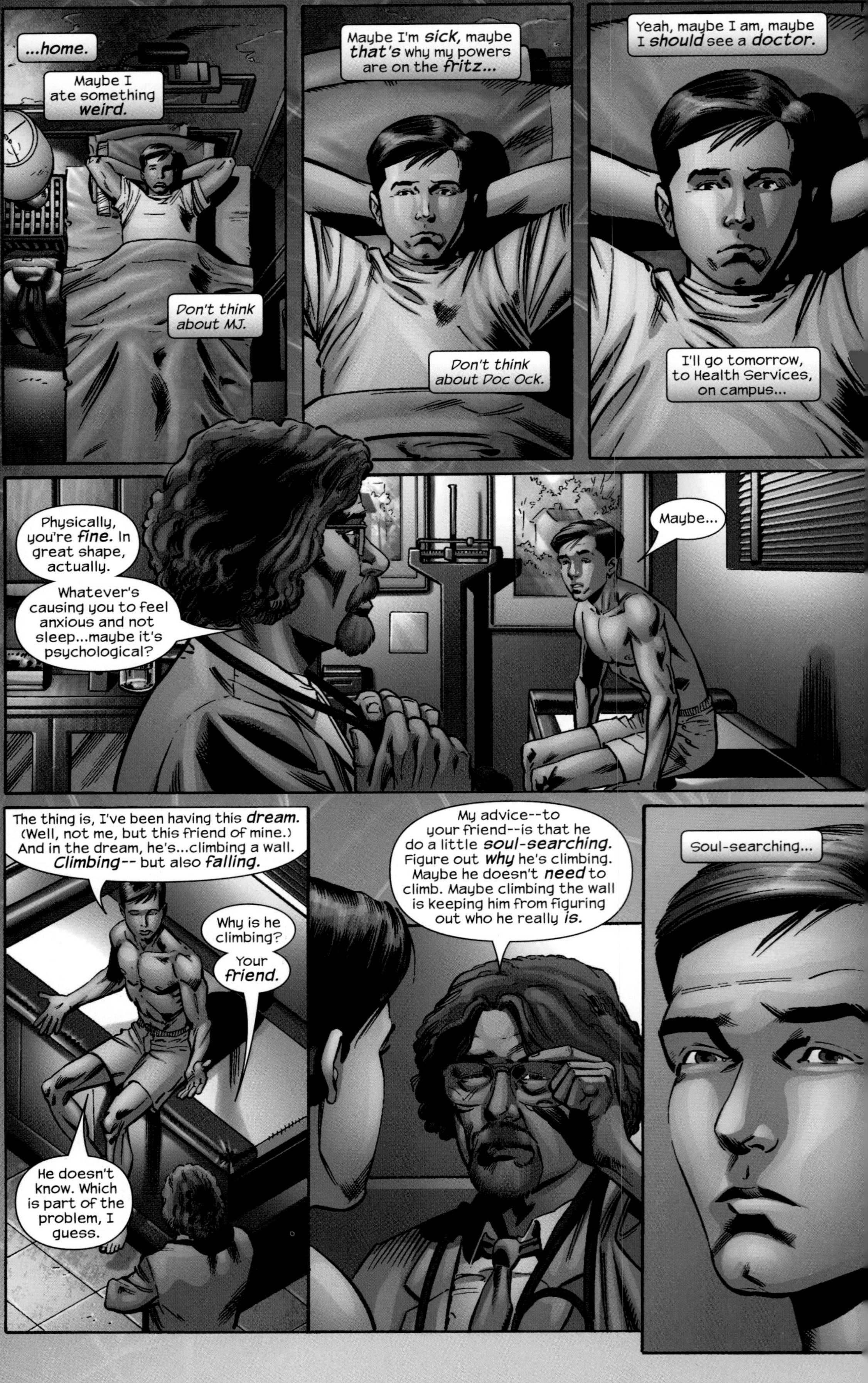

...home.
Maybe I ate something weird.
Don't think about MJ.
Maybe I'm sick, maybe that's why my powers are on the fritz...
Don't think about Doc Ock.
Yeah, maybe I am, maybe I should see a doctor.
I'll go tomorrow, to Health Services, on campus...
Physically, you're fine. In great shape, actually.
Whatever's causing you to feel anxious and not sleep...maybe it's psychological?
Maybe...
The thing is, I've been having this dream. (Well, not me, but this friend of mine.) And in the dream, he's...climbing a wall. Climbing-- but also falling.
Why is he climbing?
Your friend.
He doesn't know. Which is part of the problem, I guess.
My advice--to your friend--is that he do a little soul-searching. Figure out why he's climbing. Maybe he doesn't need to climb. Maybe climbing the wall is keeping him from figuring out who he really is.
Soul-searching...

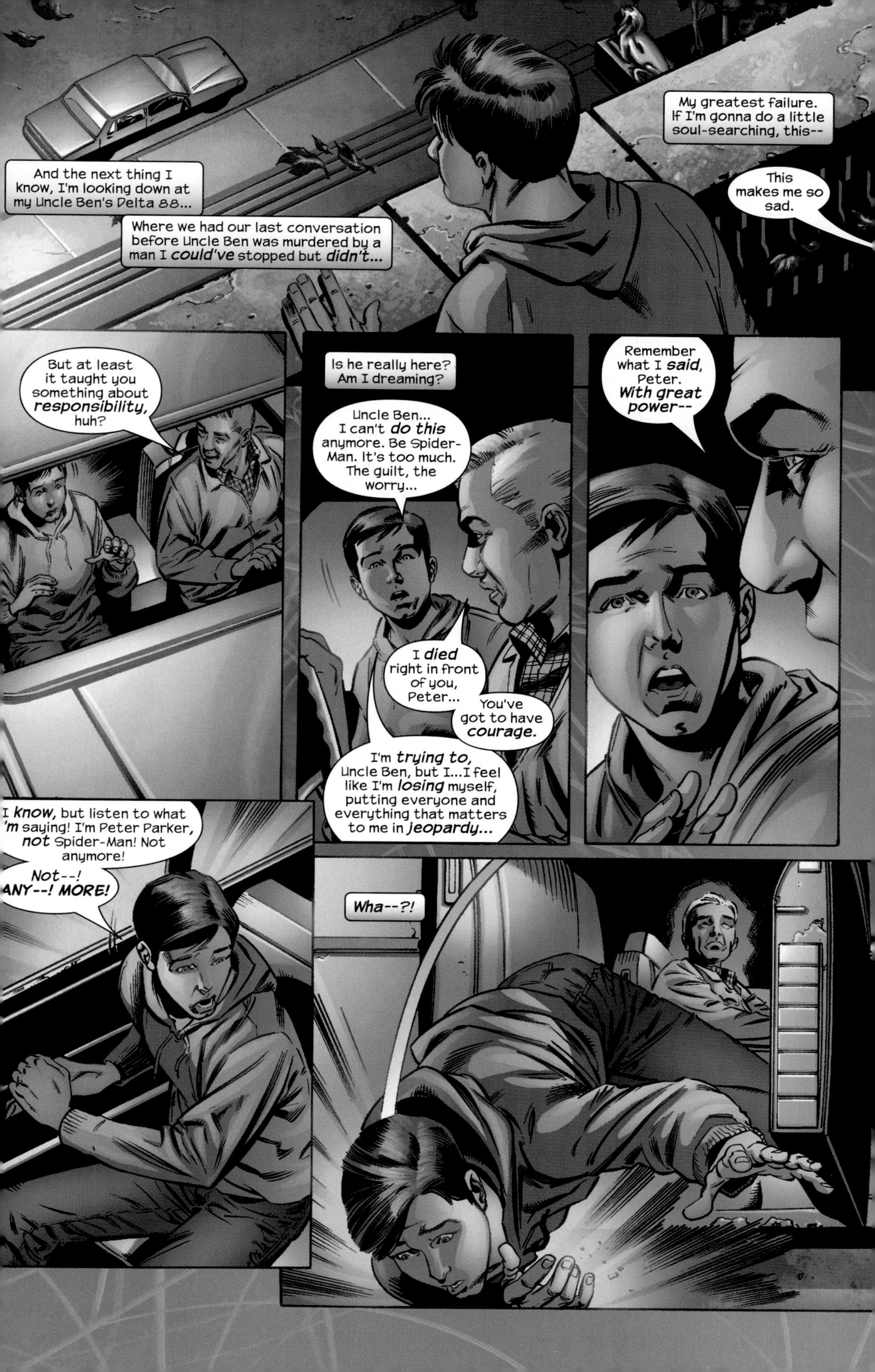
And the next thing I know, I'm looking down at my Uncle Ben's Delta 88...
Where we had our last conversation before Uncle Ben was murdered by a man I could've stopped but didn't...
My greatest failure. If I'm gonna do a little soul-searching, this--
This makes me so sad.
But at least it taught you something about responsibility, huh?
Is he really here? Am I dreaming?
Uncle Ben... I can't do this anymore. Be Spider-Man. It's too much. The guilt, the worry...
I died right in front of you, Peter...
You've got to have courage.
I'm trying to, Uncle Ben, but I...I feel like I'm losing myself, putting everyone and everything that matters to me in jeopardy...
Remember what I said, Peter. With great power--
I know, but listen to what I'm saying! I'm Peter Parker, not Spider-Man! Not anymore!
Not--! ANY--! MORE!
Wha--?!

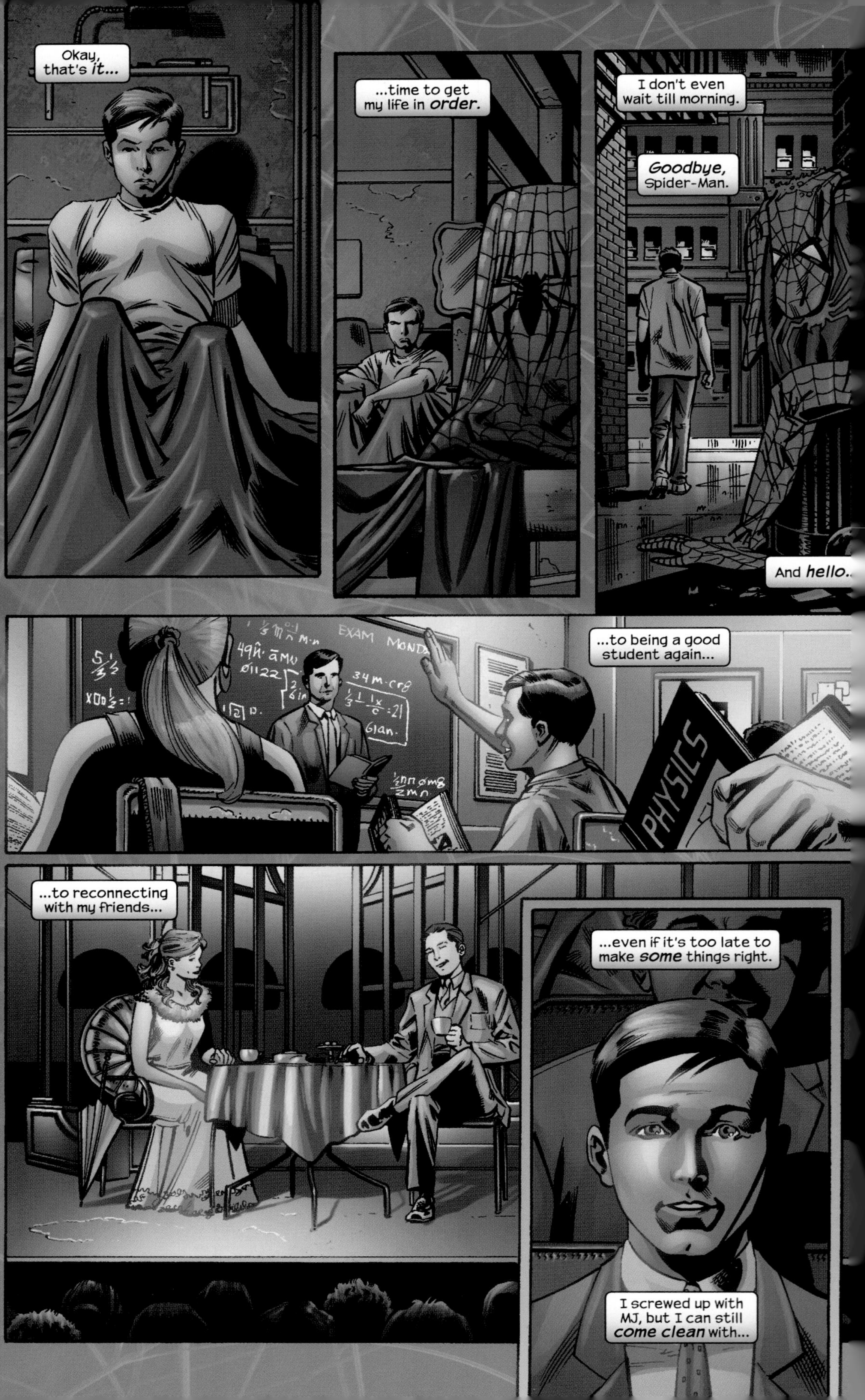
Okay, that's *it*...
...time to get my life in *order*.
I don't even wait till morning.
Goodbye, Spider-Man.
And *hello*...
...to being a good student again...
EXAM MONDA
PHYSICS
...to reconnecting with my friends...
...even if it's too late to make *some* things right.
I screwed up with MJ, but I can still *come clean* with...

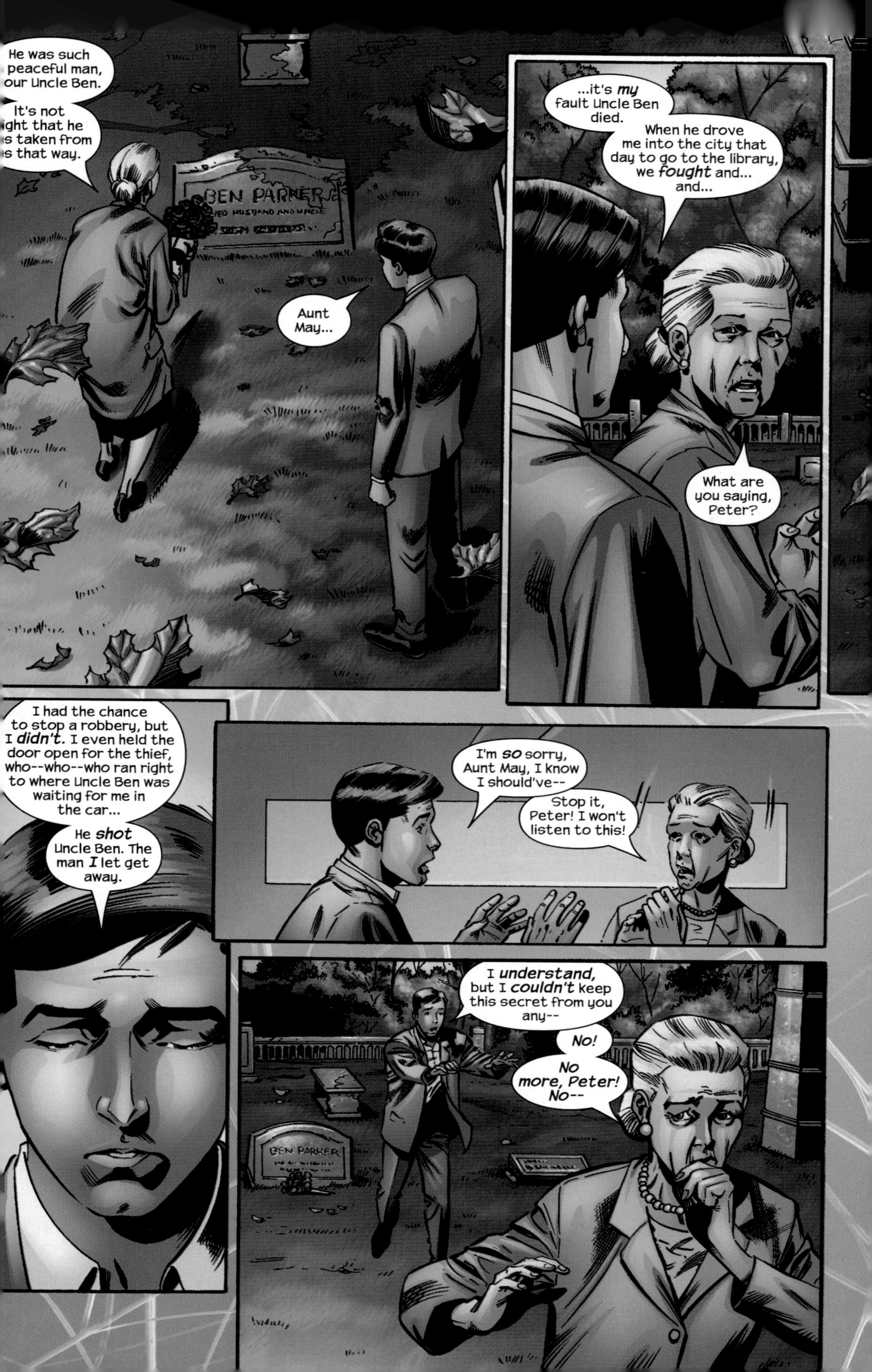
He was such peaceful man, our Uncle Ben.
It's not ight that he s taken from s that way.
BEN PARKER
Aunt May...
...it's *my* fault Uncle Ben died.
When he drove me into the city that day to go to the library, we *fought* and... and...
What are you saying, Peter?
I had the chance to stop a robbery, but I *didn't*. I even held the door open for the thief, who--who--who ran right to where Uncle Ben was waiting for me in the car...
He *shot* Uncle Ben. The man *I* let get away.
I'm *so* sorry, Aunt May, I know I should've--
Stop it, Peter! I won't listen to this!
I *understand*, but I *couldn't* keep this secret from you any--
BEN PARKER
No!
No more, Peter! No--

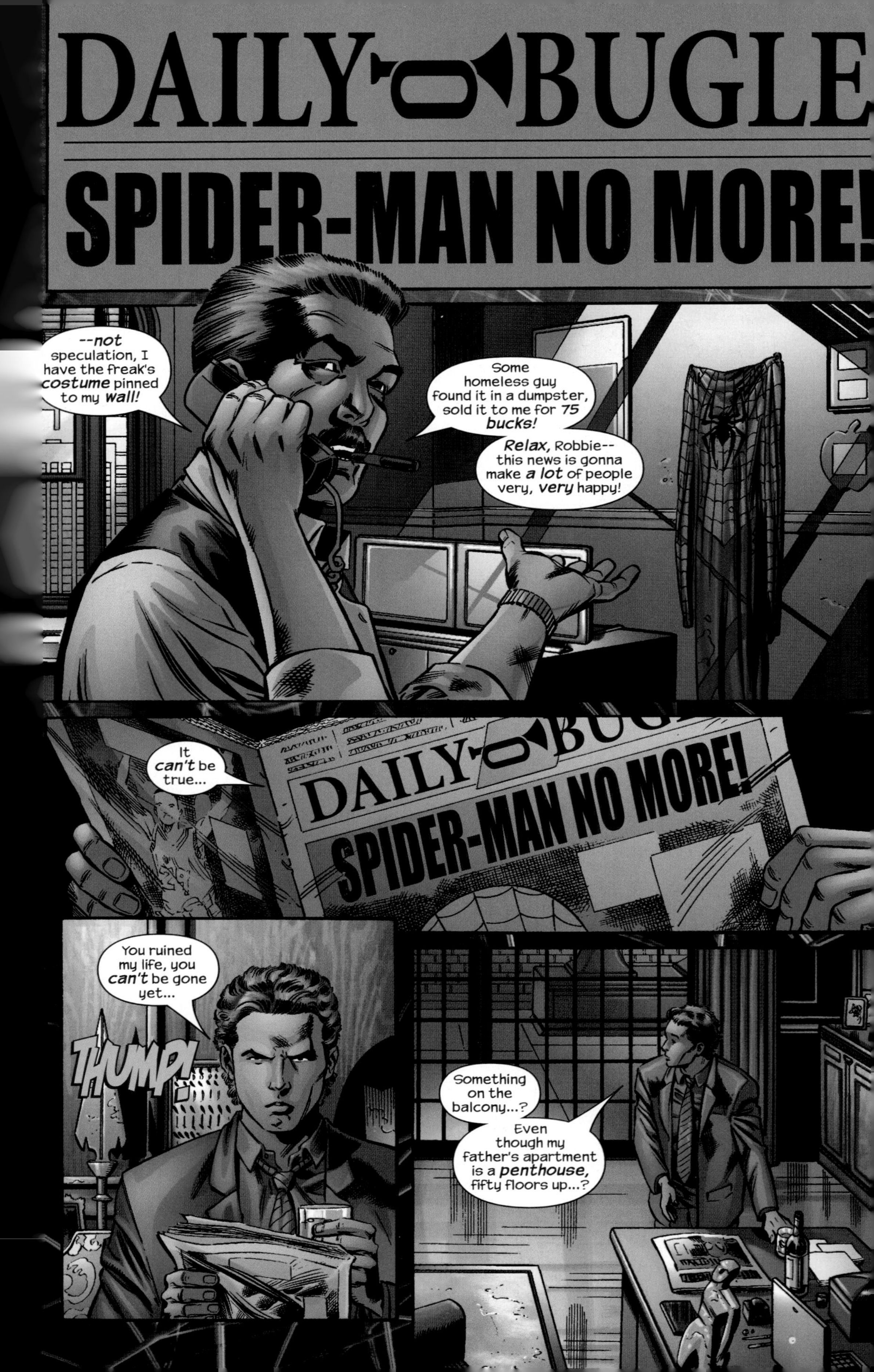

DAILY BUGLE
SPIDER-MAN NO MORE!
--not speculation, I have the freak's costume pinned to my wall!
Some homeless guy found it in a dumpster, sold it to me for 75 bucks!
Relax, Robbie-- this news is gonna make a lot of people very, very happy!
It can't be true...
DAILY BUGLE
SPIDER-MAN NO MORE!
You ruined my life, you can't be gone yet...
THUMP!
Something on the balcony...?
Even though my father's apartment is a penthouse, fifty floors up...?

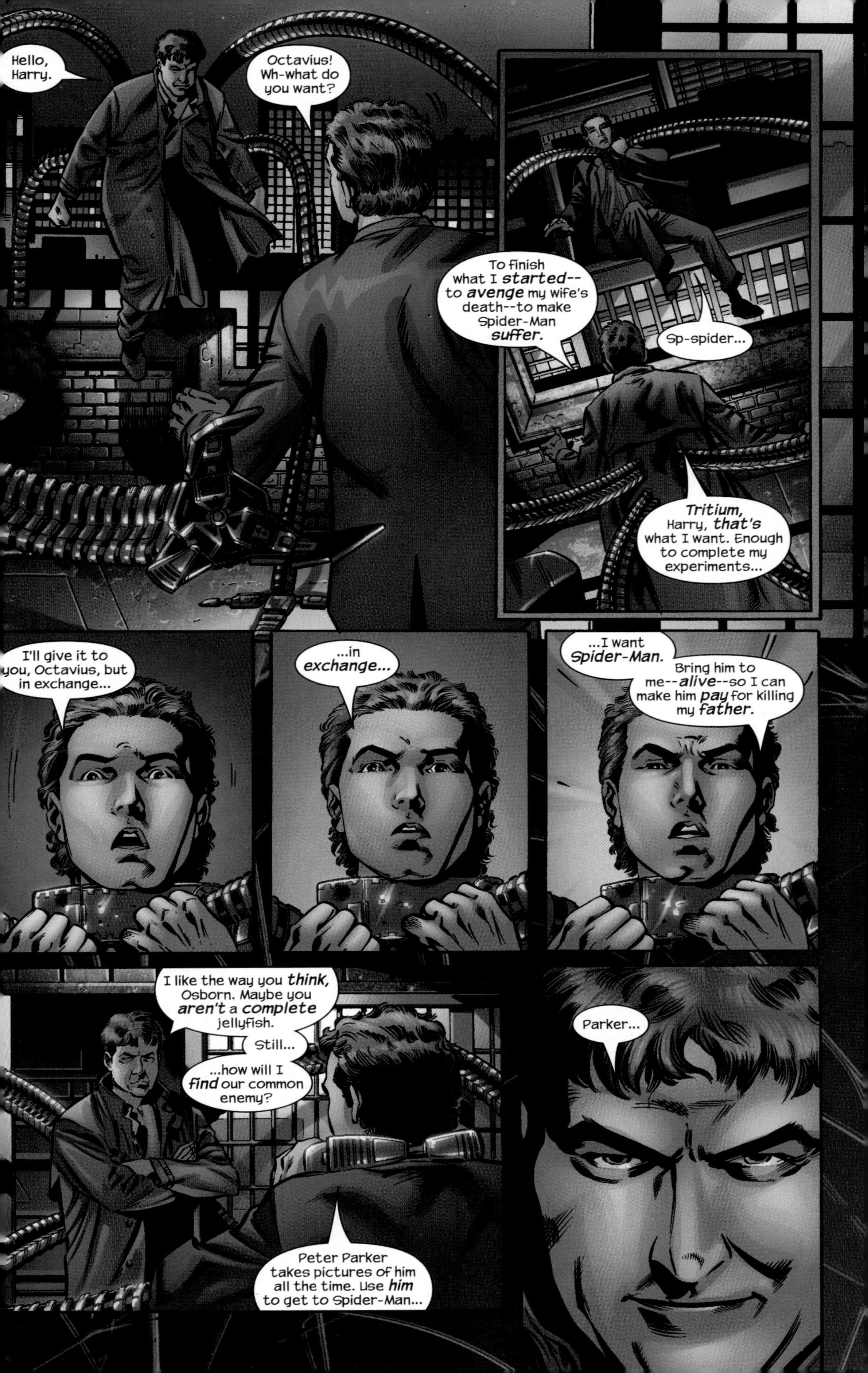

Hello, Harry.
Octavius! Wh-what do you want?
To finish what I *started*--to *avenge* my wife's death--to make Spider-Man *suffer*.
Sp-spider...
Tritium, Harry, *that's* what I want. Enough to complete my experiments...
I'll give it to you, Octavius, but in exchange...
...in *exchange*...
...I want *Spider-Man*.
Bring him to me--*alive*--so I can make him *pay* for killing my *father*.
I like the way you *think*, Osborn. Maybe you *aren't* a *complete* jellyfish.
Still...
...how will I *find* our common enemy?
Peter Parker takes pictures of him all the time. Use *him* to get to Spider-Man...
Parker...

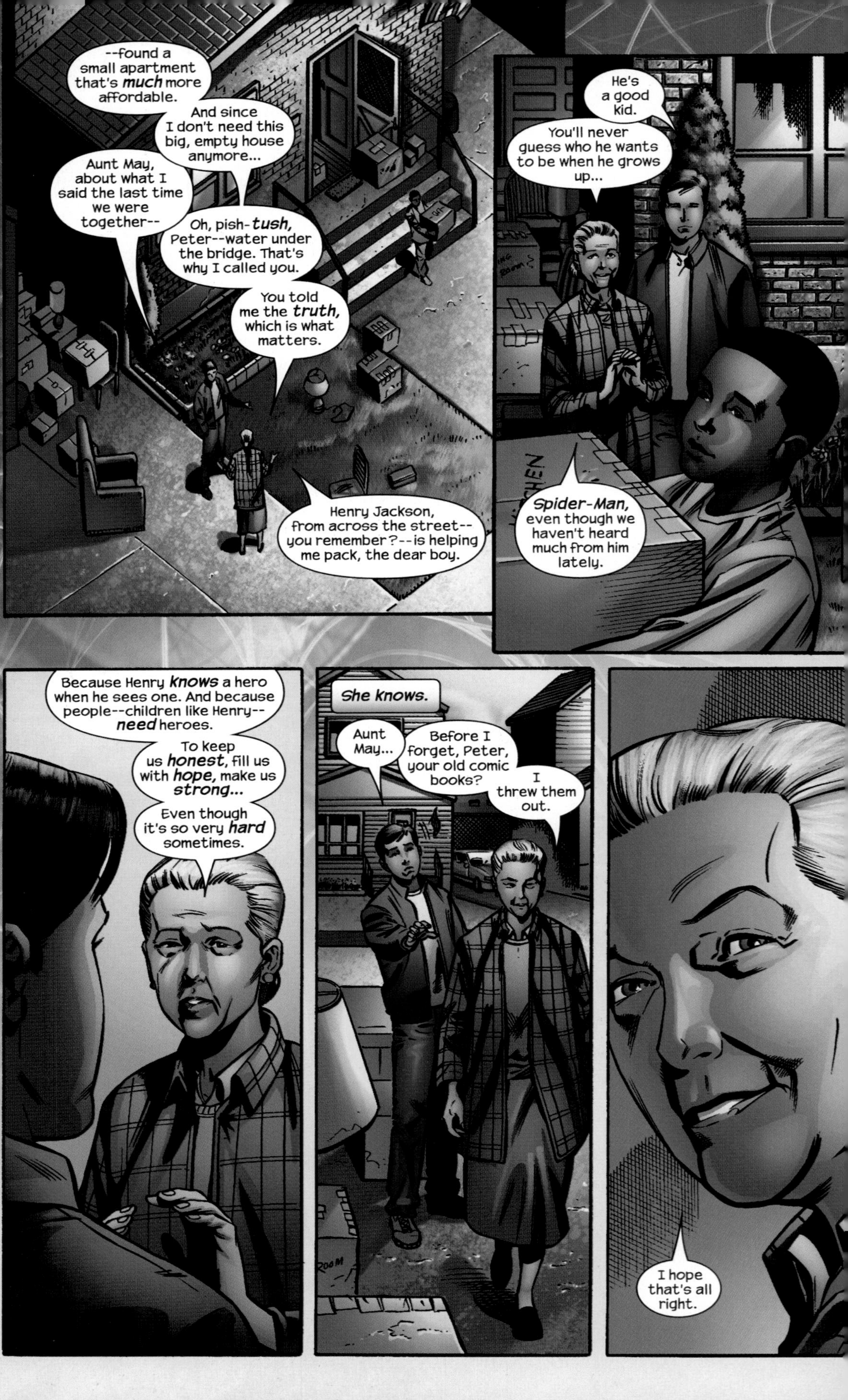
--found a small apartment that's *much* more affordable.
And since I don't need this big, empty house anymore...
Aunt May, about what I said the last time we were together--
Oh, pish-*tush,* Peter--water under the bridge. That's why I called you.
You told me the *truth,* which is what matters.
Henry Jackson, from across the street--you remember?--is helping me pack, the dear boy.
He's a good kid.
You'll never guess who he wants to be when he grows up...
Spider-Man, even though we haven't heard much from him lately.
Because Henry *knows* a hero when he sees one. And because people--children like Henry--*need* heroes.
To keep us *honest,* fill us with *hope,* make us *strong...*
Even though it's so very *hard* sometimes.
She knows.
Aunt May...
Before I forget, Peter, your old comic books?
I threw them out.
I hope that's all right.

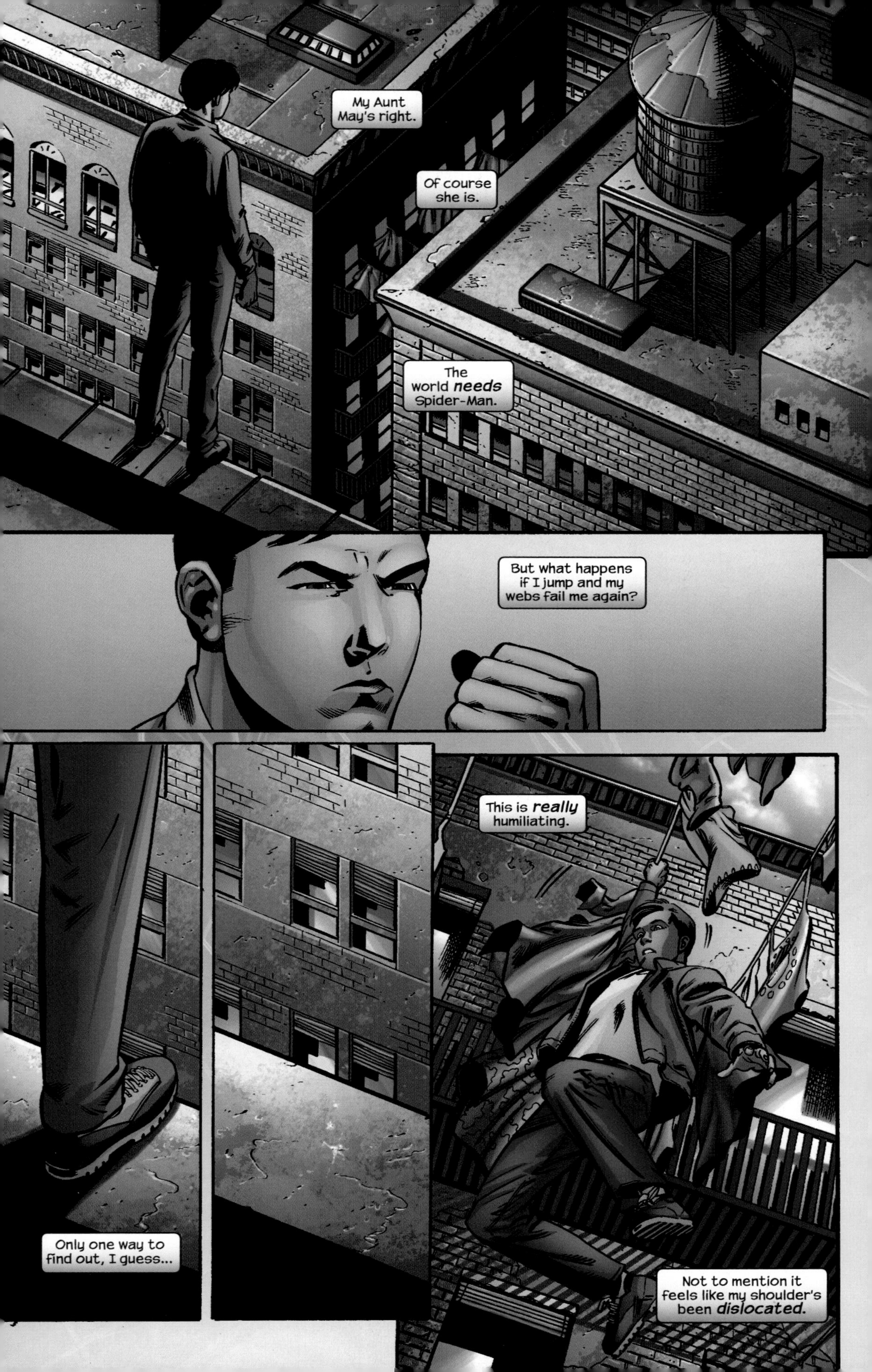
My Aunt May's right.
Of course she is.
The world *needs* Spider-Man.
But what happens if I jump and my webs fail me again?
Only one way to find out, I guess...
This is *really* humiliating.
Not to mention it feels like my shoulder's been *dislocated.*

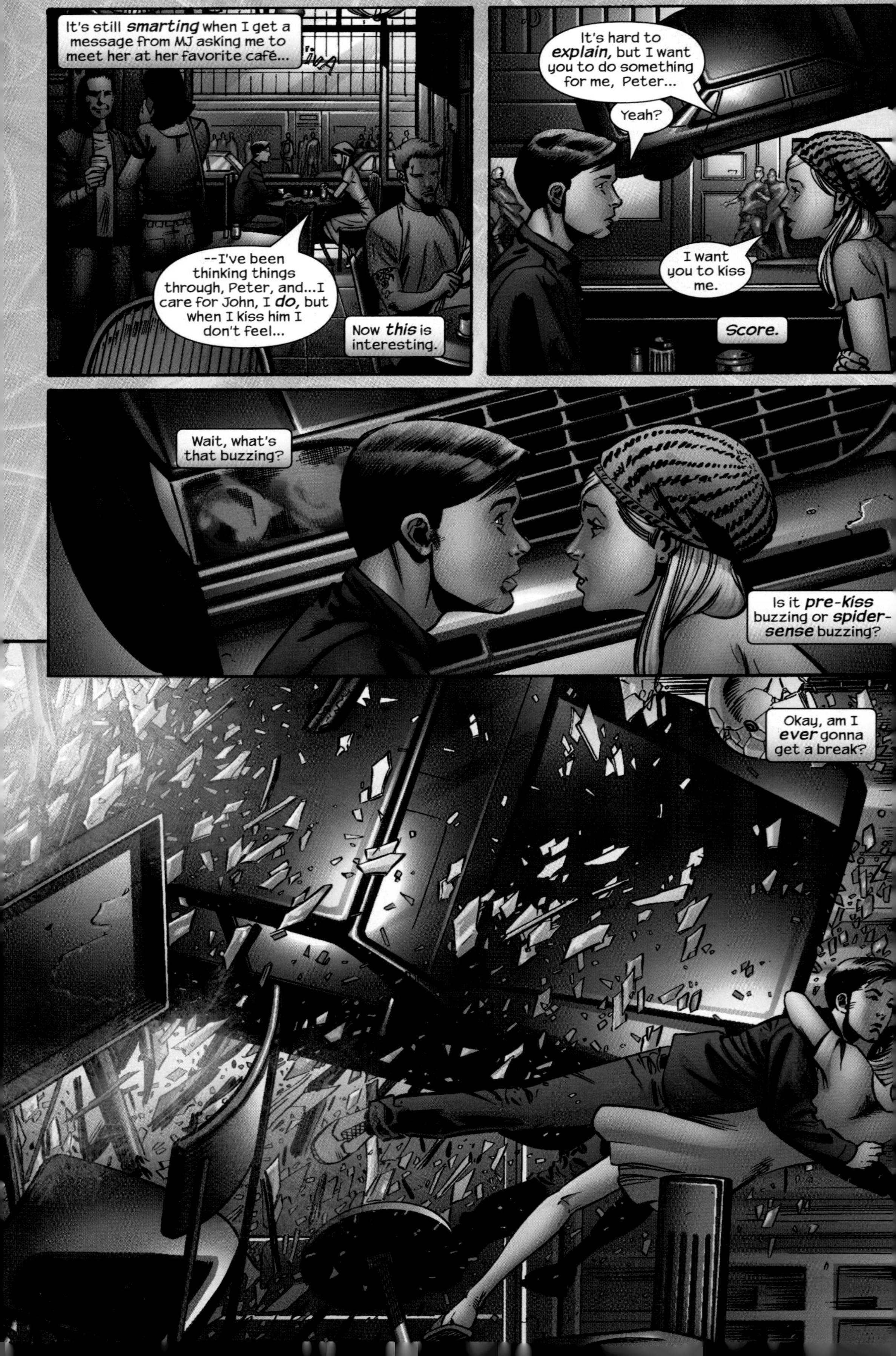

It's still *smarting* when I get a message from MJ asking me to meet her at her favorite café...
--I've been thinking things through, Peter, and...I care for John, I *do,* but when I kiss him I don't feel...
Now *this* is interesting.
It's hard to *explain,* but I want you to do something for me, Peter...
Yeah?
I want you to kiss me.
Score.
Wait, what's that buzzing?
Is it *pre-kiss* buzzing or *spider-sense* buzzing?
Okay, am I *ever* gonna get a break?

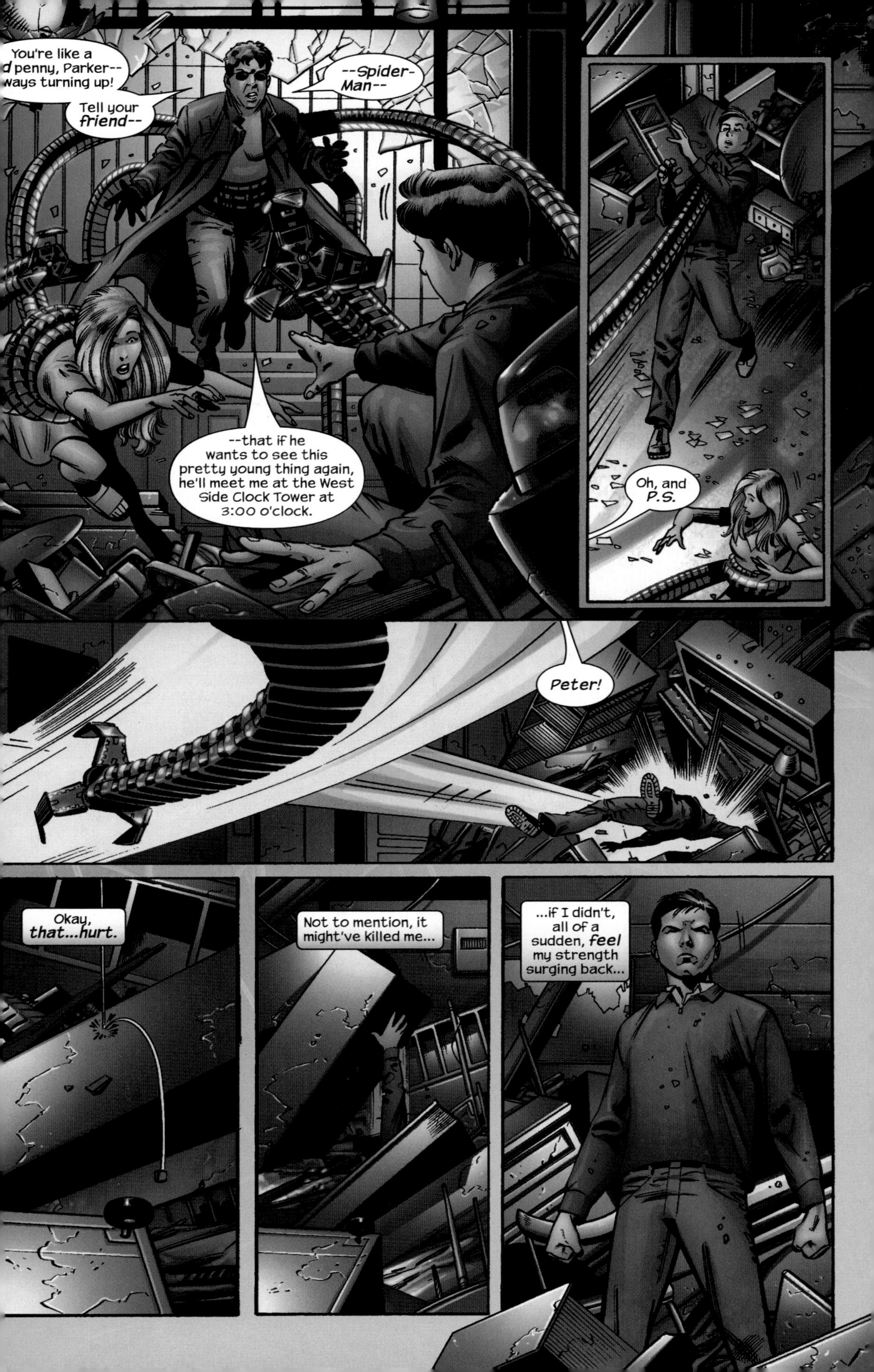
You're like a d penny, Parker-- ways turning up!
Tell your friend--
--Spider-Man--
--that if he wants to see this pretty young thing again, he'll meet me at the West Side Clock Tower at 3:00 o'clock.
Oh, and P.S.
Peter!
Okay, that...hurt.
Not to mention, it might've killed me...
...if I didn't, all of a sudden, feel my strength surging back...

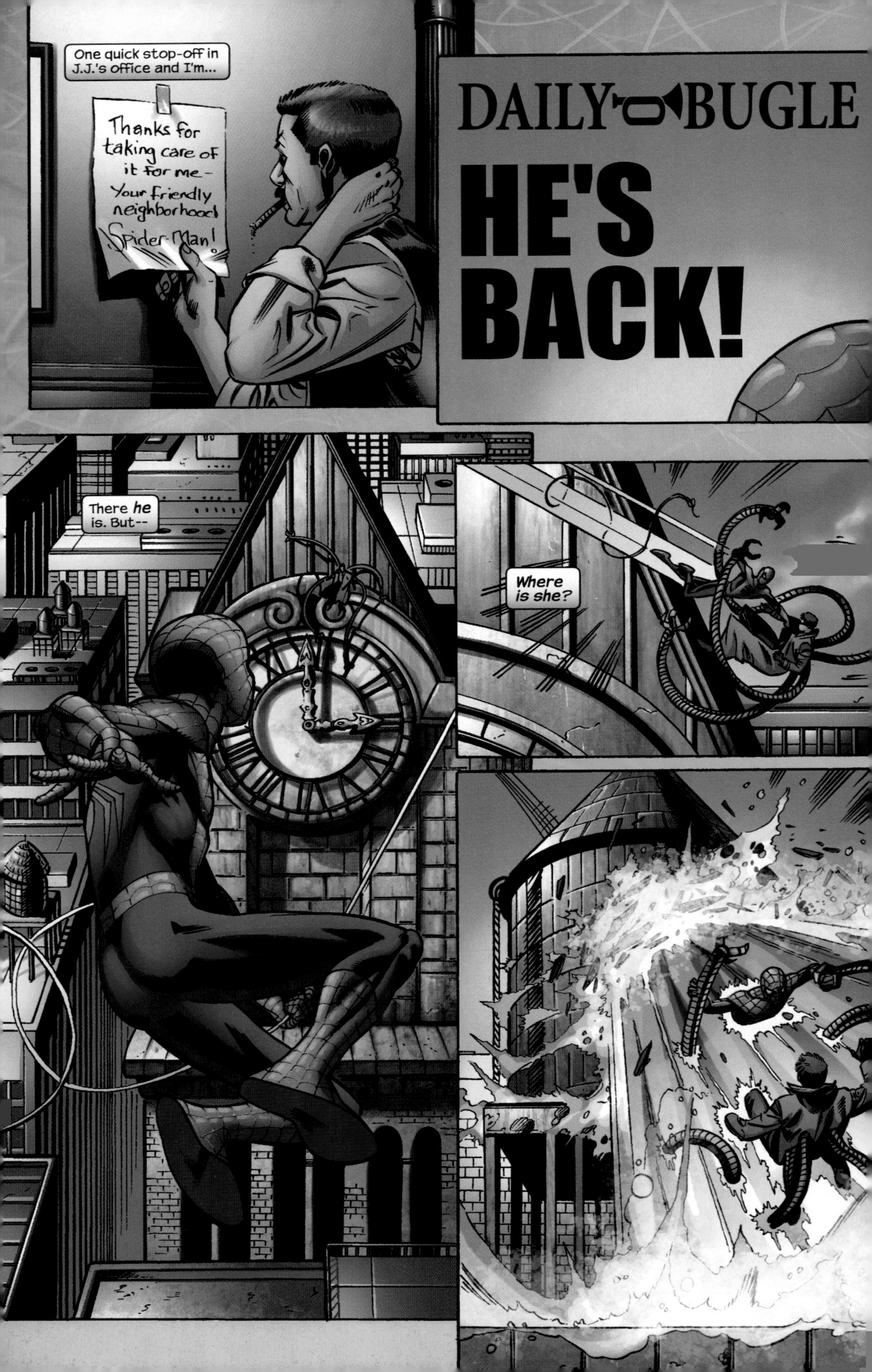
One quick stop-off in J.J.'s office and I'm...
Thanks for taking care of it for me - Your friendly neighborhood Spider-Man!
DAILY BUGLE
HE'S BACK!
There *he* is. But--
Where is she?

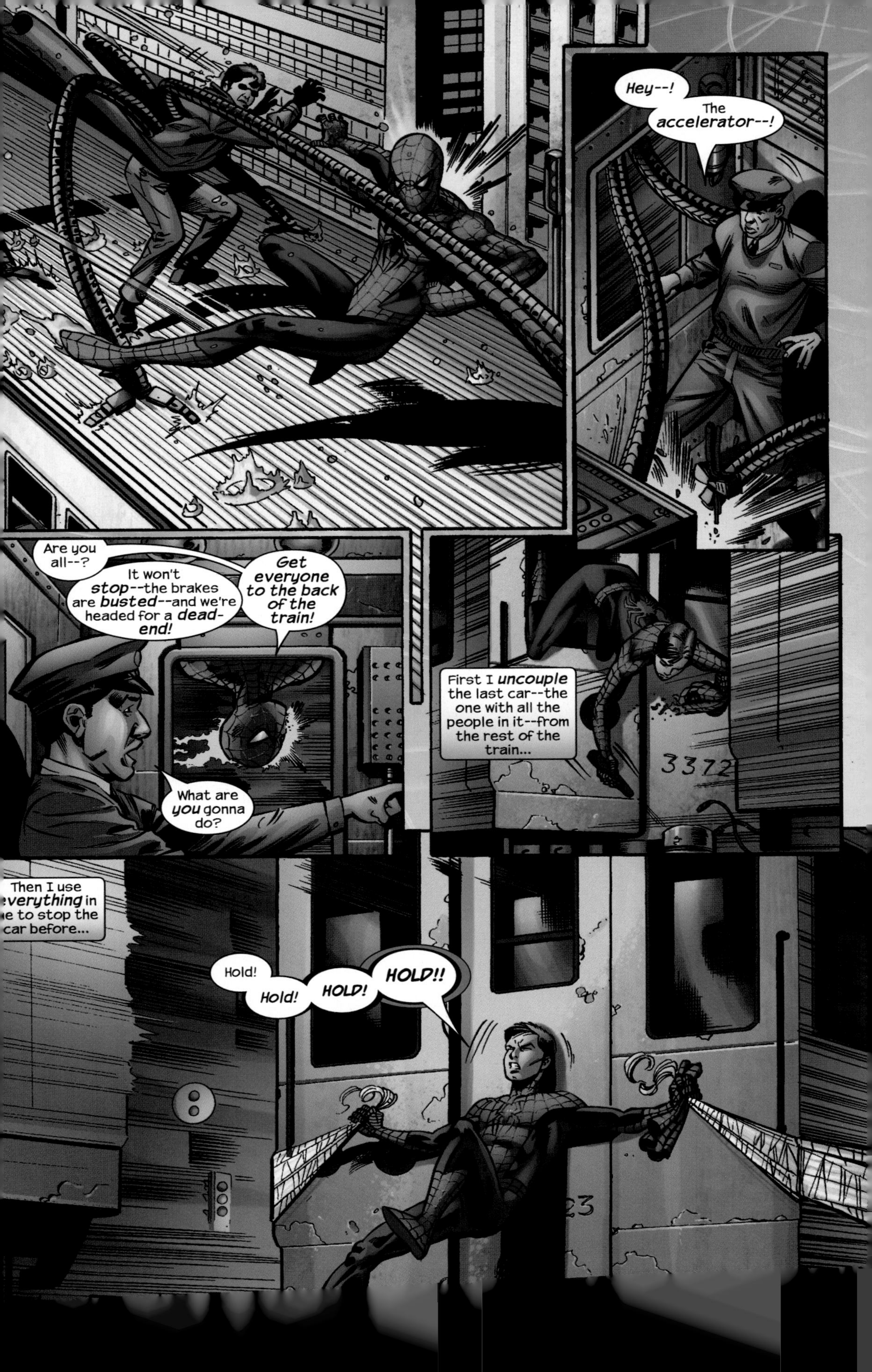
Hey--!
The accelerator--!
Are you all--?
It won't stop--the brakes are busted--and we're headed for a dead-end!
Get everyone to the back of the train!
What are you gonna do?
First I uncouple the last car--the one with all the people in it--from the rest of the train...
3372
Then I use everything in
e to stop the car before...
Hold!
Hold!
HOLD!
HOLD!!
23

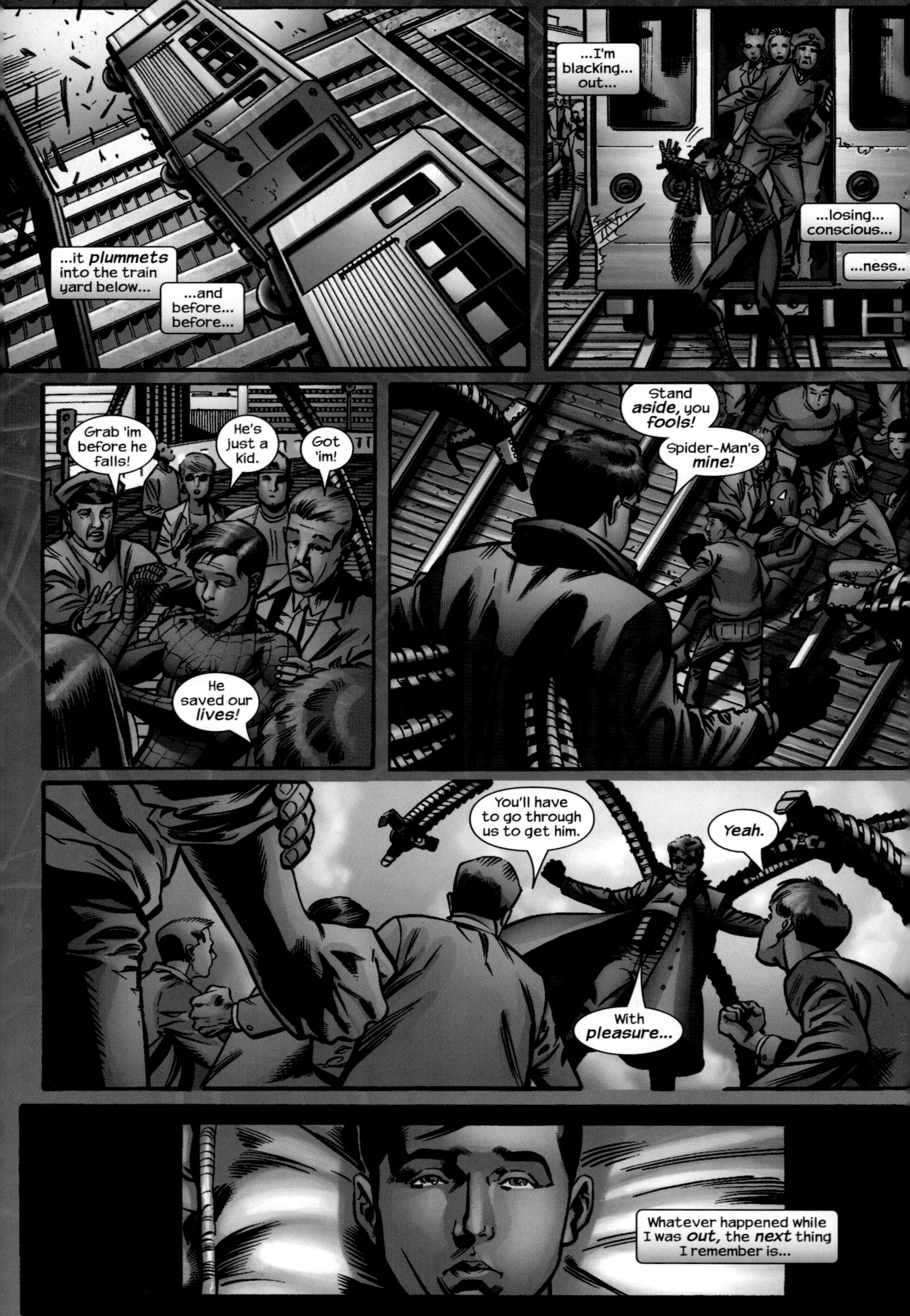
...it plummets into the train yard below...
...and before... before...
...I'm blacking... out...
...losing... conscious...
...ness...
Grab 'im before he falls!
He's just a kid.
Got 'im!
He saved our lives!
Stand aside, you fools!
Spider-Man's mine!
You'll have to go through us to get him.
Yeah.
With pleasure...
Whatever happened while I was out, the next thing I remember is...

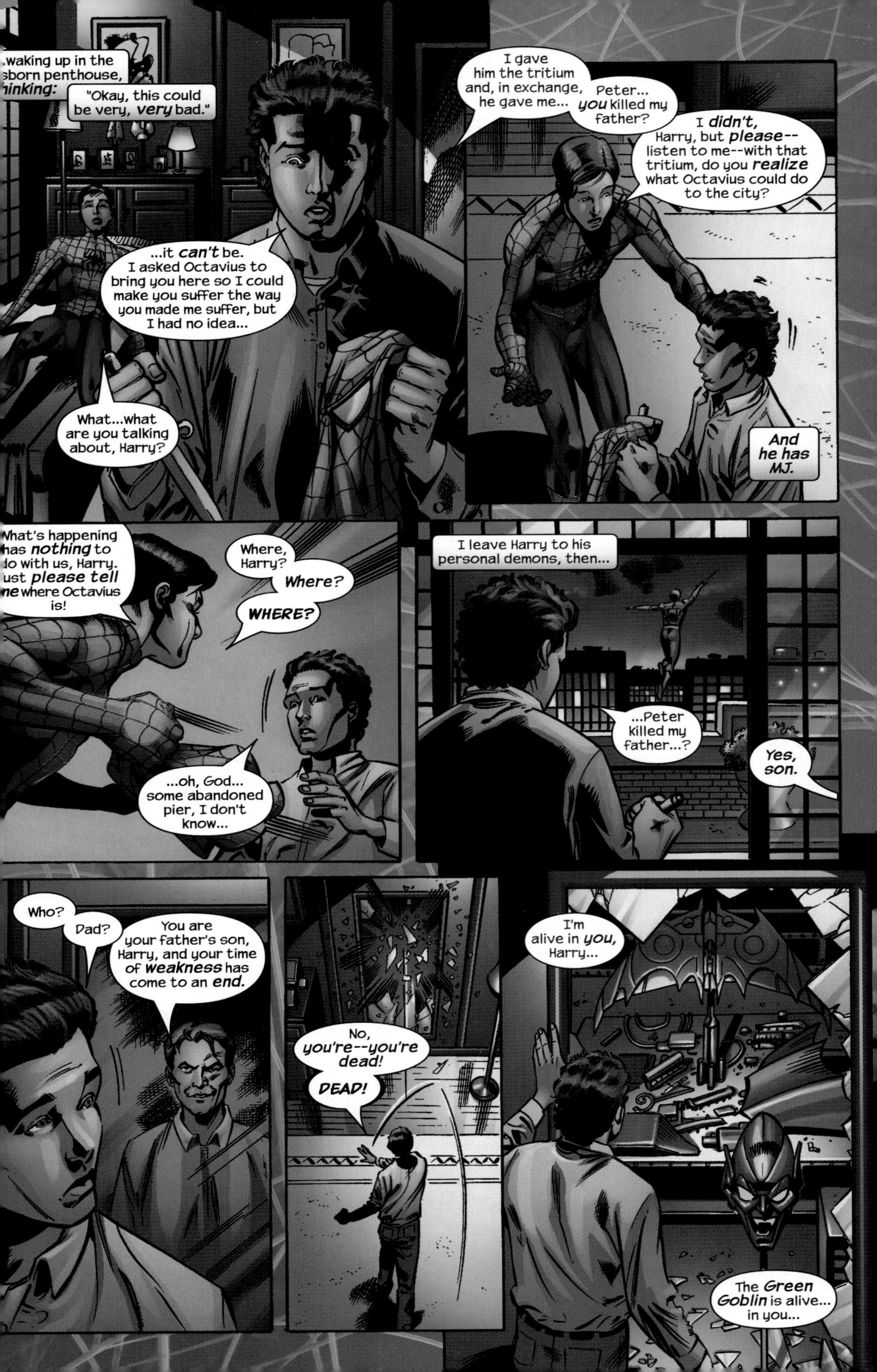

...waking up in the ...sborn penthouse, ...hinking:
"Okay, this could be very, very bad."
...it can't be. I asked Octavius to bring you here so I could make you suffer the way you made me suffer, but I had no idea...
What...what are you talking about, Harry?
I gave him the tritium and, in exchange, he gave me...
Peter... you killed my father?
I didn't, Harry, but please-- listen to me--with that tritium, do you realize what Octavius could do to the city?
And he has MJ.
...hat's happening ...has nothing to ...o with us, Harry. ...ust please tell ...ne where Octavius is!
Where, Harry?
Where?
WHERE?
...oh, God... some abandoned pier, I don't know...
I leave Harry to his personal demons, then...
...Peter killed my father...?
Yes, son.
Who?
Dad?
You are your father's son, Harry, and your time of weakness has come to an end.
No, you're--you're dead!
DEAD!
I'm alive in you, Harry...
The Green Goblin is alive... in you...

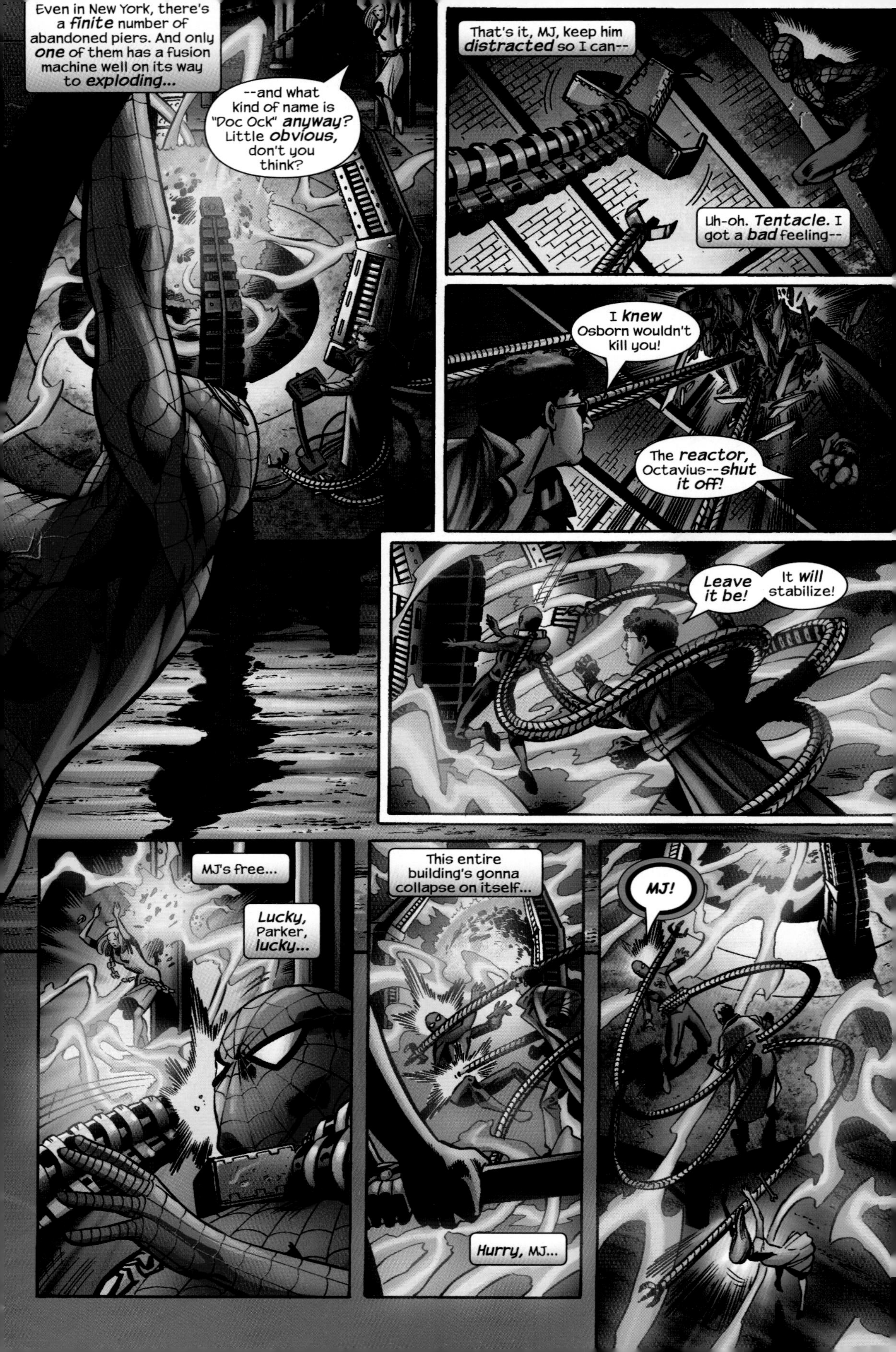

Even in New York, there's a finite number of abandoned piers. And only one of them has a fusion machine well on its way to exploding...
--and what kind of name is "Doc Ock" anyway? Little obvious, don't you think?
That's it, MJ, keep him distracted so I can--
Uh-oh. Tentacle. I got a bad feeling--
I knew Osborn wouldn't kill you!
The reactor, Octavius--shut it off!
Leave it be!
It will stabilize!
MJ's free...
Lucky, Parker, lucky...
This entire building's gonna collapse on itself...
Hurry, MJ...
MJ!

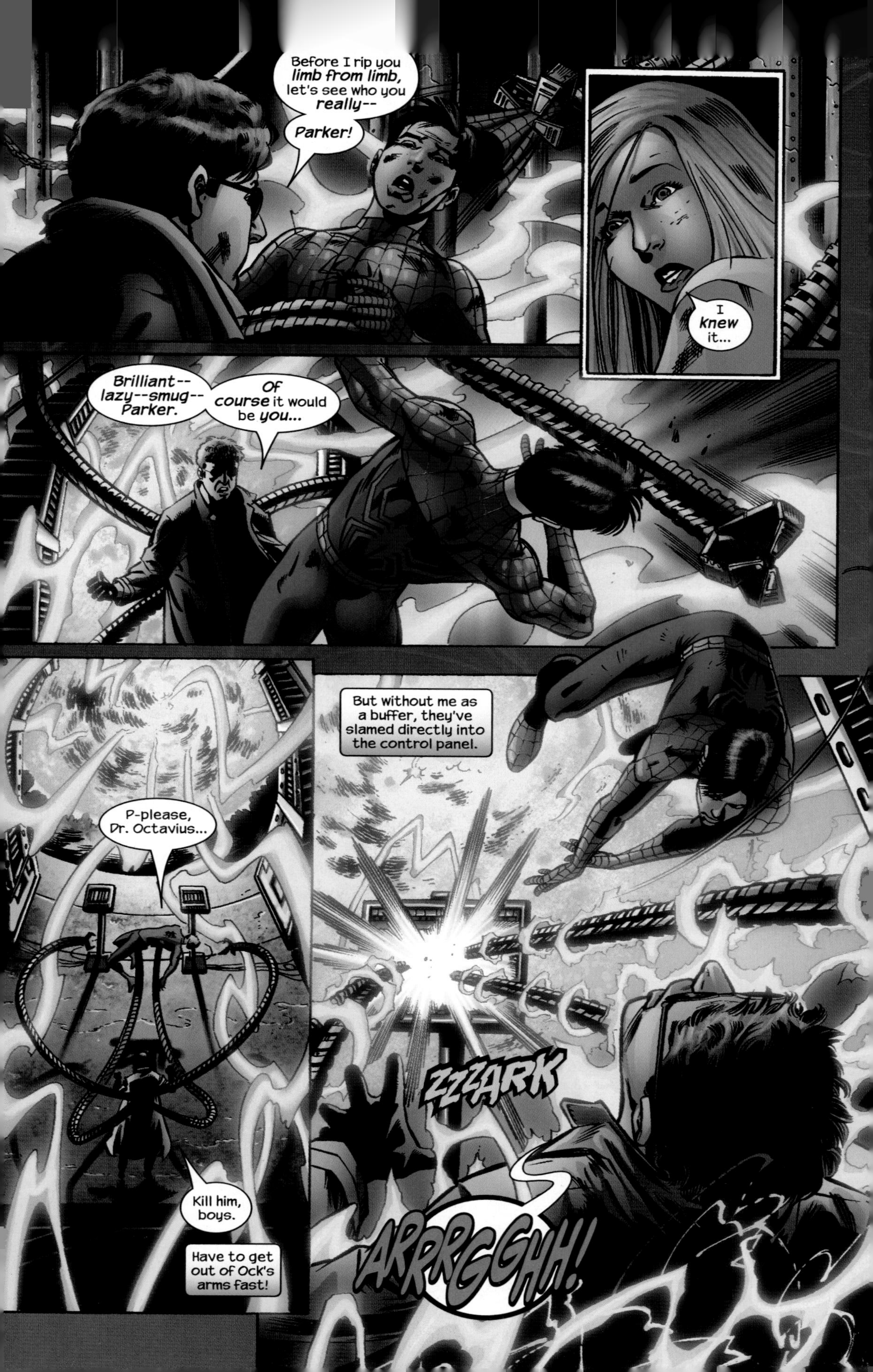
Before I rip you limb from limb, let's see who you really--
Parker!
I knew it...
Brilliant--lazy--smug--Parker.
Of course it would be you...
P-please, Dr. Octavius...
Kill him, boys.
Have to get out of Ock's arms fast!
But without me as a buffer, they've slamed directly into the control panel.
ZZZARK
ARRRGGHH!

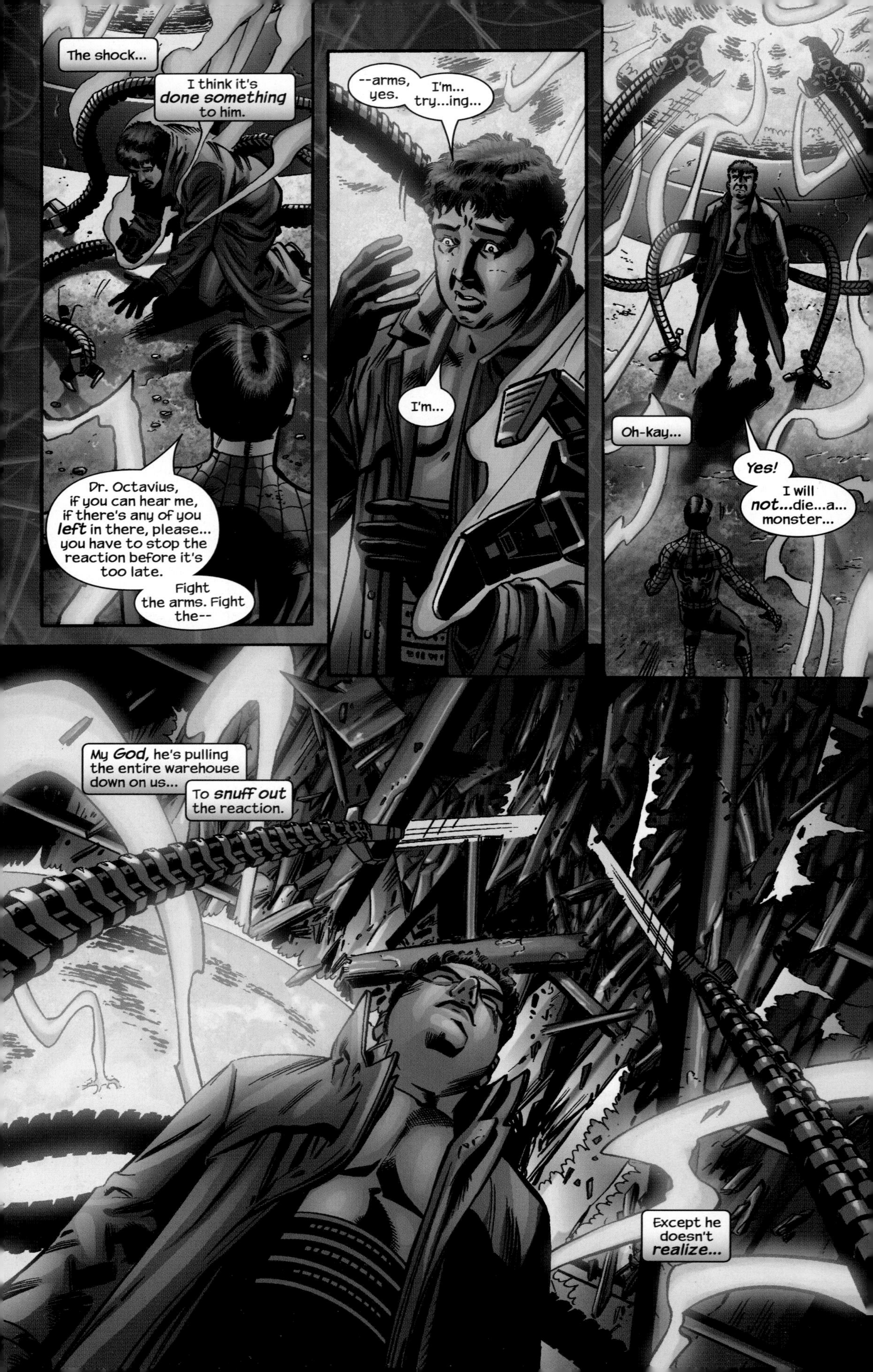
The shock...
I think it's *done something* to him.
Dr. Octavius, if you can hear me, if there's any of you *left* in there, please... you have to stop the reaction before it's too late.
Fight the arms. Fight the--
--arms, yes.
I'm... try...ing...
I'm...
Oh-kay...
Yes!
I will *not*...die...a... monster...
My *God,* he's pulling the entire warehouse down on us...
To *snuff out* the reaction.
Except he doesn't *realize*...

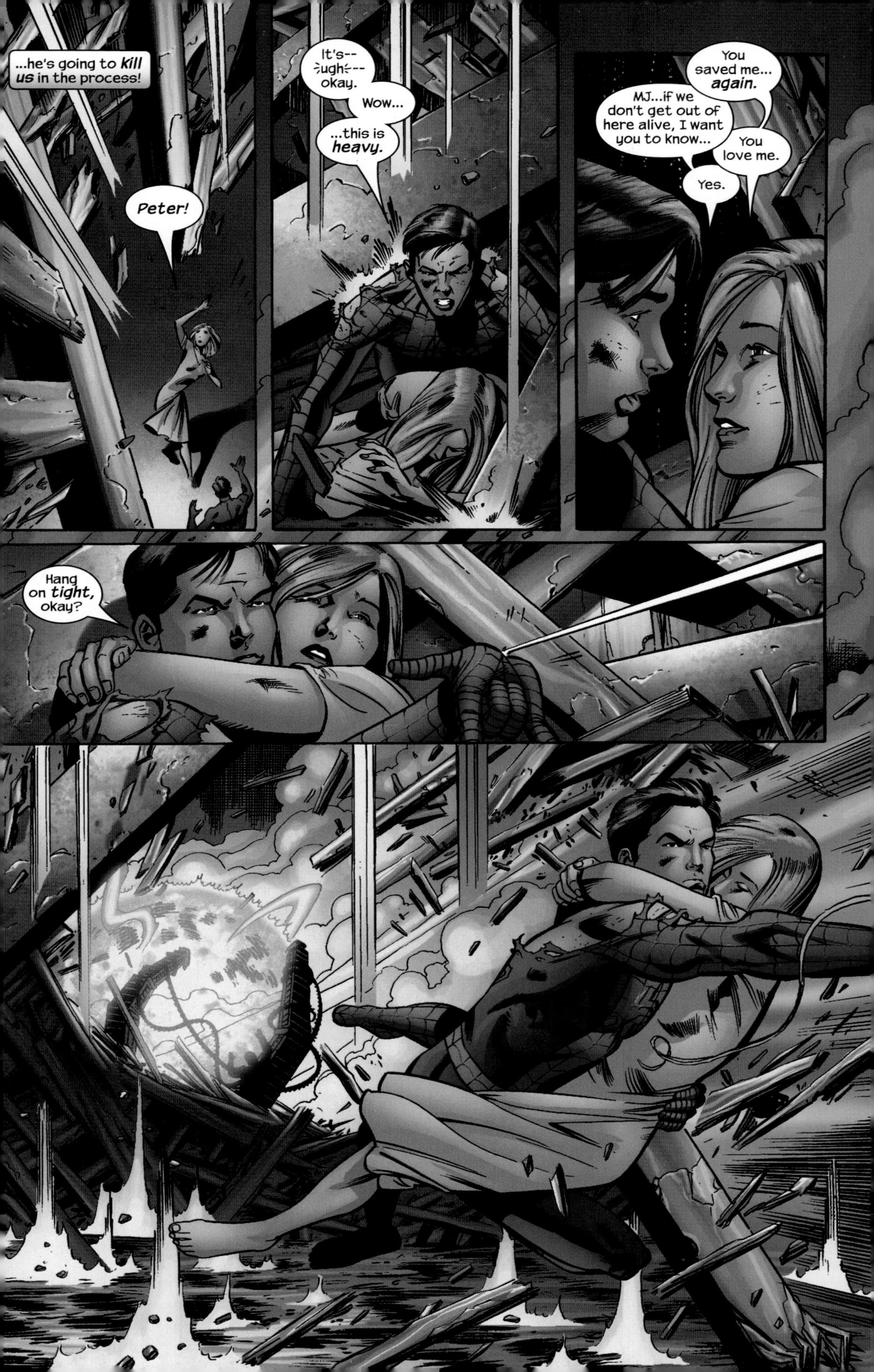
...he's going to **kill** **us** in the process!
Peter!
It's-- ugh-- okay.
Wow...
...this is **heavy.**
MJ...if we don't get out of here alive, I want you to know...
You saved me... **again.**
You love me.
Yes.
Hang on **tight,** okay?

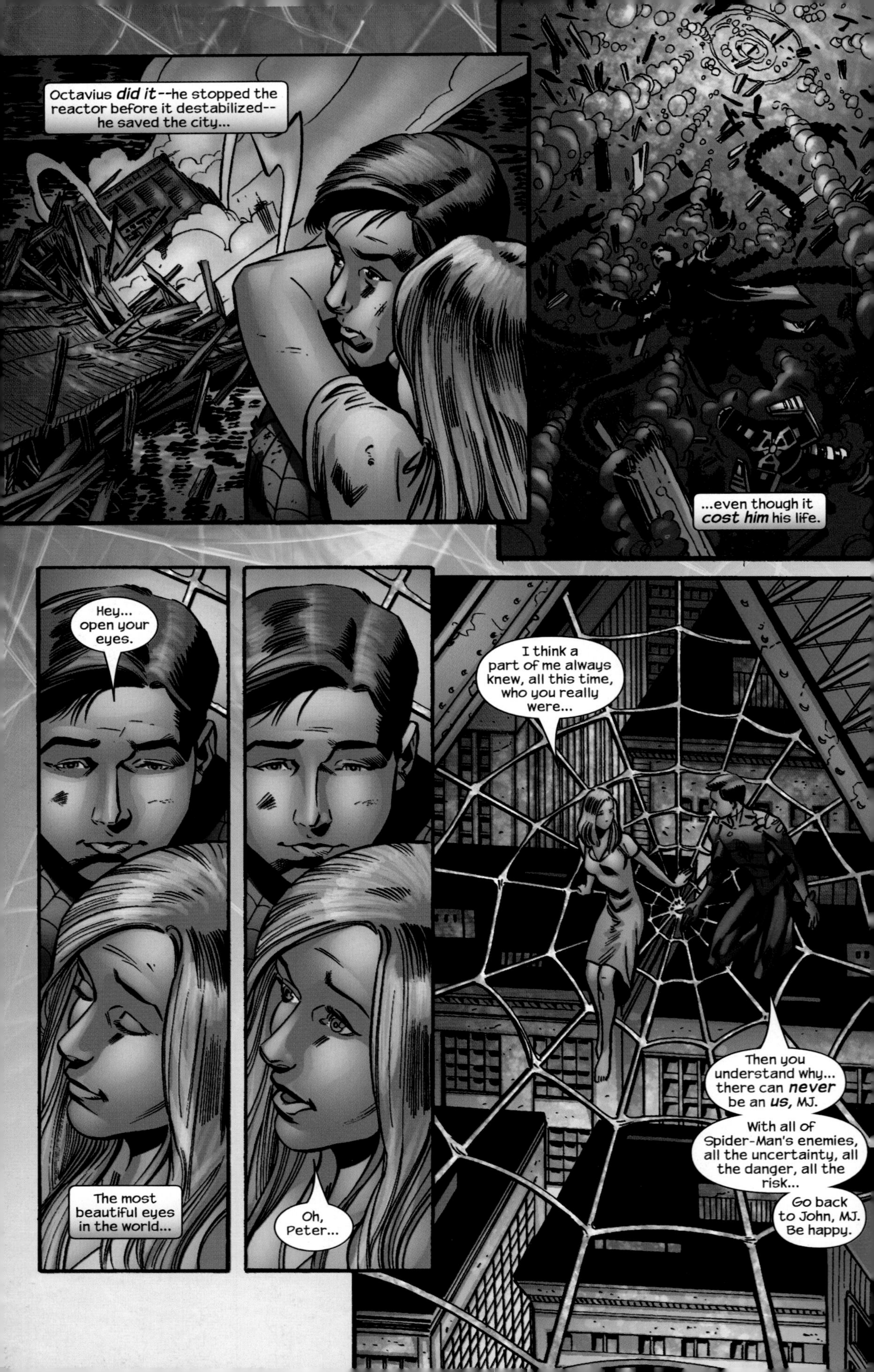
Octavius did it--he stopped the reactor before it destabilized--he saved the city...
...even though it cost him his life.
Hey... open your eyes.
The most beautiful eyes in the world...
Oh, Peter...
I think a part of me always knew, all this time, who you really were...
Then you understand why... there can never be an us, MJ.
With all of Spider-Man's enemies, all the uncertainty, all the danger, all the risk...
Go back to John, MJ. Be happy.

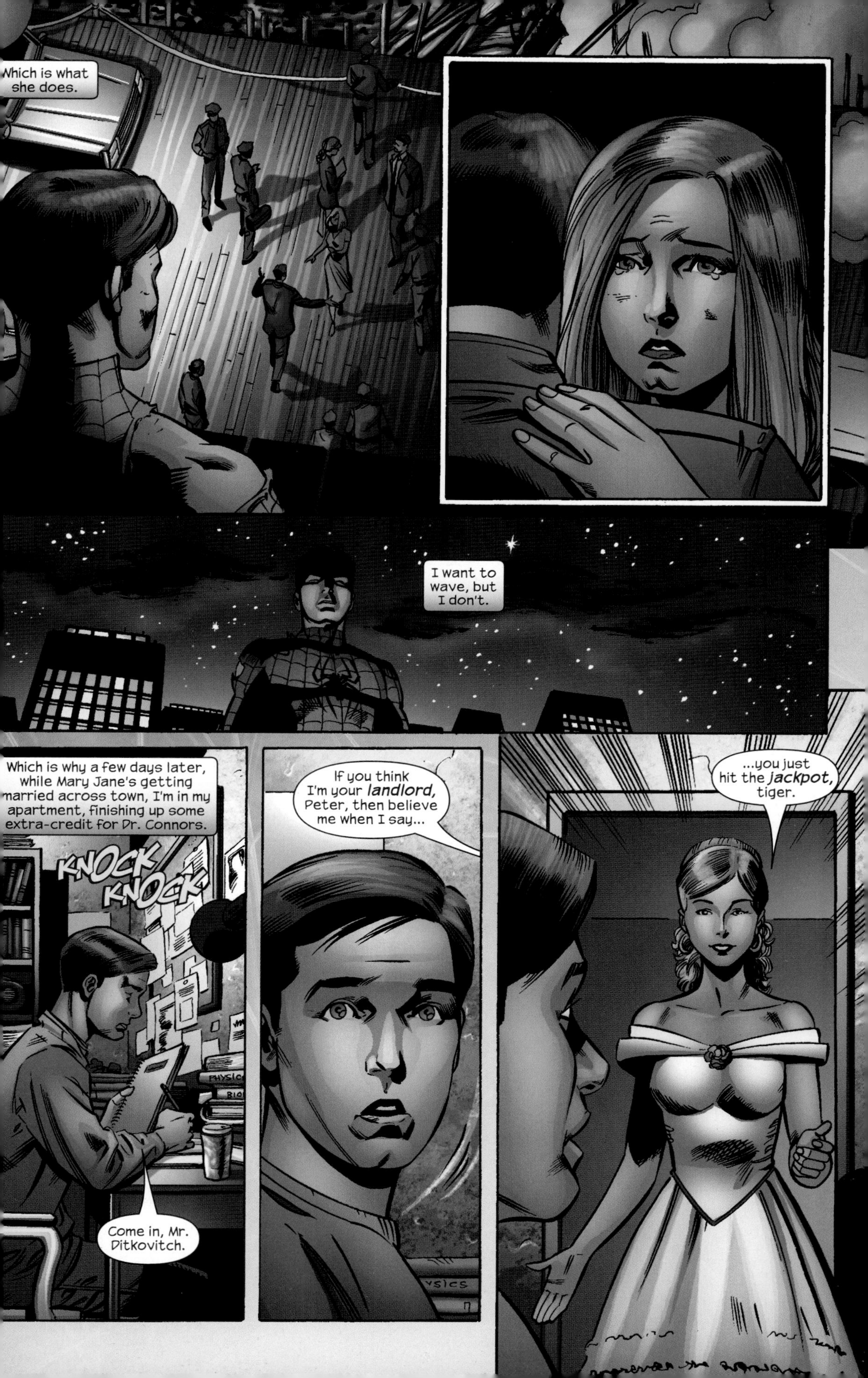
Which is what she does.
I want to wave, but I don't.
Which is why a few days later, while Mary Jane's getting married across town, I'm in my apartment, finishing up some extra-credit for Dr. Connors.
KNOCK KNOCK
Come in, Mr. Ditkovitch.
If you think I'm your landlord, Peter, then believe me when I say...
...you just hit the jackpot, tiger.

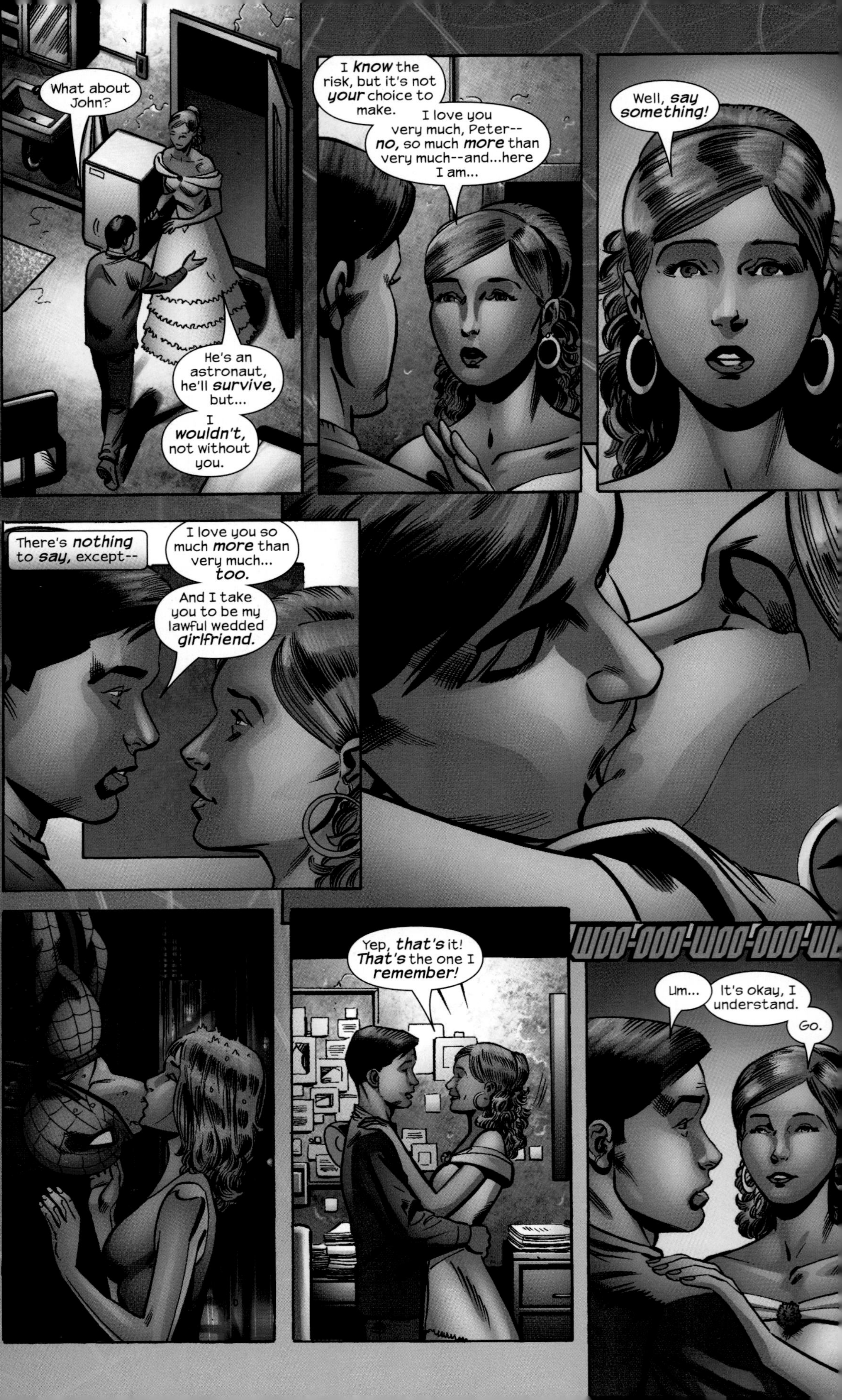
What about John?
He's an astronaut, he'll survive, but...
I wouldn't, not without you.
I know the risk, but it's not your choice to make.
I love you very much, Peter-- no, so much more than very much--and...here I am...
Well, say something!
There's nothing to say, except--
I love you so much more than very much... too.
And I take you to be my lawful wedded girlfriend.
Yep, that's it! That's the one I remember!
WOO-OOO-WOO-OOO-WE
Um...
It's okay, I understand.
Go.

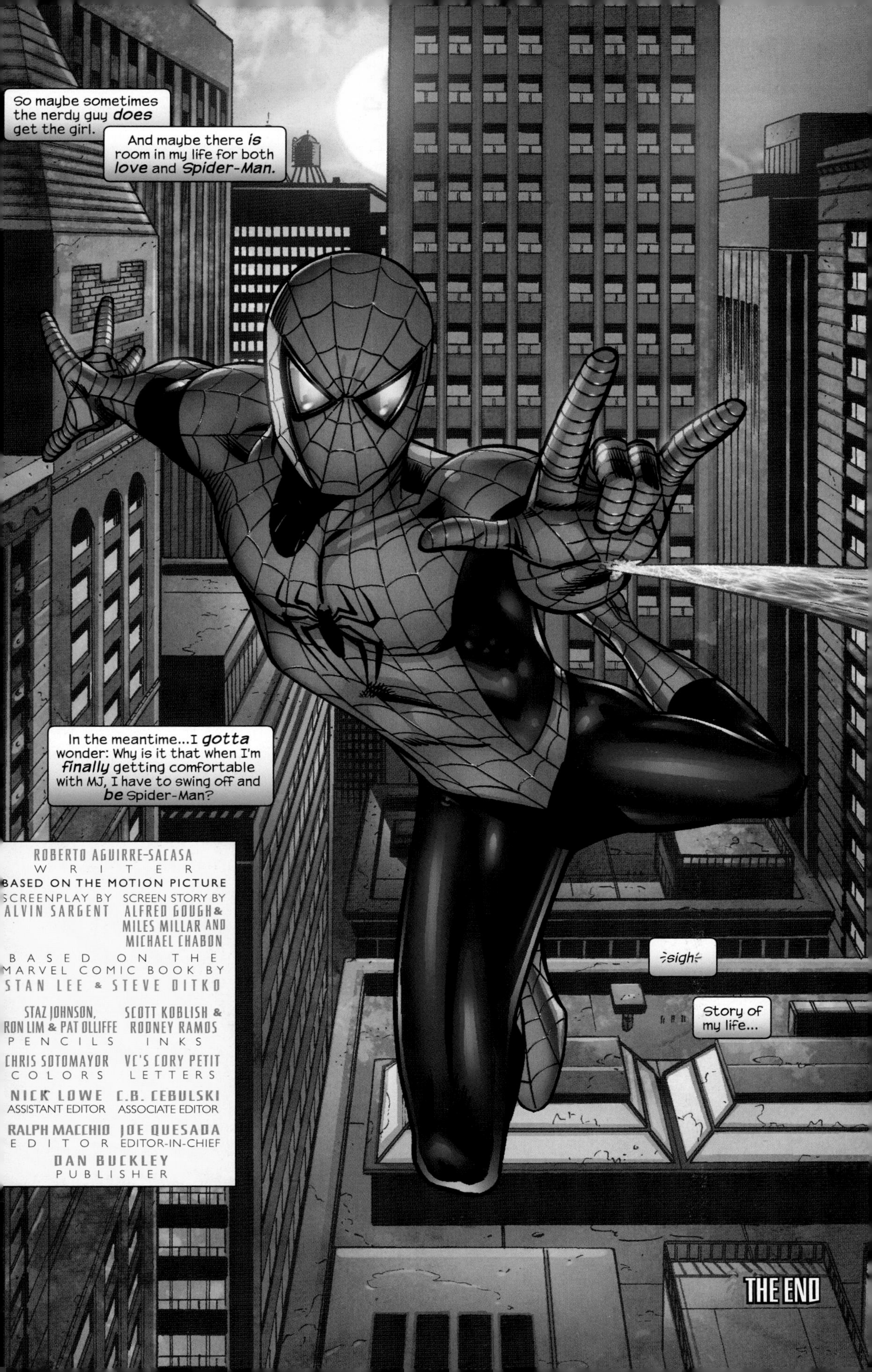
So maybe sometimes the nerdy guy does get the girl.
And maybe there is room in my life for both love and Spider-Man.
In the meantime...I gotta wonder: Why is it that when I'm finally getting comfortable with MJ, I have to swing off and be Spider-Man?
ROBERTO AGUIRRE-SACASA WRITER
BASED ON THE MOTION PICTURE
SCREENPLAY BY ALVIN SARGENT
SCREEN STORY BY ALFRED GOUGH & MILES MILLAR AND MICHAEL CHABON
BASED ON THE MARVEL COMIC BOOK BY STAN LEE & STEVE DITKO
STAZ JOHNSON, RON LIM & PAT OLLIFFE PENCILS
SCOTT KOBLISH & RODNEY RAMOS INKS
CHRIS SOTOMAYOR COLORS
VC'S CORY PETIT LETTERS
NICK LOWE ASSISTANT EDITOR
C.B. CEBULSKI ASSOCIATE EDITOR
RALPH MACCHIO EDITOR
JOE QUESADA EDITOR-IN-CHIEF
DAN BUCKLEY PUBLISHER
sigh
Story of my life...
THE END

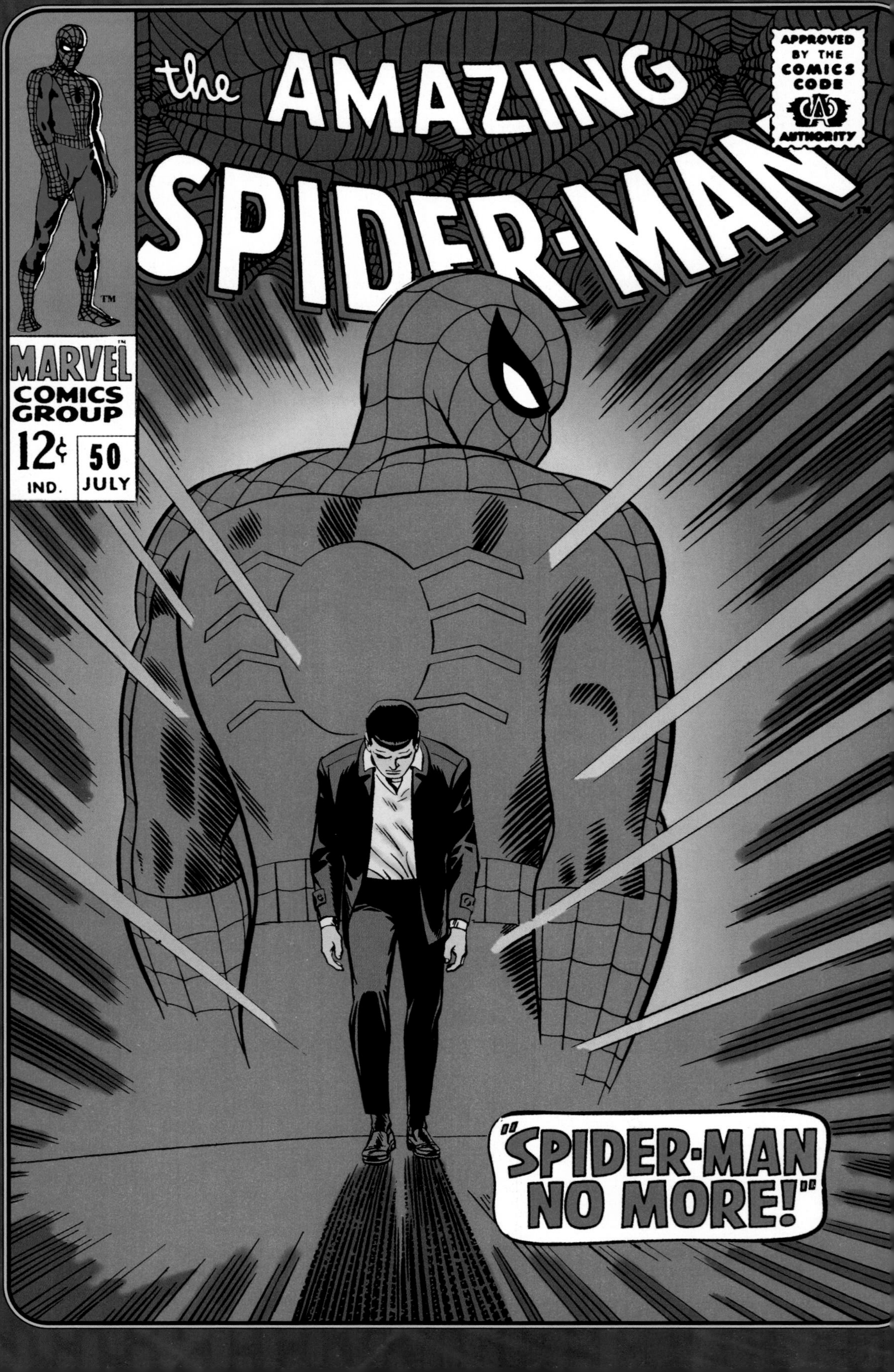
the AMAZING SPIDER-MAN
APPROVED BY THE COMICS CODE AUTHORITY
MARVEL COMICS GROUP
12¢ IND.
50 JULY
"SPIDER-MAN NO MORE!"

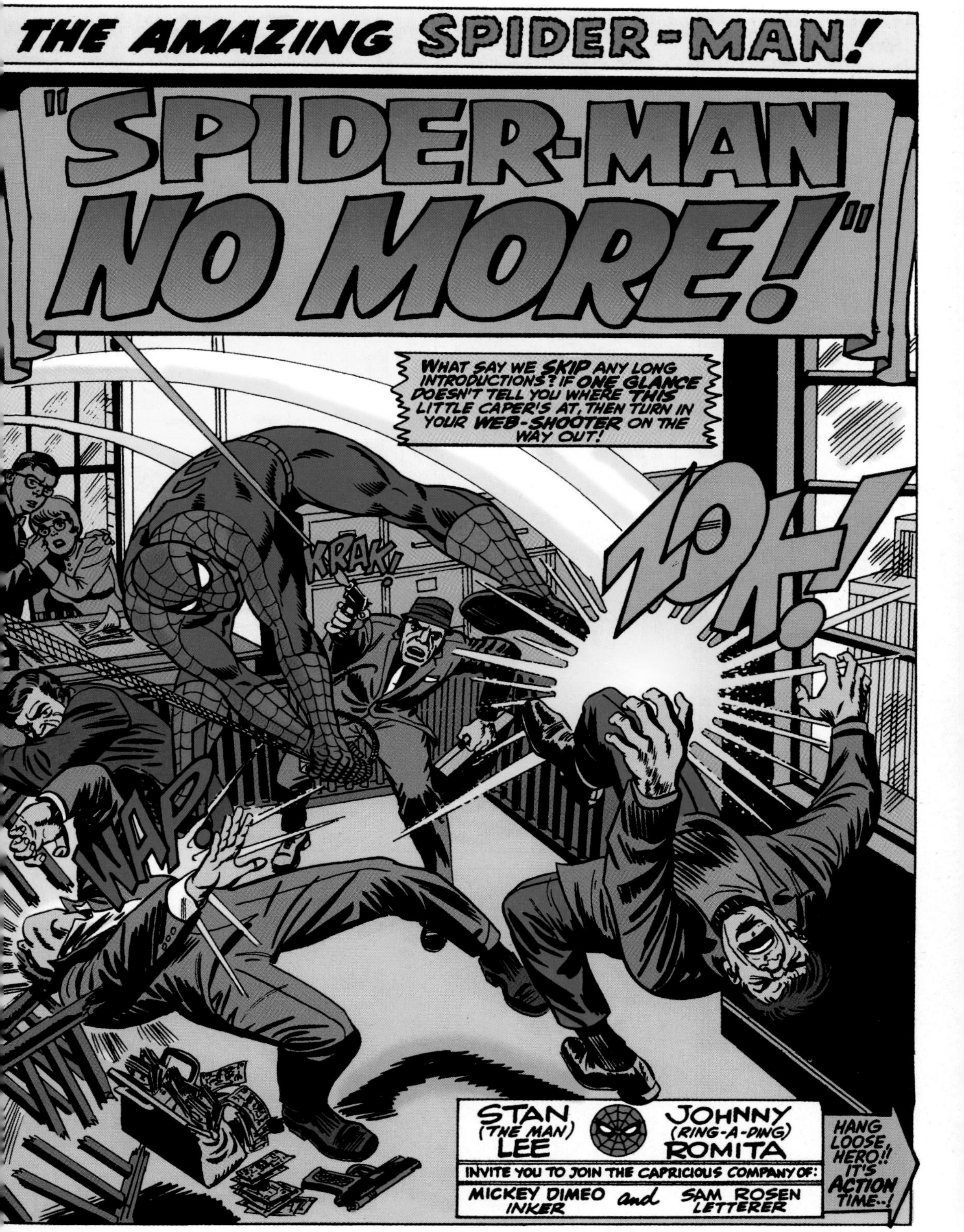
THE AMAZING SPIDER-MAN!
"SPIDER-MAN NO MORE!"
WHAT SAY WE SKIP ANY LONG INTRODUCTIONS? IF ONE GLANCE DOESN'T TELL YOU WHERE THIS LITTLE CAPER'S AT, THEN TURN IN YOUR WEB-SHOOTER ON THE WAY OUT!
KRAK!
ZOK!
WAP!
STAN (THE MAN) LEE
JOHNNY (RING-A-DING) ROMITA
INVITE YOU TO JOIN THE CAPRICIOUS COMPANY OF:
MICKEY DIMEO INKER and SAM ROSEN LETTERER
HANG LOOSE, HERO!! IT'S ACTION TIME..!

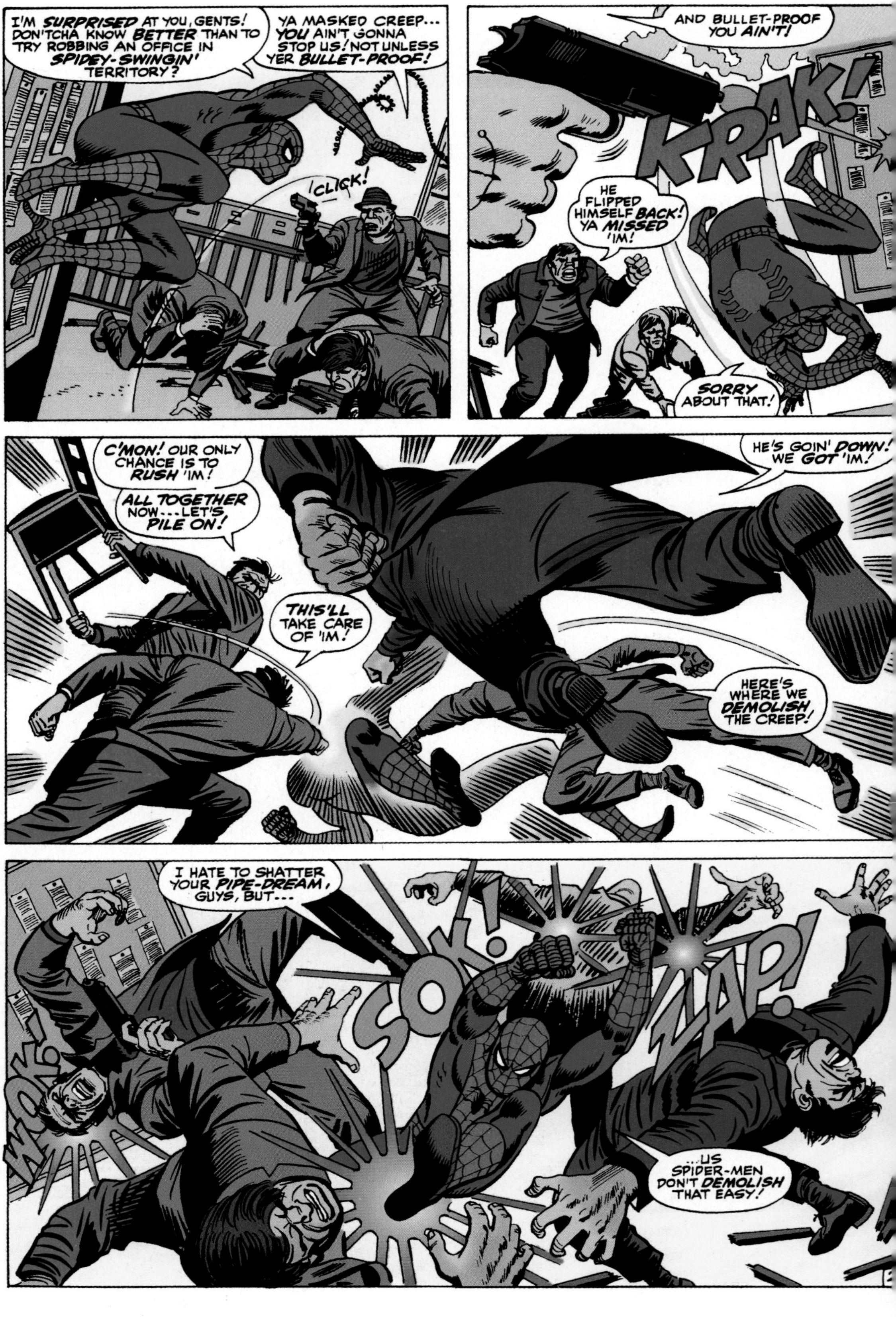
I'M SURPRISED AT YOU, GENTS! DON'TCHA KNOW BETTER THAN TO TRY ROBBING AN OFFICE IN SPIDEY-SWINGIN' TERRITORY?
YA MASKED CREEP... YOU AIN'T GONNA STOP US! NOT UNLESS YER BULLET-PROOF!
CLICK!
AND BULLET-PROOF YOU AIN'T!
KRAK!
HE FLIPPED HIMSELF BACK! YA MISSED 'IM!
SORRY ABOUT THAT!
C'MON! OUR ONLY CHANCE IS TO RUSH 'IM!
ALL TOGETHER NOW... LET'S PILE ON!
THIS'LL TAKE CARE OF 'IM!
HE'S GOIN' DOWN! WE GOT 'IM!
HERE'S WHERE WE DEMOLISH THE CREEP!
I HATE TO SHATTER YOUR PIPE-DREAM, GUYS, BUT...
SOK!
ZAP!
...US SPIDER-MEN DON'T DEMOLISH THAT EASY!

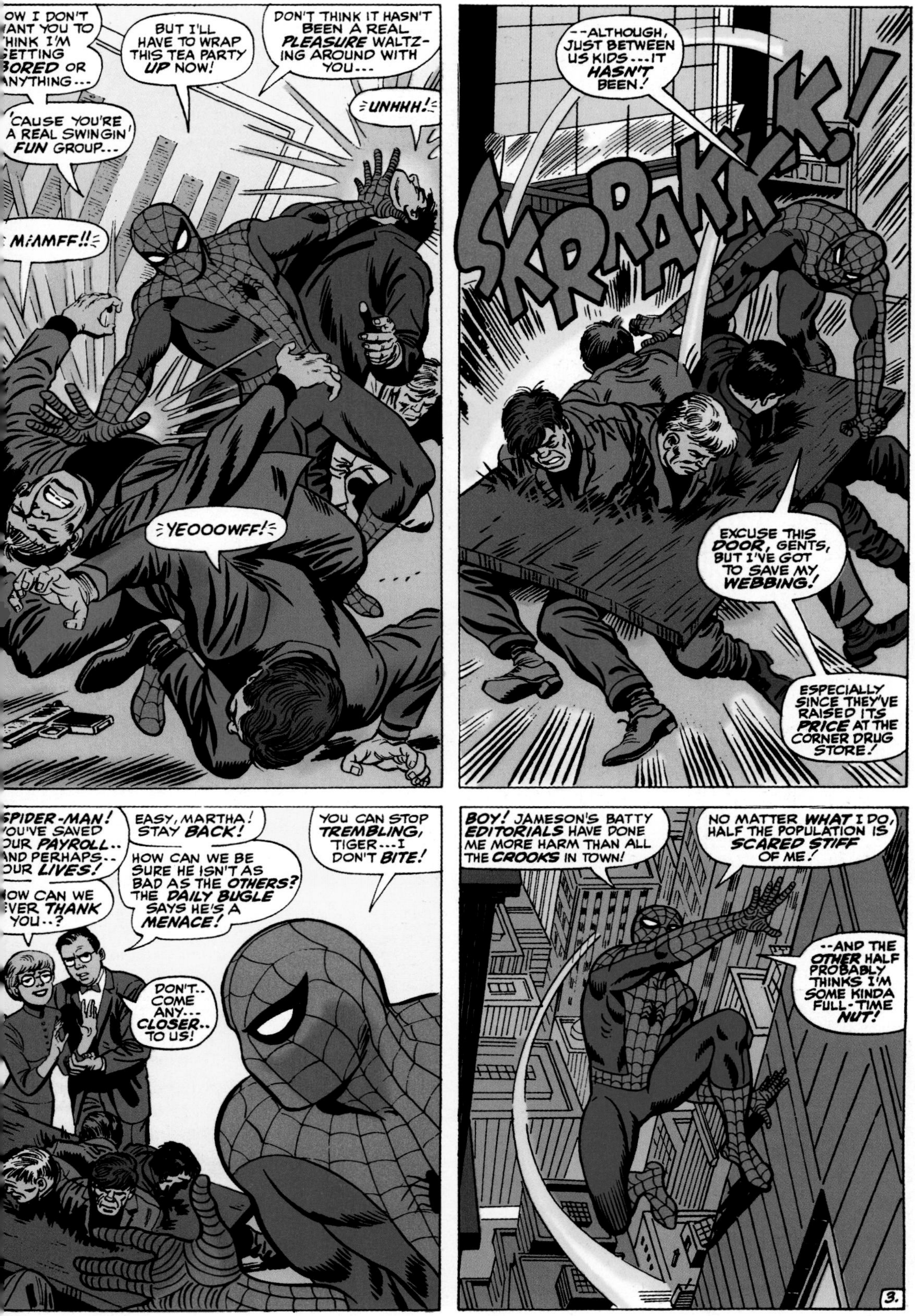

OW I DON'T WANT YOU TO THINK I'M GETTING BORED OR ANYTHING...
BUT I'LL HAVE TO WRAP THIS TEA PARTY UP NOW!
DON'T THINK IT HASN'T BEEN A REAL PLEASURE WALTZ-ING AROUND WITH YOU...
'CAUSE YOU'RE A REAL SWINGIN' FUN GROUP...
UNHHH!
M!AMFF!!
YEOOOWFF!
--ALTHOUGH, JUST BETWEEN US KIDS...IT HASN'T BEEN!
SKRRAKK-K!
EXCUSE THIS DOOR, GENTS, BUT I'VE GOT TO SAVE MY WEBBING!
ESPECIALLY SINCE THEY'VE RAISED ITS PRICE AT THE CORNER DRUG STORE!
SPIDER-MAN! YOU'VE SAVED OUR PAYROLL.. AND PERHAPS.. OUR LIVES!
HOW CAN WE EVER THANK YOU..?
EASY, MARTHA! STAY BACK!
HOW CAN WE BE SURE HE ISN'T AS BAD AS THE OTHERS? THE DAILY BUGLE SAYS HE'S A MENACE!
YOU CAN STOP TREMBLING, TIGER...I DON'T BITE!
DON'T.. COME ANY... CLOSER.. TO US!
BOY! JAMESON'S BATTY EDITORIALS HAVE DONE ME MORE HARM THAN ALL THE CROOKS IN TOWN!
NO MATTER WHAT I DO, HALF THE POPULATION IS SCARED STIFF OF ME!
--AND THE OTHER HALF PROBABLY THINKS I'M SOME KINDA FULL-TIME NUT!
3.

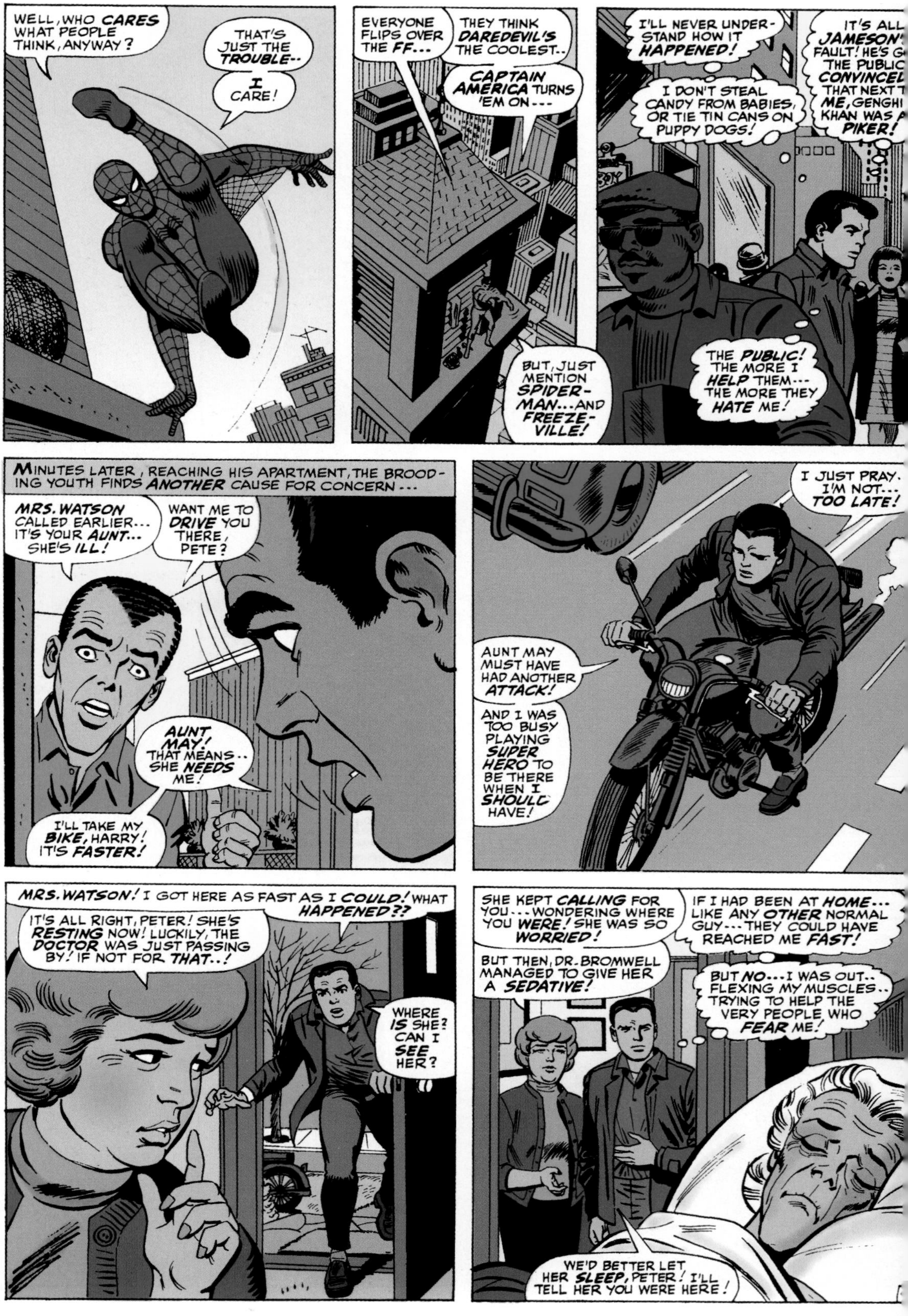
WELL, WHO CARES WHAT PEOPLE THINK, ANYWAY?
THAT'S JUST THE TROUBLE-- I CARE!
EVERYONE FLIPS OVER THE FF...
THEY THINK DAREDEVIL'S THE COOLEST..
CAPTAIN AMERICA TURNS 'EM ON---
BUT, JUST MENTION SPIDER-MAN...AND FREEZE-VILLE!
I'LL NEVER UNDER-STAND HOW IT HAPPENED!
IT'S ALL JAMESON' FAULT! HE'S G THE PUBLIC CONVINCEL THAT NEXT T ME, GENGHI KHAN WAS A PIKER!
I DON'T STEAL CANDY FROM BABIES, OR TIE TIN CANS ON PUPPY DOGS!
THE PUBLIC! THE MORE I HELP THEM--- THE MORE THEY HATE ME!
MINUTES LATER, REACHING HIS APARTMENT, THE BROODING YOUTH FINDS ANOTHER CAUSE FOR CONCERN---
MRS. WATSON CALLED EARLIER... IT'S YOUR AUNT... SHE'S ILL!
WANT ME TO DRIVE YOU THERE, PETE?
AUNT MAY! THAT MEANS.. SHE NEEDS ME!
I'LL TAKE MY BIKE, HARRY! IT'S FASTER!
I JUST PRAY. I'M NOT... TOO LATE!
AUNT MAY MUST HAVE HAD ANOTHER ATTACK!
AND I WAS TOO BUSY PLAYING SUPER HERO TO BE THERE WHEN I SHOULD HAVE!
MRS. WATSON! I GOT HERE AS FAST AS I COULD! WHAT HAPPENED??
IT'S ALL RIGHT, PETER! SHE'S RESTING NOW! LUCKILY, THE DOCTOR WAS JUST PASSING BY! IF NOT FOR THAT..!
WHERE IS SHE? CAN I SEE HER?
SHE KEPT CALLING FOR YOU... WONDERING WHERE YOU WERE! SHE WAS SO WORRIED!
BUT THEN, DR. BROMWELL MANAGED TO GIVE HER A SEDATIVE!
IF I HAD BEEN AT HOME... LIKE ANY OTHER NORMAL GUY--- THEY COULD HAVE REACHED ME FAST!
BUT NO--- I WAS OUT.. FLEXING MY MUSCLES.. TRYING TO HELP THE VERY PEOPLE WHO FEAR ME!
WE'D BETTER LET HER SLEEP, PETER! I'LL TELL HER YOU WERE HERE!

TRY NOT TO BE TOO FAR FROM THE *PHONE* TILL YOUR AUNT IS BACK ON HER FEET, SON!

I *WILL*, MRS. WATSON!

AND *THANKS*.. FOR LOOKING *AFTER* HER!

IF..ANYTHING HAD *HAPPENED* ...BEFORE I COULD HAVE REACHED HER.. I'D NEVER *FORGIVE* MYSELF!

EVER SINCE I MOVED IN WITH HARRY, I'VE HARDLY EVEN *THOUGHT* ABOUT AUNT MAY!

AFTER ALL, WHY *SHOULD* I CARE ABOUT HER?

ALL SHE EVER *DID* IS SPEND A *LIFETIME* LOOKING AFTER ME.. TREATING ME LIKE HER OWN *SON!*

THAT'S ALL...

SHE DEVOTED MOST OF HER LIFE..REPLACING THE *MOTHER*..THAT I NEVER HAD!

AND, I SHOW MY *GRATITUDE*--BY NEVER *BEING* THERE ...WHEN SHE *NEEDS* ME!

I'VE GOT A ROUGH *EXAM* TOMORROW.. BUT THERE'S NO USE TRYING TO *STUDY*...

I'D NEVER BE ABLE TO CONCENTRATE.. NOT *NOW!*

THE NEXT DAY, AT THE CONCLUSION OF THE TEST--

ANYTHING WRONG, PETE? I HARDLY SAW YOU WRITE A *THING!*

IF I *PASSED*, IT'LL BE A *MIRACLE!*

PARKER! WOULD YOU MIND *REMAINING* A FEW MINUTES AFTER CLASS?

I'D LIKE TO HAVE A *WORD* WITH YOU!

SURE, PROFESSOR WARREN!

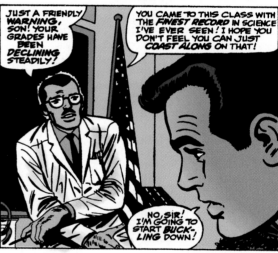

JUST A FRIENDLY WARNING, *SON!* YOUR GRADES HAVE BEEN *DECLINING* STEADILY!

YOU CAME TO THIS CLASS WITH THE *FINEST RECORD* IN SCIENCE I'VE EVER SEEN! I HOPE YOU DON'T FEEL YOU CAN JUST *COAST ALONG* ON THAT!

NO, SIR! I'M GOING TO START *BUCK- LING* DOWN!

OH, *PETER!* I'M HAVING A LITTLE *GET- TOGETHER* AT HOME TONIGHT!

I'D LOVE YOU TO *BE* THERE, IF YOU CAN!

I'VE BEEN *WAITING* FOR GWEN TO ASK ME! BUT WITH AUNT MAY SO ILL...AND MY GRADES SO LOW...

GEE, I'M *SORRY*, GWEN! WOULD YOU MIND IF I TAKE A *RAIN CHECK*, INSTEAD?

'COURSE NOT, PETE! THOUGH I AM *DIS- APPOINTED!*

EXIT

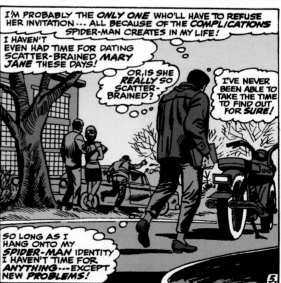

I'M PROBABLY THE *ONLY ONE* WHO'LL HAVE TO REFUSE HER INVITATION ... ALL BECAUSE OF THE *COMPLICATIONS* SPIDER-MAN CREATES IN MY LIFE!

I HAVEN'T EVEN HAD TIME FOR DATING SCATTER-BRAINED *MARY JANE* THESE DAYS!

OR, IS SHE *REALLY* SO *SCATTER- BRAINED?*

I'VE NEVER BEEN ABLE TO TAKE THE TIME TO FIND OUT FOR *SURE!*

SO LONG AS I HANG ONTO MY *SPIDER-MAN* IDENTITY I HAVEN'T TIME FOR *ANYTHING*----EXCEPT NEW *PROBLEMS!*

5.

ALL THE WAY HOME, THE TROUBLED YOUTH'S THOUGHTS KEEP TUMBLING TORTUOUSLY IN HIS BRAIN, UNTIL...

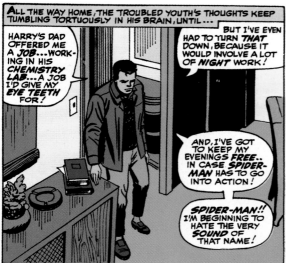

HARRY'S DAD OFFERED ME A *JOB*...WORKING IN HIS *CHEMISTRY LAB*...A JOB I'D GIVE MY *EYE TEETH* FOR!

BUT I'VE EVEN HAD TO TURN *THAT* DOWN, BECAUSE IT WOULD INVOLVE A LOT OF *NIGHT* WORK!

AND, I'VE GOT TO KEEP MY EVENINGS *FREE*.. IN CASE *SPIDER-MAN* HAS TO GO INTO ACTION!

SPIDER-MAN!! I'M BEGINNING TO HATE THE VERY *SOUND* OF THAT NAME!

BUT, HATE IT OR NOT, NO SOONER DOES HE TURN ON THE T.V., THAN THAT SOBRIQUET *CONTINUES* TO HAUNT THE BROODING ADVENTURER...

MAYBE IF I HEAR THE *NEWS* FOR A WHILE, I'LL--OH *NO!*

...AND MY *NEWSPAPER* CHALLENGES *ANYONE* TO PROVE THAT *SPIDER-MAN* ISN'T A *PUBLIC ENEMY!*

IT'S *JAMESON* AGAIN...USING THE *SHOW* HE SPONSORS TO STIR UP THE PEOPLE *AGAINST* ME!

SOME MISGUIDED FOOLS CALL HIM A *SUPER HERO!* BUT, WHY DOES HE OPERATE *OUTSIDE* THE LAW? WHY DOES HE CLOAK HIS IDENTITY BEHIND THAT UGLY *FRIGHT MASK?!!*

LET ME *TELL* YOU WHY...

BECAUSE HE'S REALLY AN *EGOMANIAC*...A NEUROTIC *TROUBLE-MAKER*, FLAUNTING HIS POWER BEFORE THE ORDINARY CITIZENS WHOM HE *DESPISES!*

FOR ALL WE KNOW, HE *HIMSELF* PROVOKES THE CRIMINALS WHOM HE LATER SEEMS TO *DEFEAT!*

DO WE WANT OUR YOUNGSTERS TO MAKE AN *IDOL* OF A *MENTALLY-DISTURBED MENACE??*

I SAY *NO!!* WE MUST *FIND* HIM... *UNMASK* HIM--AND THEN...*DESTROY* HIM!!

AS PUBLISHER OF THE *DAILY BUGLE*, I OFFER *ONE THOUSAND DOLLARS* FOR THE CAPTURE AND *CONVICTION* OF THAT WEB-SLINGING, WALL-CRAWLING MOCKERY OF A MAN...

A *THOUSAND DOLLARS REWARD*... JUST FOR *ME?!*

HE..*HATES* ME..FAR *MORE* THAN I *THOUGHT*..!

MAGNAVOX

THE TIME HAS COME TO *RID* OURSELVES OF THAT FALSE FACED FREAK WHO *HIDES* BY DAY AND TRIES TO TAKE THE LAW INTO HIS *OWN* HANDS UNDER COVER OF *NIGHT!*

THE TERRIBLE THING IS...HE *MEANS* IT! HE ACTUALLY *BELIEVES* WHAT HE SAYS! HE SINCERELY THINKS I *AM* A THREAT TO SOCIETY!

56

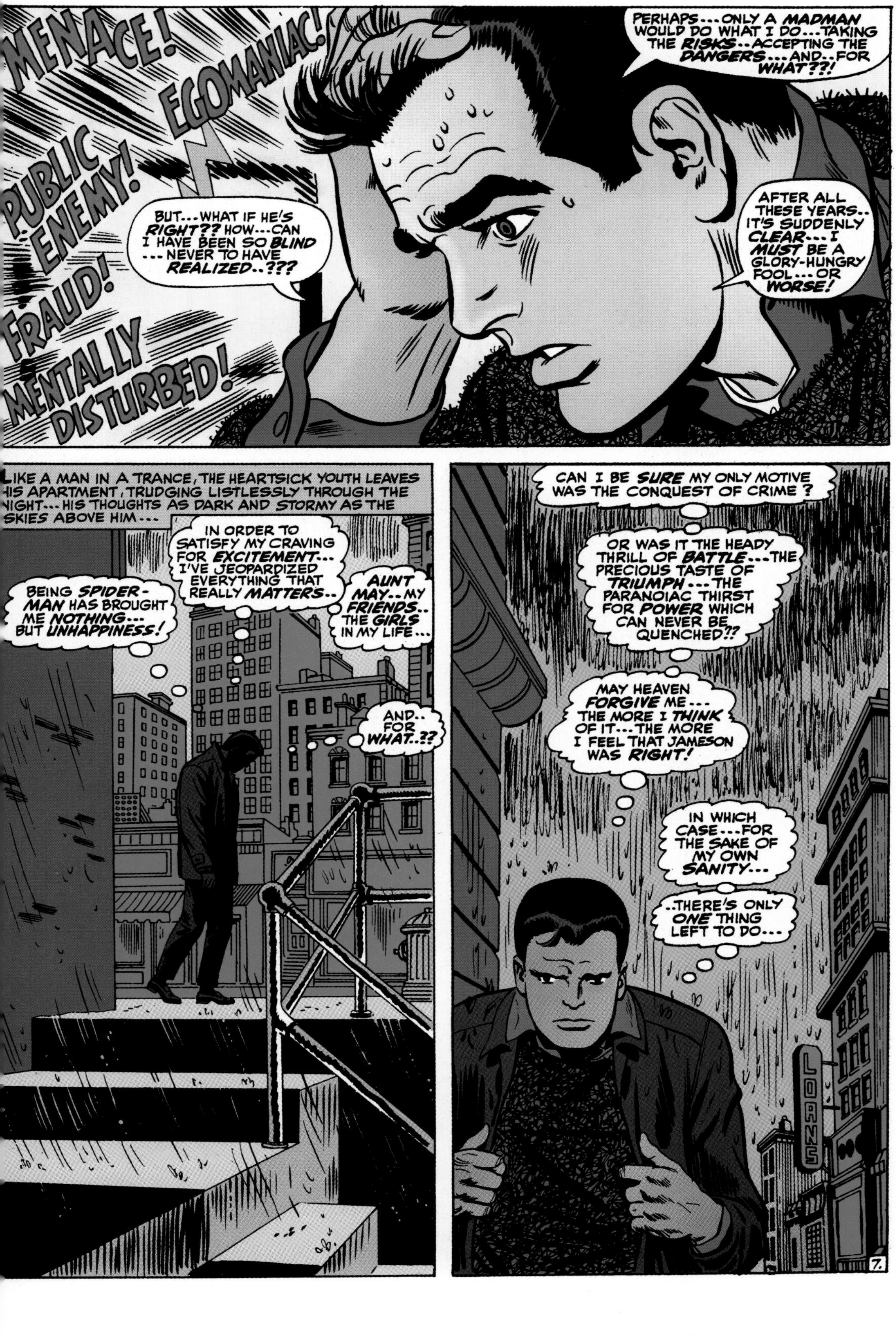
MENACE!
EGOMANIAC!
PUBLIC ENEMY!
FRAUD!
MENTALLY DISTURBED!
PERHAPS... ONLY A MADMAN WOULD DO WHAT I DO... TAKING THE RISKS.. ACCEPTING THE DANGERS... AND.. FOR WHAT??!
BUT... WHAT IF HE'S RIGHT?? HOW... CAN I HAVE BEEN SO BLIND ... NEVER TO HAVE REALIZED..???
AFTER ALL THESE YEARS.. IT'S SUDDENLY CLEAR... I MUST BE A GLORY-HUNGRY FOOL... OR WORSE!
LIKE A MAN IN A TRANCE, THE HEARTSICK YOUTH LEAVES HIS APARTMENT, TRUDGING LISTLESSLY THROUGH THE NIGHT... HIS THOUGHTS AS DARK AND STORMY AS THE SKIES ABOVE HIM...
BEING SPIDER-MAN HAS BROUGHT ME NOTHING... BUT UNHAPPINESS!
IN ORDER TO SATISFY MY CRAVING FOR EXCITEMENT... I'VE JEOPARDIZED EVERYTHING THAT REALLY MATTERS..
AUNT MAY.. MY FRIENDS.. THE GIRLS IN MY LIFE...
AND.. FOR WHAT..??
CAN I BE SURE MY ONLY MOTIVE WAS THE CONQUEST OF CRIME?
OR WAS IT THE HEADY THRILL OF BATTLE... THE PRECIOUS TASTE OF TRIUMPH... THE PARANOIAC THIRST FOR POWER WHICH CAN NEVER BE QUENCHED??
MAY HEAVEN FORGIVE ME... THE MORE I THINK OF IT... THE MORE I FEEL THAT JAMESON WAS RIGHT!
IN WHICH CASE... FOR THE SAKE OF MY OWN SANITY...
..THERE'S ONLY ONE THING LEFT TO DO...
LOANS
7.

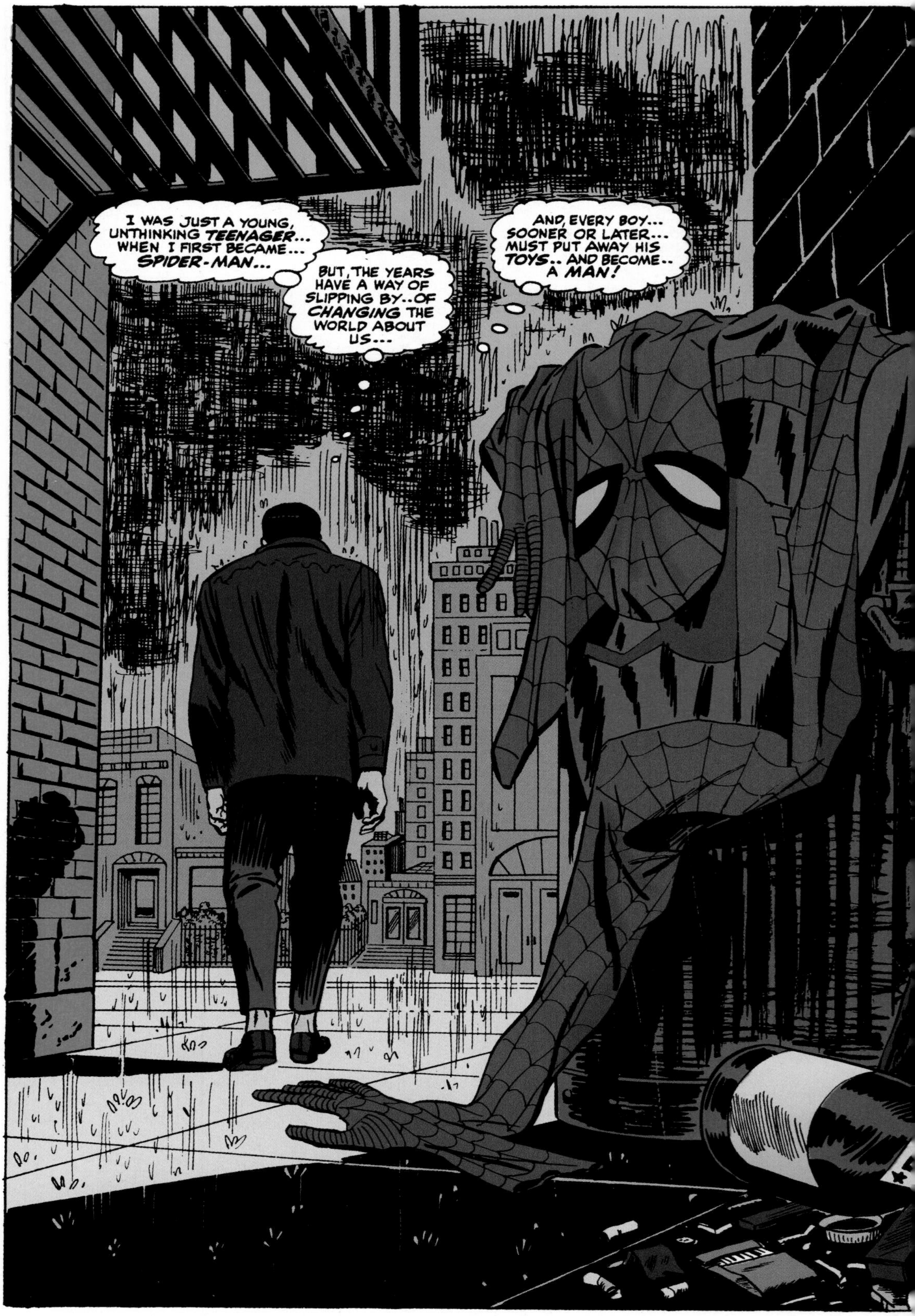
I WAS JUST A YOUNG, UNTHINKING TEENAGER... WHEN I FIRST BECAME... SPIDER-MAN...
BUT, THE YEARS HAVE A WAY OF SLIPPING BY..OF CHANGING THE WORLD ABOUT US...
AND, EVERY BOY... SOONER OR LATER... MUST PUT AWAY HIS TOYS.. AND BECOME.. A MAN!

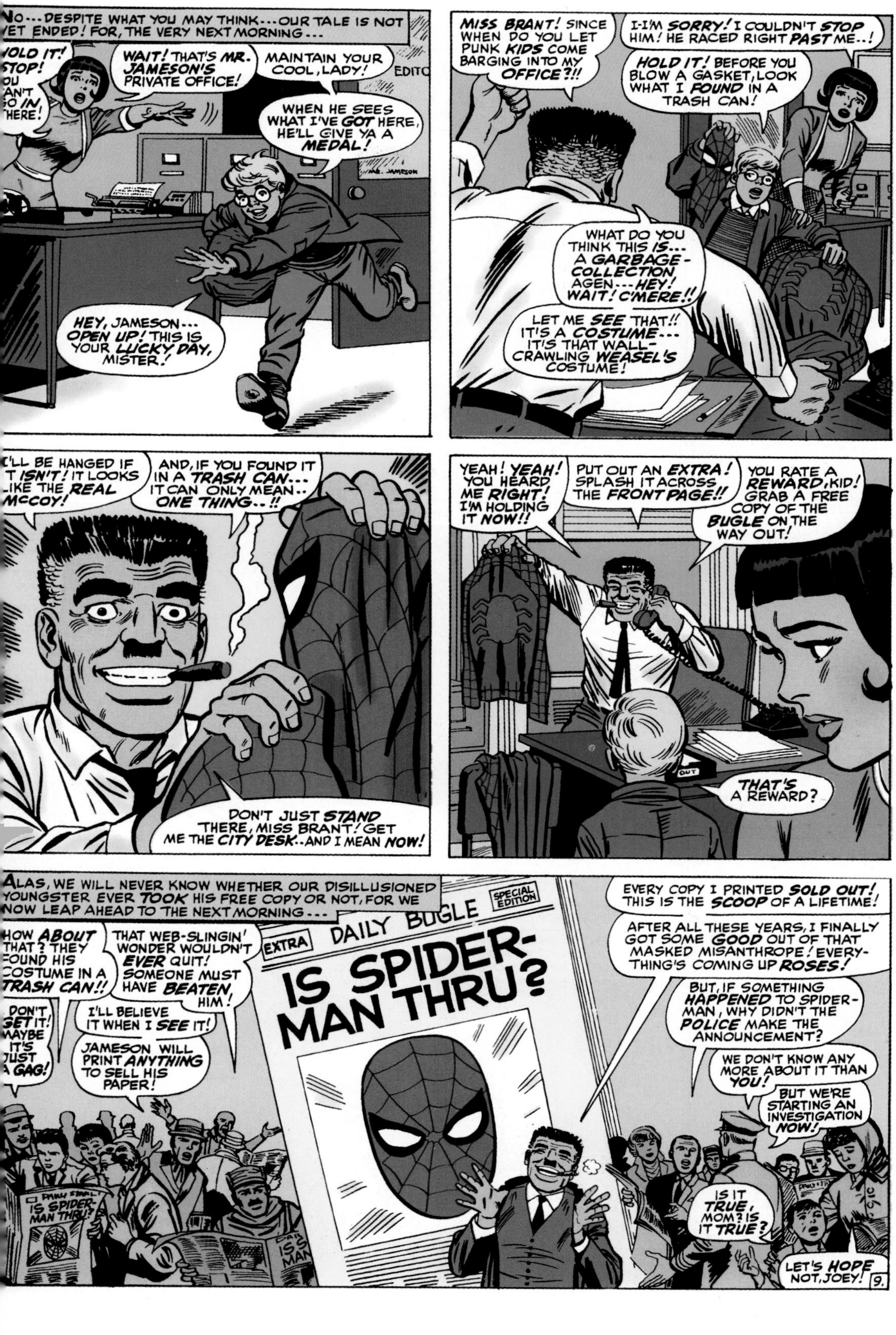

NO... DESPITE WHAT YOU MAY THINK... OUR TALE IS NOT YET ENDED! FOR, THE VERY NEXT MORNING...
HOLD IT! STOP! YOU CAN'T GO IN THERE!
WAIT! THAT'S MR. JAMESON'S PRIVATE OFFICE!
MAINTAIN YOUR COOL, LADY!
WHEN HE SEES WHAT I'VE GOT HERE, HE'LL GIVE YA A MEDAL!
HEY, JAMESON... OPEN UP! THIS IS YOUR LUCKY DAY, MISTER!
MISS BRANT! SINCE WHEN DO YOU LET PUNK KIDS COME BARGING INTO MY OFFICE?!!
I-I'M SORRY! I COULDN'T STOP HIM! HE RACED RIGHT PAST ME...!
HOLD IT! BEFORE YOU BLOW A GASKET, LOOK WHAT I FOUND IN A TRASH CAN!
WHAT DO YOU THINK THIS IS... A GARBAGE-COLLECTION AGEN--- HEY! WAIT! C'MERE!!
LET ME SEE THAT!! IT'S A COSTUME--- IT'S THAT WALL-CRAWLING WEASEL'S COSTUME!
I'LL BE HANGED IF IT ISN'T! IT LOOKS LIKE THE REAL McCOY!
AND, IF YOU FOUND IT IN A TRASH CAN... IT CAN ONLY MEAN.. ONE THING..!!
DON'T JUST STAND THERE, MISS BRANT! GET ME THE CITY DESK..AND I MEAN NOW!
YEAH! YEAH! YOU HEARD ME RIGHT! I'M HOLDING IT NOW!!
PUT OUT AN EXTRA! SPLASH IT ACROSS THE FRONT PAGE!!
YOU RATE A REWARD, KID! GRAB A FREE COPY OF THE BUGLE ON THE WAY OUT!
THAT'S A REWARD?
ALAS, WE WILL NEVER KNOW WHETHER OUR DISILLUSIONED YOUNGSTER EVER TOOK HIS FREE COPY OR NOT, FOR WE NOW LEAP AHEAD TO THE NEXT MORNING...
DAILY BUGLE
SPECIAL EDITION
EXTRA
IS SPIDER-MAN THRU?
HOW ABOUT THAT? THEY FOUND HIS COSTUME IN A TRASH CAN!!
THAT WEB-SLINGIN' WONDER WOULDN'T EVER QUIT! SOMEONE MUST HAVE BEATEN HIM!
I DON'T GET IT! MAYBE IT'S JUST A GAG!
I'LL BELIEVE IT WHEN I SEE IT!
JAMESON WILL PRINT ANYTHING TO SELL HIS PAPER!
IS SPIDER-MAN THRU?
EVERY COPY I PRINTED SOLD OUT! THIS IS THE SCOOP OF A LIFETIME!
AFTER ALL THESE YEARS, I FINALLY GOT SOME GOOD OUT OF THAT MASKED MISANTHROPE! EVERY-THING'S COMING UP ROSES!
BUT, IF SOMETHING HAPPENED TO SPIDER-MAN, WHY DIDN'T THE POLICE MAKE THE ANNOUNCEMENT?
WE DON'T KNOW ANY MORE ABOUT IT THAN YOU!
BUT WE'RE STARTING AN INVESTIGATION NOW!
IS IT TRUE, MOM? IS IT TRUE?
LET'S HOPE NOT, JOEY!
9.

NEEDLESS TO SAY, IT DOESN'T TAKE LONG FOR THE *T.V. NETWORKS* TO COVER THE BIGGEST HUMAN-INTEREST STORY OF THE YEAR--!

I'LL GIVE THE FOLKS A *CLOSE-UP VIEW* OF IT, JOHNNY!

LET'S NOT FORGET TO MENTION THAT IT WAS MY *DAILY BUGLE* THAT FIRST PUBLISHED THE NEWS!

AS A *PUBLIC SERVICE*, OF COURSE!

WE'RE OFFERING A *BARGAIN SUBSCRIPTION RATE* RIGHT NOW!

SUPPOSE WE GET THE CONVERSATION BACK TO *SPIDER-MAN*, MR. JAMESON--!

NATURALLY! *NATURALLY!* YOU DON'T THINK I WAS TRYING FOR A FREE *PLUG*, DO YOU?

OH, PERISH FORBID!

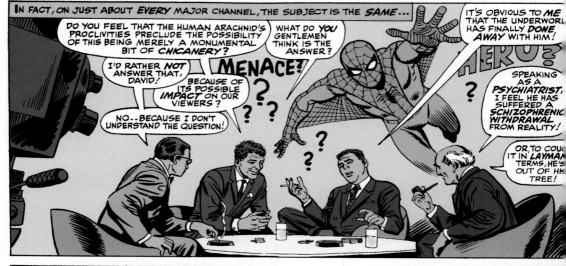

IN FACT, ON JUST ABOUT *EVERY* MAJOR CHANNEL, THE SUBJECT IS THE *SAME*...

DO YOU FEEL THAT THE HUMAN ARACHNID'S PROCLIVITIES PRECLUDE THE POSSIBILITY OF THIS BEING MERELY A MONUMENTAL BIT OF *CHICANERY?*

I'D RATHER *NOT* ANSWER THAT, DAVID!

BECAUSE OF ITS POSSIBLE *IMPACT* ON OUR VIEWERS?

NO--BECAUSE I DON'T UNDERSTAND THE QUESTION!

MENACE?

WHAT DO *YOU* GENTLEMEN THINK IS THE ANSWER?

IT'S OBVIOUS TO *ME* THAT THE UNDERWORLD HAS FINALLY *DONE AWAY* WITH HIM!

HERO?

SPEAKING AS A *PSYCHIATRIST*, I FEEL HE HAS SUFFERED A *SCHIZOPHRENIC WITHDRAWAL* FROM REALITY!

OR, TO COUCH IT IN *LAYMAN* TERMS, HE'S OUT OF HIS TREE!

AND, AMONGST THE HIGHEST ECHELONS OF THE *UNDERWORLD*, THE REACTION IS EQUALLY FAST AND FAR-REACHING..

THIS IS THE MOMENT WE'VE BEEN *WAITING* FOR!

WITH *SPIDER-MAN* GONE, MY PLANS CAN NOW REACH *FRUITION!*

TELL THE BOYS TO START SPREADING THE WORD...

I WANT EVERY MOB IN THE CITY TO KNOW...THE *KINGPIN* IS READY TO *TAKE OVER!*

WILL DO, KINGPIN!

WE'LL HAVE A *SUMMIT MEETIN'* THAT'LL MAKE *APPALACHIN* LOOK LIKE A TEA PARTY!

AS THE LONG, FATEFUL HOURS TICK BY, *ONE MAN* BECOMES INCREASINGLY AWARE OF A NEW *MOOD* AMONG THE CITY'S CRIMINAL ELEMENT...

SOMETHING'S IN THE AIR! I CAN SEE IT...FEEL IT... I CAN ALMOST REACH OUT AND *TOUCH* IT!

MOBSTERS WHO WOULDN'T BE CAUGHT WITHIN *MILES* OF EACH OTHER--DEADLY ENEMIES-- ARE MEETING----AND WHISPERING--!

WHATEVER IT *IS* THAT'S IN THE WIND... ONE THING'S FOR SURE... IT'S SOMETHING *BIG!*

...D IT WON'T BE [L]ONG BEFORE [P]ATCH, THE [S]TOOL PIGEON, [FI]NDS OUT [W]HAT'S GOING ON!

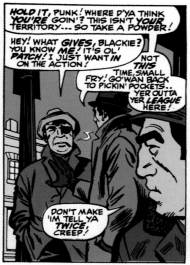

HOLD IT, PUNK! WHERE D'YA THINK *YOU'RE* GOIN'? THIS ISN'T *YOUR* TERRITORY... SO TAKE A POWDER!

HEY! WHAT *GIVES*, BLACKIE? YOU KNOW *ME!* IT'S OL' *PATCH!* I JUST WANT *IN* ON THE ACTION!

NOT *THIS* TIME, SMALL FRY! GO'WAN BACK.. TO PICKIN' POCKETS.. YER OUTTA YER *LEAGUE* HERE!

DON'T MAKE 'IM TELL YA *TWICE,* CREEP!

I WAS *RIGHT!* SOME OF THE BIGGEST MOBSTERS IN THE EAST ARE GETTING TOGETHER!

AND THEY'RE NOT DOING IT JUST BECAUSE THEY'RE *LONELY!*

I'D BETTER TAKE OFF AND MAKE MY *OWN* PLANS BEFORE THEY GET *SUSPICIOUS* OF ME!

...AND, AS THE THOUGHTFUL STOOLIE SLOWLY [FA]DES INTO THE DEEPENING SHADOWS...

WITH *SPIDER-MAN* GONE, THE *KINGPIN* IS READY TO TAKE OVER AS *HEAD MAN* OF THE MOBS!

ANY *QUESTIONS?*

WHY DON'T HE TELL US *HIM-SELF?* I DON'T DEAL WITH *STOOGES!*

RELAX, SHORTY! YOU KNOW THE KINGPIN LIKES TO STAY IN THE *BACKGROUND!*

IF *ANYONE* IS GONNA TAKE CONTROL AROUND HERE, THE *KINGPIN'S* OUR BOY!

UP TO NOW, I ALWAYS BEEN MY OWN *BOSS!* I DON'T *LIKE* IT!

THEN *START* LIKIN' IT, MISTER! WHAT THE KINGPIN *SAYS* AROUND HERE.. *GOES!*

...WHILE, IN A SMALL FURNISHED APART-[M]ENT ON THE OTHER SIDE OF TOWN...

[YOU] DON'T HAVE TO [B]E A *GENIUS* [T]O FIGURE OUT [W]HAT'S GOING ON!

SPIDER-MAN HELPED TO KEEP THE *UNDERWORLD* ON THE RUN! THEY WERE DISORGANIZED.. FEARFUL.. CAUTIOUS! BUT *NOW,* IT'S DIFFERENT!

WITH THE WEB-SLINGER *OUT OF ACTION,* THEY'RE READY TO *POOL* THEIR FORCES...

JUDGING BY THE ONES I'VE *SEEN,* IT COULD BE THE MOST *POWERFUL* ARMY OF CRIME EVER ASSEMBLED!

AND, SINCE *SOMEBODY* WILL HAVE TO *LEAD* THEM... WHY COULDN'T IT BE... THE MAN CALLED *PATCH?!!*

NOT A MAN *ALIVE* KNOWS THAT I'M *REALLY* FREDRICK FOSWELL!

THE NEXT MORNING...

AS *FOSWELL,* I'M JUST A TWO-BIT REPORTER...BUT, IF I COULD BECOME THE KING OF *CRIME* ONCE AGAIN...*

NOW THAT I'VE GONE *STRAIGHT,* EVERYONE *TRUSTS* ME! THEY'D NEVER SUSPECT!

HEY, FOSWELL! COME HERE... I WANNA *SHOW* YOU SOME-THING!

YES, SIR, MR. JAMESON!

* REMEMBER WHEN JJJ GAVE FOSWELL A JOB AFTER HIS PAROLE? HE HAD BEEN KNOWN AS *THE BIG MAN*--TILL SPIDEY CAUGHT HIM! ...*SUPER-MEMORY STAN.*

11.

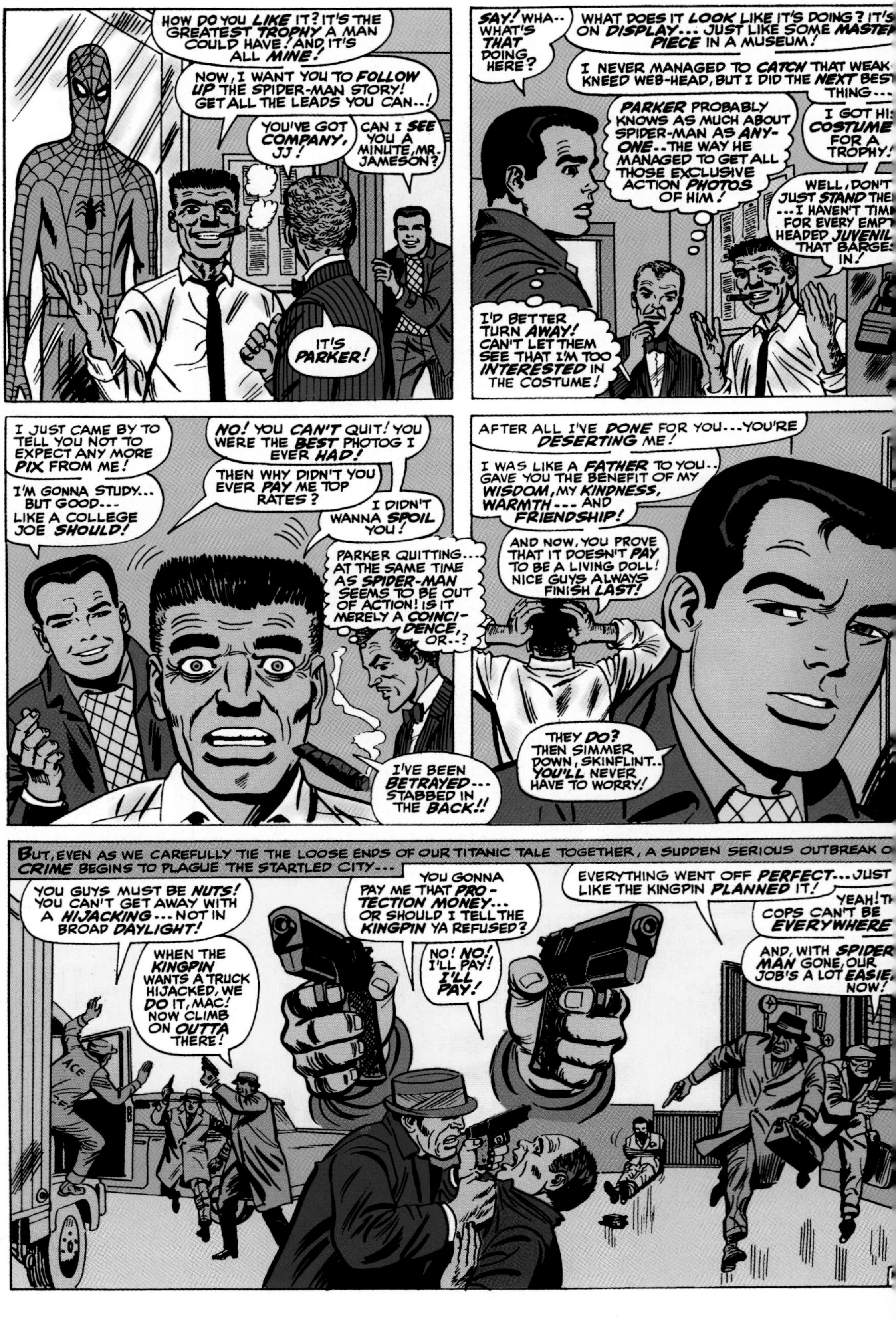

HOW DO YOU LIKE IT? IT'S THE GREATEST TROPHY A MAN COULD HAVE! AND IT'S ALL MINE!
NOW, I WANT YOU TO FOLLOW UP THE SPIDER-MAN STORY! GET ALL THE LEADS YOU CAN..!
YOU'VE GOT COMPANY, JJ!
CAN I SEE YOU A MINUTE, MR. JAMESON?
IT'S PARKER!
SAY! WHA.. WHAT'S THAT DOING HERE?
WHAT DOES IT LOOK LIKE IT'S DOING? IT'S ON DISPLAY... JUST LIKE SOME MASTER PIECE IN A MUSEUM!
I NEVER MANAGED TO CATCH THAT WEAK KNEED WEB-HEAD, BUT I DID THE NEXT BEST THING...
I GOT HIS COSTUME FOR A TROPHY!
PARKER PROBABLY KNOWS AS MUCH ABOUT SPIDER-MAN AS ANY-ONE..THE WAY HE MANAGED TO GET ALL THOSE EXCLUSIVE ACTION PHOTOS OF HIM!
WELL, DON'T JUST STAND THERE ...I HAVEN'T TIME FOR EVERY EMPTY HEADED JUVENILE THAT BARGES IN!
I'D BETTER TURN AWAY! CAN'T LET THEM SEE THAT I'M TOO INTERESTED IN THE COSTUME!
I JUST CAME BY TO TELL YOU NOT TO EXPECT ANY MORE PIX FROM ME!
I'M GONNA STUDY... BUT GOOD--- LIKE A COLLEGE JOE SHOULD!
NO! YOU CAN'T QUIT! YOU WERE THE BEST PHOTOG I EVER HAD!
THEN WHY DIDN'T YOU EVER PAY ME TOP RATES?
I DIDN'T WANNA SPOIL YOU!
PARKER QUITTING... AT THE SAME TIME AS SPIDER-MAN SEEMS TO BE OUT OF ACTION! IS IT MERELY A COINCI-DENCE, OR..?
I'VE BEEN BETRAYED... STABBED IN THE BACK!!
AFTER ALL I'VE DONE FOR YOU...YOU'RE DESERTING ME!
I WAS LIKE A FATHER TO YOU.. GAVE YOU THE BENEFIT OF MY WISDOM, MY KINDNESS, WARMTH --- AND FRIENDSHIP!
AND NOW, YOU PROVE THAT IT DOESN'T PAY TO BE A LIVING DOLL! NICE GUYS ALWAYS FINISH LAST!
THEY DO? THEN SIMMER DOWN, SKINFLINT.. YOU'LL NEVER HAVE TO WORRY!
BUT, EVEN AS WE CAREFULLY TIE THE LOOSE ENDS OF OUR TITANIC TALE TOGETHER, A SUDDEN SERIOUS OUTBREAK OF CRIME BEGINS TO PLAGUE THE STARTLED CITY...
YOU GUYS MUST BE NUTS! YOU CAN'T GET AWAY WITH A HIJACKING... NOT IN BROAD DAYLIGHT!
WHEN THE KINGPIN WANTS A TRUCK HIJACKED, WE DO IT, MAC! NOW CLIMB ON OUTTA THERE!
YOU GONNA PAY ME THAT PRO-TECTION MONEY... OR SHOULD I TELL THE KINGPIN YA REFUSED?
NO! NO! I'LL PAY! I'LL PAY!
EVERYTHING WENT OFF PERFECT... JUST LIKE THE KINGPIN PLANNED IT!
YEAH! TH COPS CAN'T BE EVERYWHERE
AND, WITH SPIDER MAN GONE, OUR JOB'S A LOT EASIE NOW!
ACE

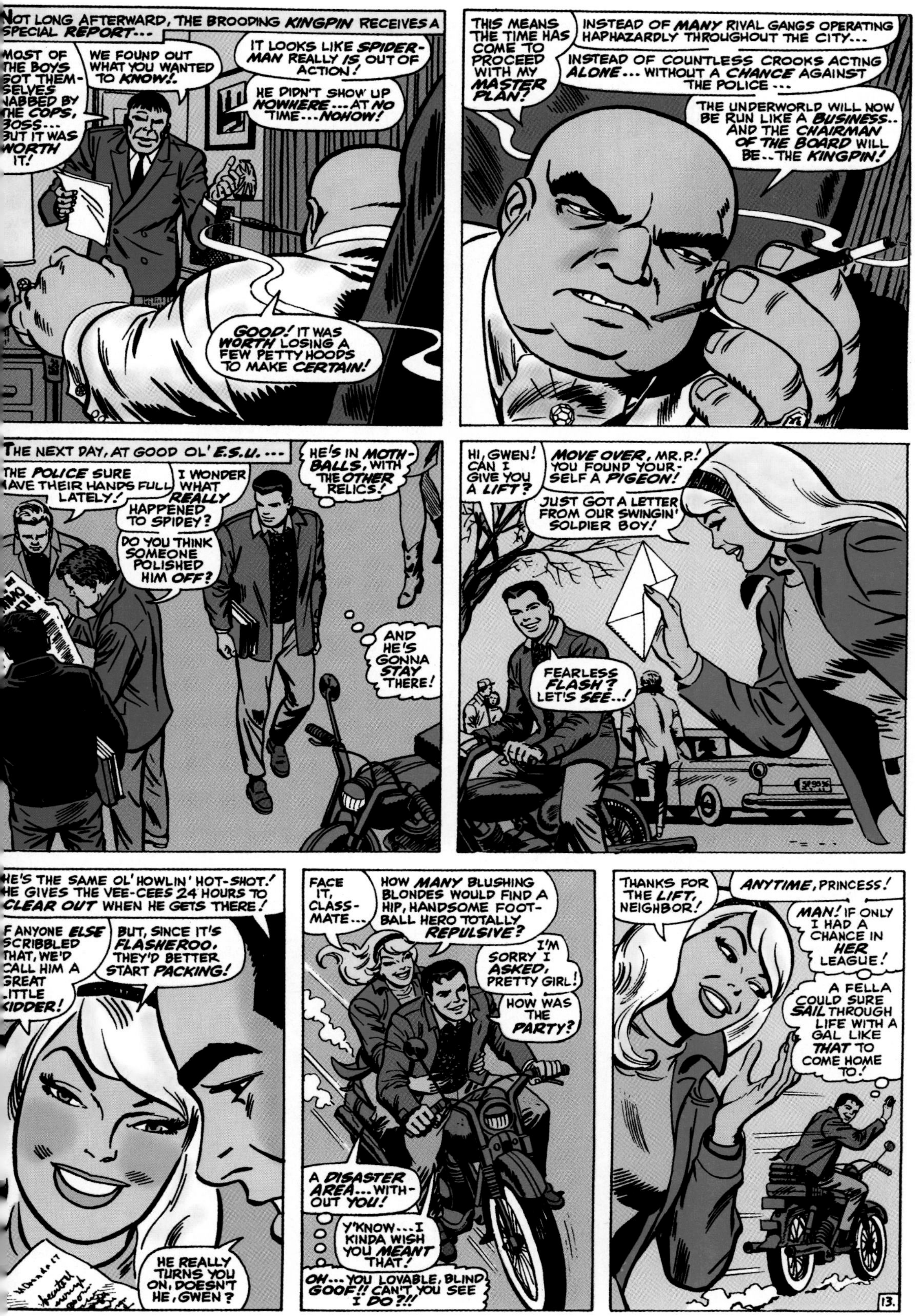

NOT LONG AFTERWARD, THE BROODING KINGPIN RECEIVES A SPECIAL REPORT...
MOST OF THE BOYS GOT THEM-SELVES NABBED BY THE COPS, BOSS... BUT IT WAS WORTH IT!
WE FOUND OUT WHAT YOU WANTED TO KNOW!.
IT LOOKS LIKE SPIDER-MAN REALLY IS OUT OF ACTION!
HE DIDN'T SHOW UP NOWHERE... AT NO TIME... NOHOW!
GOOD! IT WAS WORTH LOSING A FEW PETTY HOODS TO MAKE CERTAIN!
THIS MEANS THE TIME HAS COME TO PROCEED WITH MY MASTER PLAN!
INSTEAD OF MANY RIVAL GANGS OPERATING HAPHAZARDLY THROUGHOUT THE CITY...
INSTEAD OF COUNTLESS CROOKS ACTING ALONE... WITHOUT A CHANCE AGAINST THE POLICE...
THE UNDERWORLD WILL NOW BE RUN LIKE A BUSINESS.. AND THE CHAIRMAN OF THE BOARD WILL BE.. THE KINGPIN!
THE NEXT DAY, AT GOOD OL' E.S.U. ...
THE POLICE SURE HAVE THEIR HANDS FULL LATELY!
I WONDER WHAT REALLY HAPPENED TO SPIDEY?
DO YOU THINK SOMEONE POLISHED HIM OFF?
HE'S IN MOTH-BALLS, WITH THE OTHER RELICS!
AND HE'S GONNA STAY THERE!
HI, GWEN! CAN I GIVE YOU A LIFT?
MOVE OVER, MR. P.! YOU FOUND YOUR-SELF A PIGEON!
JUST GOT A LETTER FROM OUR SWINGIN' SOLDIER BOY!
FEARLESS FLASH? LET'S SEE...!
HE'S THE SAME OL' HOWLIN' HOT-SHOT! HE GIVES THE VEE-CEES 24 HOURS TO CLEAR OUT WHEN HE GETS THERE!
IF ANYONE ELSE SCRIBBLED THAT, WE'D CALL HIM A GREAT LITTLE KIDDER!
BUT, SINCE IT'S FLASHEROO, THEY'D BETTER START PACKING!
HE REALLY TURNS YOU ON, DOESN'T HE, GWEN?
FACE IT, CLASS-MATE...
HOW MANY BLUSHING BLONDES WOULD FIND A HIP, HANDSOME FOOT-BALL HERO TOTALLY REPULSIVE?
I'M SORRY I ASKED, PRETTY GIRL!
HOW WAS THE PARTY?
A DISASTER AREA... WITH-OUT YOU!
Y'KNOW... I KINDA WISH YOU MEANT THAT!
OH... YOU LOVABLE, BLIND GOOF!! CAN'T YOU SEE I DO?!!
THANKS FOR THE LIFT, NEIGHBOR!
ANYTIME, PRINCESS!
MAN! IF ONLY I HAD A CHANCE IN HER LEAGUE!
A FELLA COULD SURE SAIL THROUGH LIFE WITH A GAL LIKE THAT TO COME HOME TO!
13.

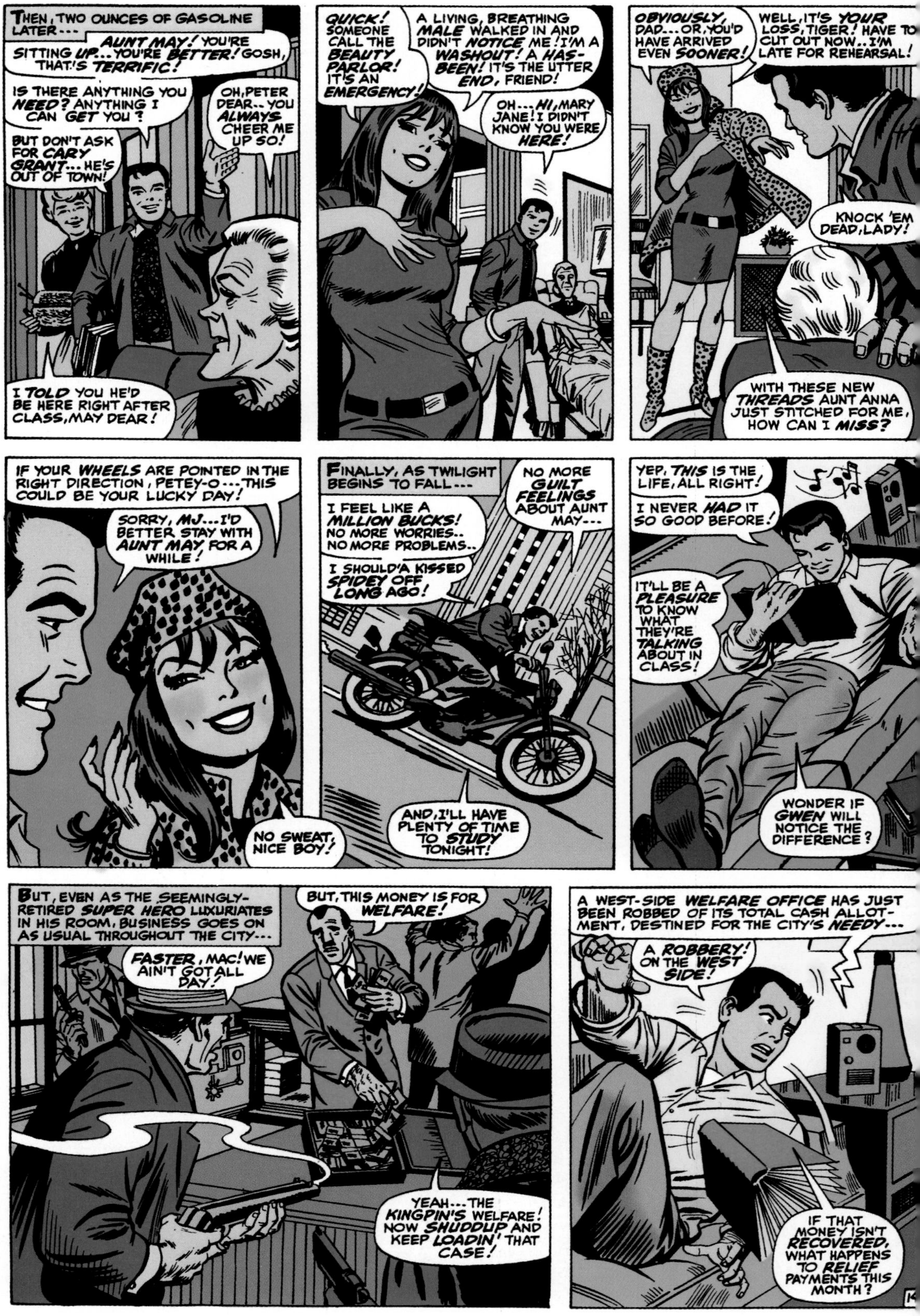
THEN, TWO OUNCES OF GASOLINE LATER---
AUNT MAY! YOU'RE SITTING UP...YOU'RE BETTER! GOSH, THAT'S TERRIFIC!
IS THERE ANYTHING YOU NEED? ANYTHING I CAN GET YOU?
BUT DON'T ASK FOR CARY GRANT...HE'S OUT OF TOWN!
OH, PETER DEAR.. YOU ALWAYS CHEER ME UP SO!
I TOLD YOU HE'D BE HERE RIGHT AFTER CLASS, MAY DEAR!
QUICK! SOMEONE CALL THE BEAUTY PARLOR! IT'S AN EMERGENCY!
A LIVING, BREATHING MALE WALKED IN AND DIDN'T NOTICE ME! I'M A WASHOUT! A HAS-BEEN! IT'S THE UTTER END, FRIEND!
OH... HI, MARY JANE! I DIDN'T KNOW YOU WERE HERE!
OBVIOUSLY, DAD...OR, YOU'D HAVE ARRIVED EVEN SOONER!
WELL, IT'S YOUR LOSS, TIGER! HAVE TO CUT OUT NOW...I'M LATE FOR REHEARSAL!
KNOCK 'EM DEAD, LADY!
WITH THESE NEW THREADS AUNT ANNA JUST STITCHED FOR ME, HOW CAN I MISS?
IF YOUR WHEELS ARE POINTED IN THE RIGHT DIRECTION, PETEY-O---THIS COULD BE YOUR LUCKY DAY!
SORRY, MJ...I'D BETTER STAY WITH AUNT MAY FOR A WHILE!
NO SWEAT, NICE BOY!
FINALLY, AS TWILIGHT BEGINS TO FALL---
I FEEL LIKE A MILLION BUCKS! NO MORE WORRIES.. NO MORE PROBLEMS..
I SHOULD'A KISSED SPIDEY OFF LONG AGO!
NO MORE GUILT FEELINGS ABOUT AUNT MAY---
AND, I'LL HAVE PLENTY OF TIME TO STUDY TONIGHT!
YEP, THIS IS THE LIFE, ALL RIGHT!
I NEVER HAD IT SO GOOD BEFORE!
IT'LL BE A PLEASURE TO KNOW WHAT THEY'RE TALKING ABOUT IN CLASS!
WONDER IF GWEN WILL NOTICE THE DIFFERENCE?
BUT, EVEN AS THE SEEMINGLY-RETIRED SUPER HERO LUXURIATES IN HIS ROOM, BUSINESS GOES ON AS USUAL THROUGHOUT THE CITY---
FASTER, MAC! WE AIN'T GOT ALL DAY!
BUT, THIS MONEY IS FOR WELFARE!
YEAH...THE KINGPIN'S WELFARE! NOW SHUDDUP AND KEEP LOADIN' THAT CASE!
A WEST-SIDE WELFARE OFFICE HAS JUST BEEN ROBBED OF ITS TOTAL CASH ALLOTMENT, DESTINED FOR THE CITY'S NEEDY---
A ROBBERY! ON THE WEST SIDE!
IF THAT MONEY ISN'T RECOVERED, WHAT HAPPENS TO RELIEF PAYMENTS THIS MONTH?

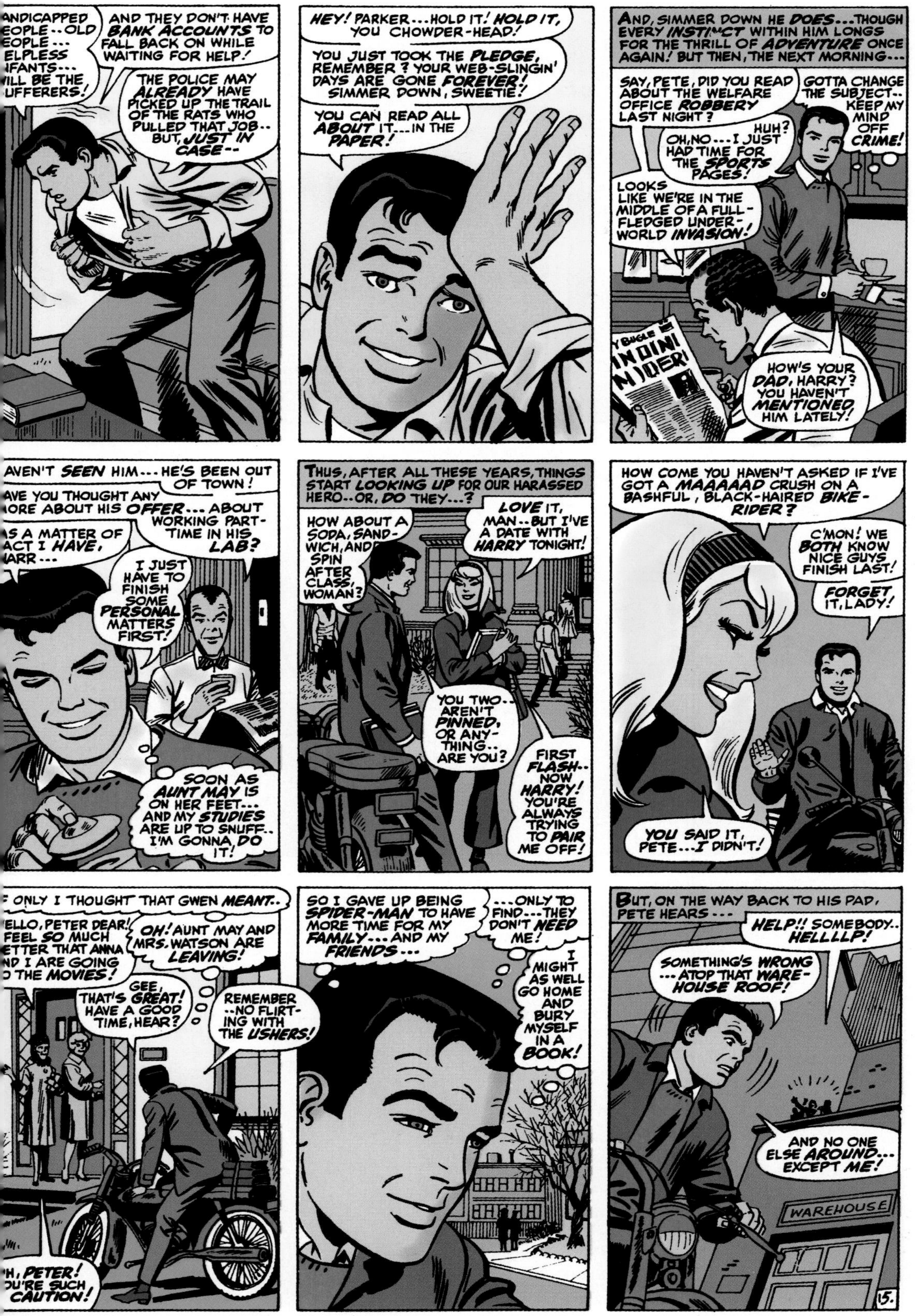
ANDICAPPED EOPLE..OLD EOPLE... ELPLESS NFANTS... VILL BE THE UFFERERS!
AND THEY DON'T HAVE BANK ACCOUNTS TO FALL BACK ON WHILE WAITING FOR HELP!
THE POLICE MAY ALREADY HAVE PICKED UP THE TRAIL OF THE RATS WHO PULLED THAT JOB.. BUT, JUST IN CASE--
HEY! PARKER...HOLD IT! HOLD IT, YOU CHOWDER-HEAD!
YOU JUST TOOK THE PLEDGE, REMEMBER? YOUR WEB-SLINGIN' DAYS ARE GONE FOREVER! SIMMER DOWN, SWEETIE!
YOU CAN READ ALL ABOUT IT...IN THE PAPER!
AND, SIMMER DOWN HE DOES...THOUGH EVERY INSTINCT WITHIN HIM LONGS FOR THE THRILL OF ADVENTURE ONCE AGAIN! BUT THEN, THE NEXT MORNING...
SAY, PETE, DID YOU READ ABOUT THE WELFARE OFFICE ROBBERY LAST NIGHT?
GOTTA CHANGE THE SUBJECT.. KEEP MY MIND OFF CRIME!
HUH? OH, NO...I JUST HAD TIME FOR THE SPORTS PAGES!
LOOKS LIKE WE'RE IN THE MIDDLE OF A FULL-FLEDGED UNDER-WORLD INVASION!
HOW'S YOUR DAD, HARRY? YOU HAVEN'T MENTIONED HIM LATELY!
AVEN'T SEEN HIM...HE'S BEEN OUT OF TOWN!
AVE YOU THOUGHT ANY ORE ABOUT HIS OFFER...ABOUT WORKING PART-TIME IN HIS LAB?
S A MATTER OF ACT I HAVE, ARR...
I JUST HAVE TO FINISH SOME PERSONAL MATTERS FIRST!
SOON AS AUNT MAY IS ON HER FEET... AND MY STUDIES ARE UP TO SNUFF.. I'M GONNA DO IT!
THUS, AFTER ALL THESE YEARS, THINGS START LOOKING UP FOR OUR HARASSED HERO..OR, DO THEY...?
HOW ABOUT A SODA, SAND-WICH, AND SPIN AFTER CLASS, WOMAN?
LOVE IT, MAN..BUT I'VE A DATE WITH HARRY TONIGHT!
YOU TWO.. AREN'T PINNED, OR ANY-THING.. ARE YOU?
FIRST FLASH.. NOW HARRY! YOU'RE ALWAYS TRYING TO PAIR ME OFF!
HOW COME YOU HAVEN'T ASKED IF I'VE GOT A MAAAAAD CRUSH ON A BASHFUL, BLACK-HAIRED BIKE-RIDER?
C'MON! WE BOTH KNOW NICE GUYS FINISH LAST!
FORGET IT, LADY!
YOU SAID IT, PETE...I DIDN'T!
F ONLY I THOUGHT THAT GWEN MEANT..
ELLO, PETER DEAR! FEEL SO MUCH ETTER THAT ANNA ND I ARE GOING O THE MOVIES!
OH! AUNT MAY AND MRS. WATSON ARE LEAVING!
GEE, THAT'S GREAT! HAVE A GOOD TIME, HEAR?
REMEMBER --NO FLIRT-ING WITH THE USHERS!
H, PETER! OU'RE SUCH CAUTION!
SO I GAVE UP BEING SPIDER-MAN TO HAVE MORE TIME FOR MY FAMILY...AND MY FRIENDS...
...ONLY TO FIND...THEY DON'T NEED ME!
I MIGHT AS WELL GO HOME AND BURY MYSELF IN A BOOK!
BUT, ON THE WAY BACK TO HIS PAD, PETE HEARS...
HELP!! SOMEBODY.. HELLLLP!
SOMETHING'S WRONG ...ATOP THAT WARE-HOUSE ROOF!
AND NO ONE ELSE AROUND... EXCEPT ME!
WAREHOUSE
15.

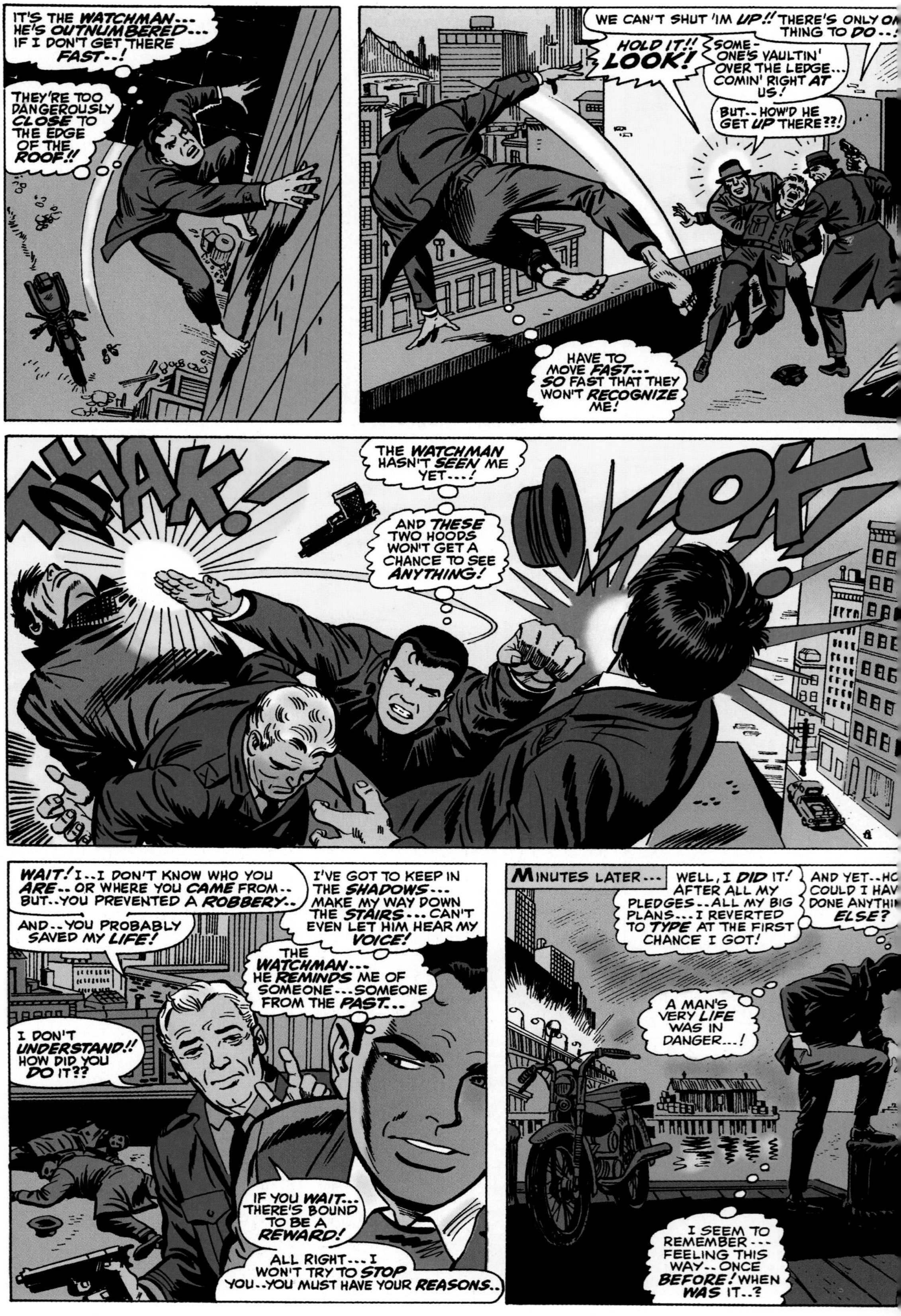

IT'S THE WATCHMAN... HE'S OUTNUMBERED... IF I DON'T GET THERE FAST..!
THEY'RE TOO DANGEROUSLY CLOSE TO THE EDGE OF THE ROOF!!
WE CAN'T SHUT 'IM UP!! THERE'S ONLY ON THING TO DO..!
HOLD IT!! LOOK!
SOME-ONE'S VAULTIN' OVER THE LEDGE... COMIN' RIGHT AT US!
BUT.. HOW'D HE GET UP THERE??!
HAVE TO MOVE FAST... SO FAST THAT THEY WON'T RECOGNIZE ME!
THAK!
THE WATCHMAN HASN'T SEEN ME YET...!
AND THESE TWO HOODS WON'T GET A CHANCE TO SEE ANYTHING!
WOK!
WAIT! I..I DON'T KNOW WHO YOU ARE.. OR WHERE YOU CAME FROM.. BUT.. YOU PREVENTED A ROBBERY..
AND.. YOU PROBABLY SAVED MY LIFE!
I'VE GOT TO KEEP IN THE SHADOWS... MAKE MY WAY DOWN THE STAIRS... CAN'T EVEN LET HIM HEAR MY VOICE!
THE WATCHMAN... HE REMINDS ME OF SOMEONE... SOMEONE FROM THE PAST...
I DON'T UNDERSTAND!! HOW DID YOU DO IT??
IF YOU WAIT... THERE'S BOUND TO BE A REWARD!
ALL RIGHT... I WON'T TRY TO STOP YOU.. YOU MUST HAVE YOUR REASONS..
MINUTES LATER...
WELL, I DID IT! AFTER ALL MY PLEDGES.. ALL MY BIG PLANS.. I REVERTED TO TYPE AT THE FIRST CHANCE I GOT!
AND YET.. HO COULD I HAV DONE ANYTHIN ELSE?
A MAN'S VERY LIFE WAS IN DANGER...!
I SEEM TO REMEMBER... FEELING THIS WAY.. ONCE BEFORE! WHEN WAS IT..?

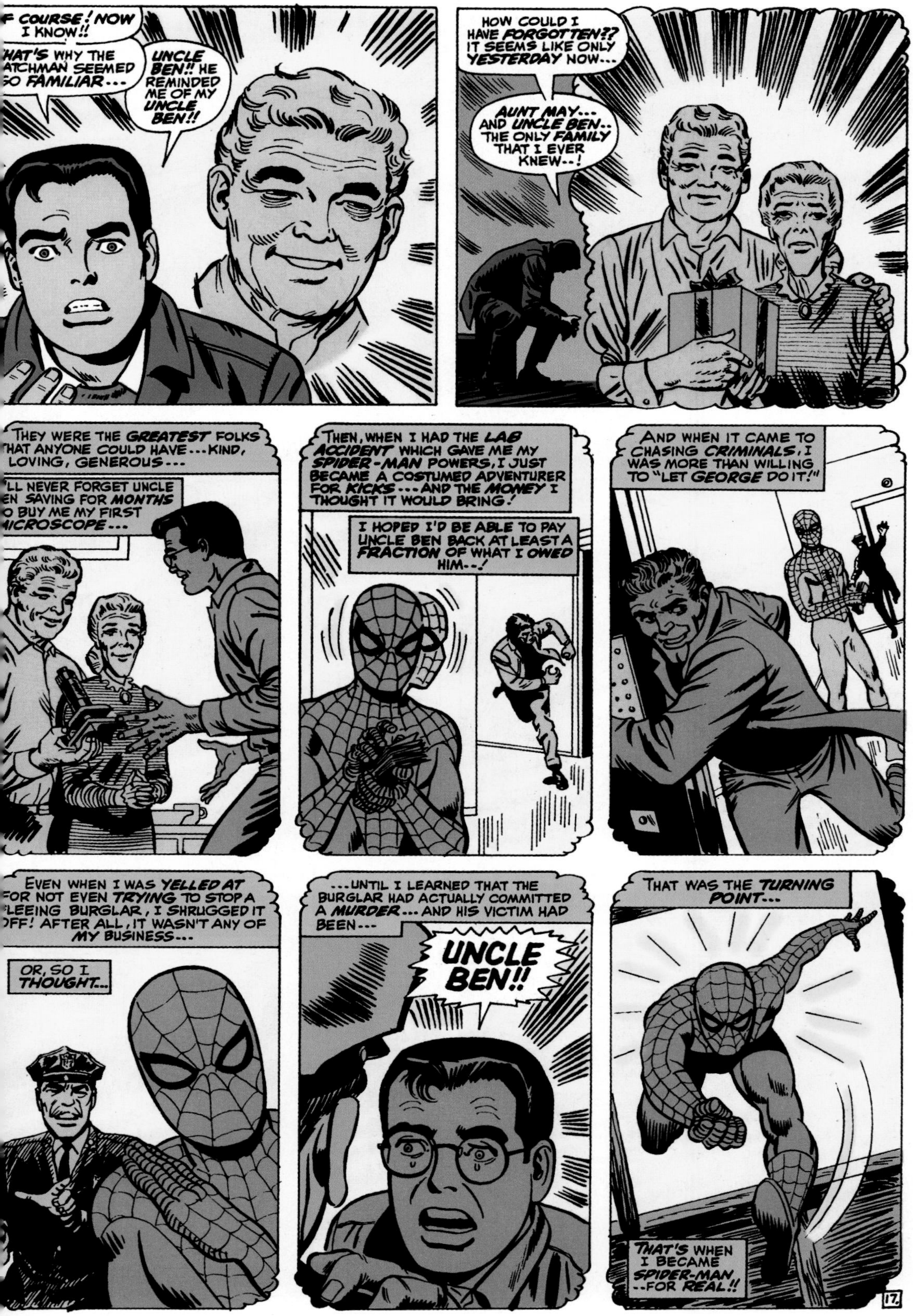

F COURSE! NOW I KNOW!!
HAT'S WHY THE ATCHMAN SEEMED O FAMILIAR...
UNCLE BEN!! HE REMINDED ME OF MY UNCLE BEN!!
HOW COULD I HAVE FORGOTTEN?? IT SEEMS LIKE ONLY YESTERDAY NOW...
AUNT MAY... AND UNCLE BEN.. THE ONLY FAMILY THAT I EVER KNEW--!
THEY WERE THE GREATEST FOLKS HAT ANYONE COULD HAVE...KIND, LOVING, GENEROUS...
LL NEVER FORGET UNCLE EN SAVING FOR MONTHS O BUY ME MY FIRST ICROSCOPE...
THEN, WHEN I HAD THE LAB ACCIDENT WHICH GAVE ME MY SPIDER-MAN POWERS, I JUST BECAME A COSTUMED ADVENTURER FOR KICKS...AND THE MONEY I THOUGHT IT WOULD BRING!
I HOPED I'D BE ABLE TO PAY UNCLE BEN BACK AT LEAST A FRACTION OF WHAT I OWED HIM--!
AND WHEN IT CAME TO CHASING CRIMINALS, I WAS MORE THAN WILLING TO "LET GEORGE DO IT!"
EVEN WHEN I WAS YELLED AT FOR NOT EVEN TRYING TO STOP A LEEING BURGLAR, I SHRUGGED IT FF! AFTER ALL, IT WASN'T ANY OF MY BUSINESS...
OR, SO I THOUGHT...
...UNTIL I LEARNED THAT THE BURGLAR HAD ACTUALLY COMMITTED A MURDER... AND HIS VICTIM HAD BEEN---
UNCLE BEN!!
THAT WAS THE TURNING POINT...
THAT'S WHEN I BECAME SPIDER-MAN --FOR REAL!!

ONE OF THE FIRST *VICTORIES* IN MY CRIME-BUSTING CAREER CAME A SHORT TIME LATER, WHEN I CORNERED AN *ARMED ROBBER*..

EVEN WITH HIS *GUN*, HE WAS NO MATCH FOR MY *SPIDER-POWERS*... AND I DUSTED HIM OFF FAST AND EASY...!

BUT, A MINUTE LATER, I GOT THE *NEXT* GREAT SURPRISE OF MY LIFE...

IT'S *HIM*!! HE'S THE ONE...WHO KILLED..*UNCLE BEN*!!

AND, THEN, I WAS SUDDENLY HIT BY THE *SHOCKING* REALIZATION WHICH HAS *HAUNTED* ME...FROM THAT MOMENT ON—

I HAD A CHANCE TO *STOP* HIM...WHEN HE RAN *PAST* ME THAT DAY...AND I *DIDN'T!*

BUT, IF ONLY I *HAD* DONE SO...

UNCLE BEN WOULD BE ALIVE TODAY!

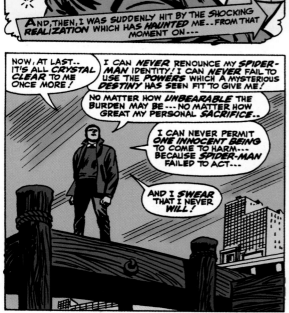

NOW, AT LAST.. IT'S ALL *CRYSTAL CLEAR* TO ME ONCE MORE!

I CAN *NEVER* RENOUNCE MY *SPIDER-MAN* IDENTITY! I CAN *NEVER* FAIL TO USE THE *POWERS* WHICH A MYSTERIOUS *DESTINY* HAS SEEN FIT TO GIVE ME!

NO MATTER HOW *UNBEARABLE* THE BURDEN MAY BE --- NO MATTER HOW GREAT MY PERSONAL *SACRIFICE*..

I CAN NEVER PERMIT *ONE INNOCENT BEING* TO COME TO HARM... BECAUSE *SPIDER-MAN* FAILED TO ACT...

AND I *SWEAR* THAT I NEVER *WILL!*

WHILE, AT THE PALATIAL HEADQUARTERS OF THE COLD-BLOODED *KINGPIN*, WE FIND---

EVER HEAR OF THE *BIG MAN*, MISTER?

YOU'RE *LOOKING* AT HIM!

I *RAN* THE RACKETS IN THIS TOWN...BEFORE *SPIDER-MAN* PUT ME ON ICE!

BUT THE WEB-SLINGER'S *GONE* NOW, SO I'M AIMING TO RUN THINGS *AGAIN!*

I *REMEMBER* YOU, FOSWELL! I THOUGHT YOU HAD GONE *STRAIGHT!*

SO DID *I*! BUT I CAN'T STAND BY AND WATCH SOMEONE *ELSE* PICK UP WHERE *I* LEFT OFF!

IF *ANYONE'S* GONNA ORGANIZE THE MOBS... IT'S GOTTA BE *ME!*

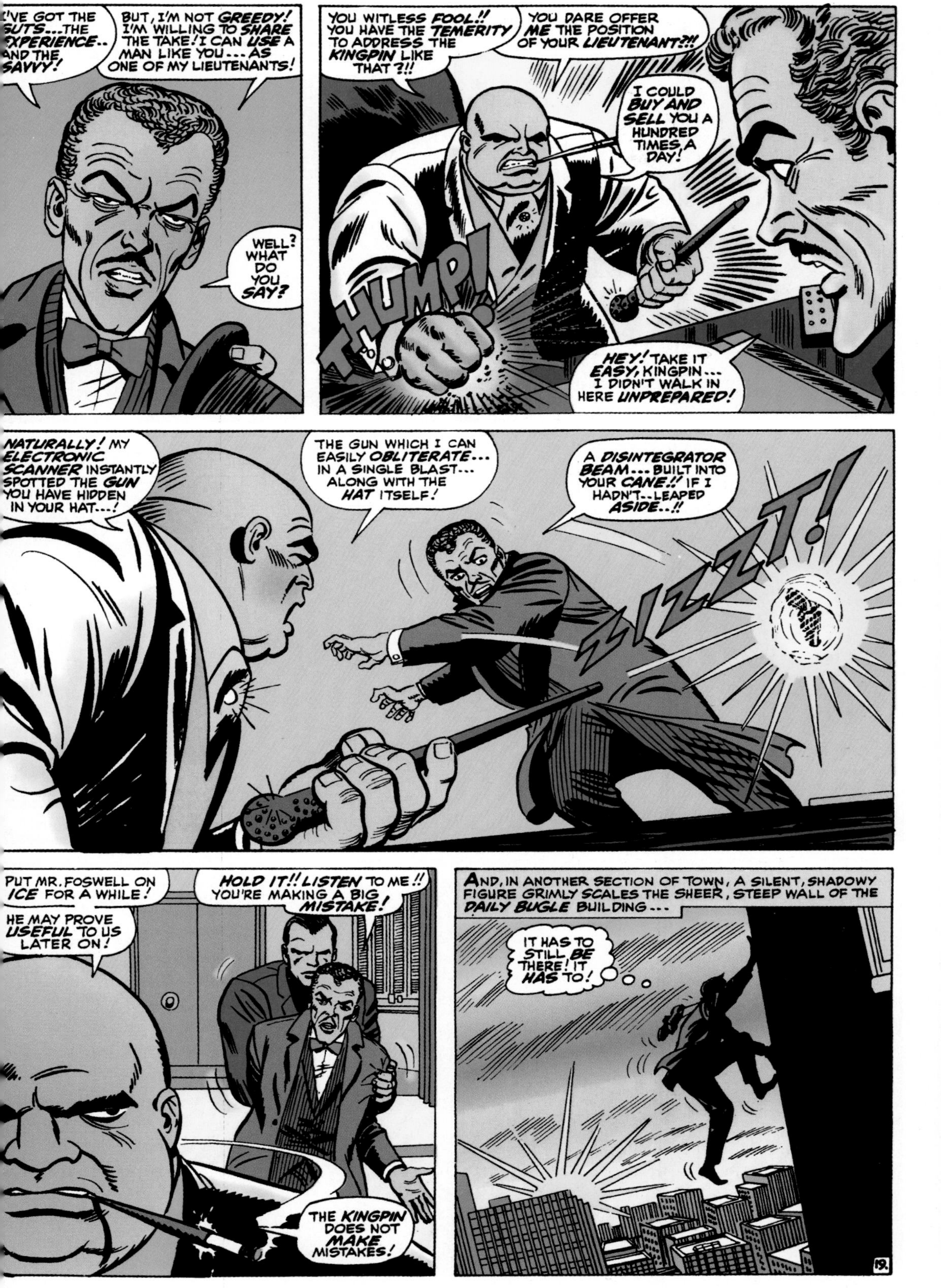
I'VE GOT THE GUTS... THE EXPERIENCE.. AND THE SAVVY!
BUT, I'M NOT GREEDY! I'M WILLING TO SHARE THE TAKE! I CAN USE A MAN LIKE YOU... AS ONE OF MY LIEUTENANTS!
WELL? WHAT DO YOU SAY?
YOU WITLESS FOOL!! YOU HAVE THE TEMERITY TO ADDRESS THE KINGPIN LIKE THAT?!!
YOU DARE OFFER ME THE POSITION OF YOUR LIEUTENANT?!!
I COULD BUY AND SELL YOU A HUNDRED TIMES A DAY!
THUMP!
HEY! TAKE IT EASY, KINGPIN... I DIDN'T WALK IN HERE UNPREPARED!
NATURALLY! MY ELECTRONIC SCANNER INSTANTLY SPOTTED THE GUN YOU HAVE HIDDEN IN YOUR HAT...!
THE GUN WHICH I CAN EASILY OBLITERATE... IN A SINGLE BLAST... ALONG WITH THE HAT ITSELF!
A DISINTEGRATOR BEAM... BUILT INTO YOUR CANE!! IF I HADN'T--LEAPED ASIDE..!!
ZIZZZT!
PUT MR. FOSWELL ON ICE FOR A WHILE!
HE MAY PROVE USEFUL TO US LATER ON!
HOLD IT!! LISTEN TO ME!! YOU'RE MAKING A BIG MISTAKE!
THE KINGPIN DOES NOT MAKE MISTAKES!
AND, IN ANOTHER SECTION OF TOWN, A SILENT, SHADOWY FIGURE GRIMLY SCALES THE SHEER, STEEP WALL OF THE DAILY BUGLE BUILDING...
IT HAS TO STILL BE THERE! IT HAS TO!
19.

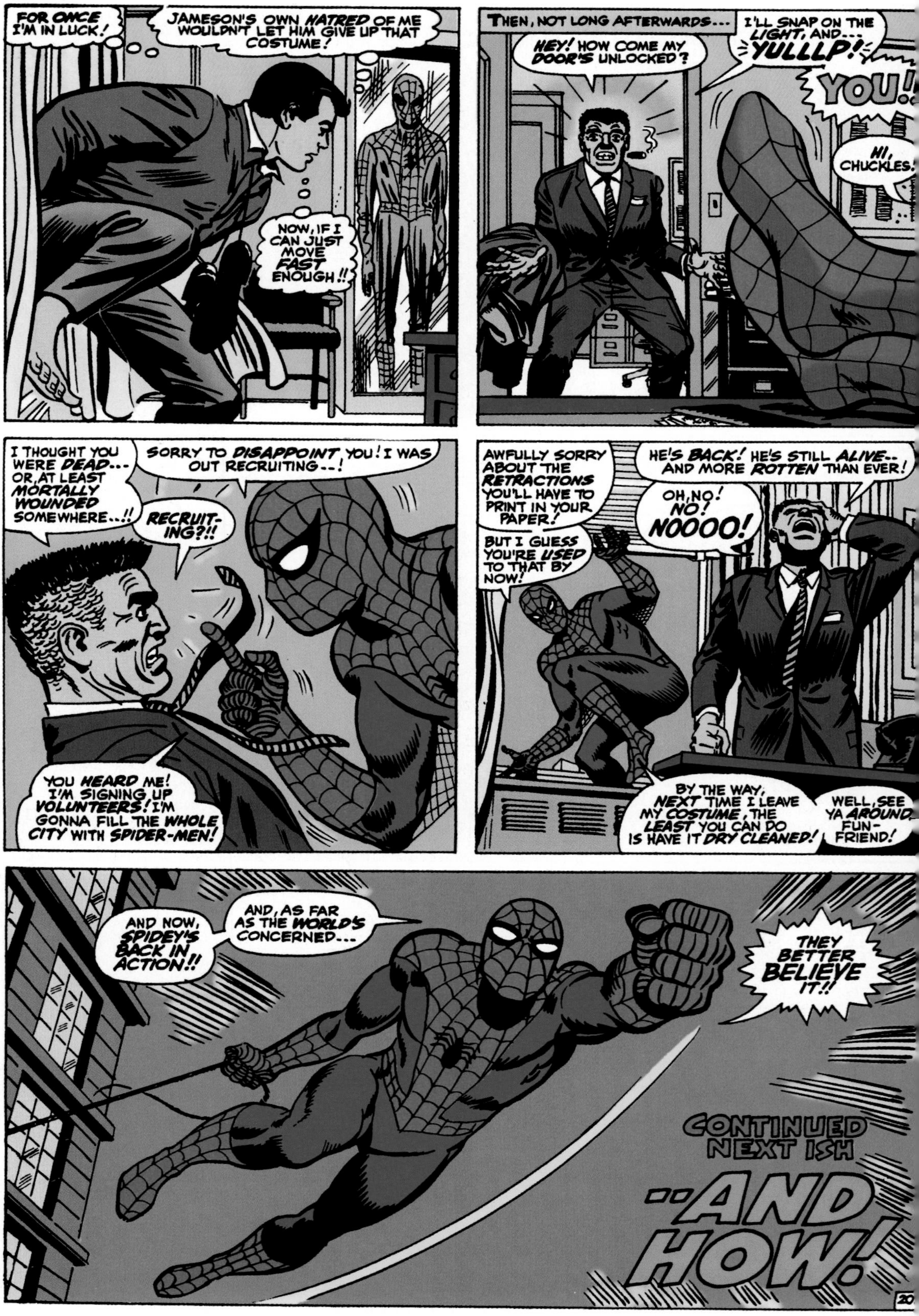

FOR ONCE I'M IN LUCK!
JAMESON'S OWN HATRED OF ME WOULDN'T LET HIM GIVE UP THAT COSTUME!
NOW, IF I CAN JUST MOVE FAST ENOUGH!!
THEN, NOT LONG AFTERWARDS...
HEY! HOW COME MY DOOR'S UNLOCKED?
I'LL SNAP ON THE LIGHT, AND... YULLLP!
YOU!!
HI, CHUCKLES!
I THOUGHT YOU WERE DEAD... OR, AT LEAST MORTALLY WOUNDED SOMEWHERE...!!
SORRY TO DISAPPOINT YOU! I WAS OUT RECRUITING--!
RECRUIT-ING?!!
YOU HEARD ME! I'M SIGNING UP VOLUNTEERS! I'M GONNA FILL THE WHOLE CITY WITH SPIDER-MEN!
AWFULLY SORRY ABOUT THE RETRACTIONS YOU'LL HAVE TO PRINT IN YOUR PAPER!
BUT I GUESS YOU'RE USED TO THAT BY NOW!
HE'S BACK! HE'S STILL ALIVE-- AND MORE ROTTEN THAN EVER!
OH, NO! NO! NOOOO!
BY THE WAY, NEXT TIME I LEAVE MY COSTUME, THE LEAST YOU CAN DO IS HAVE IT DRY CLEANED!
WELL, SEE YA AROUND, FUN-FRIEND!
AND NOW, SPIDEY'S BACK IN ACTION!!
AND, AS FAR AS THE WORLD'S CONCERNED...
THEY BETTER BELIEVE IT!!
CONTINUED NEXT ISH
--AND HOW!
20

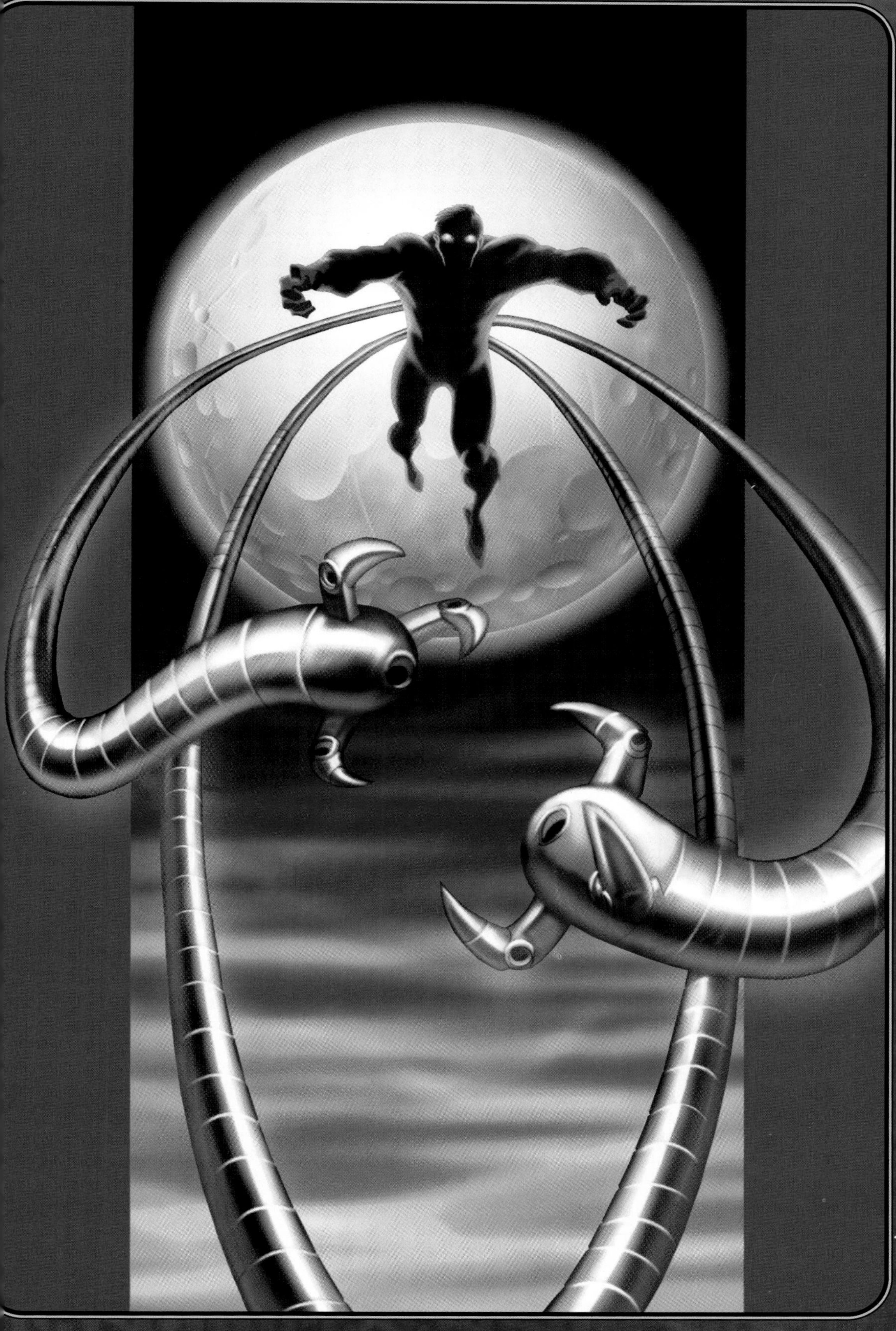

SPIDEY RECAP

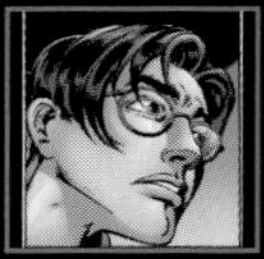
Peter Parker

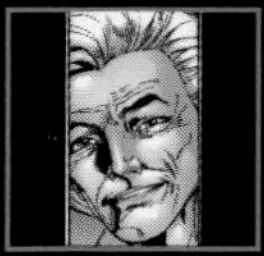
Aunt May

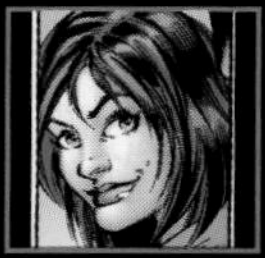
Mary Jane Watson

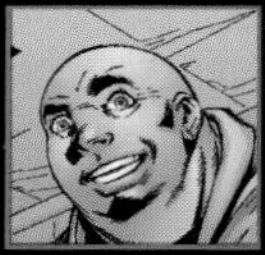
Kong

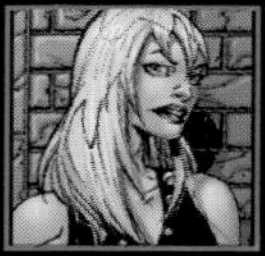
Gwen Stacy

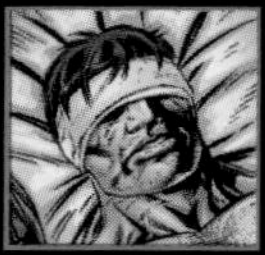
Doctor Octopus

PREVIOUSLY IN ULTIMATE SPIDER-MAN...
Previously

FAN MAIL!
Fan Mail

Stan Lee PRESENTS:

ULTIMATE SPIDER-MAN

BRIAN MICHAEL BENDIS scrip
MARK BAGLEY pencil
ART THIBERT ink
TRANSPARENCY DIGITAL color
SHARPEFONT'
DAVE SHARPE letter
BRIAN SMITH assistant edito
RALPH MACCHIO edito
JOE QUESADA editor in chie
BILL JEMAS president and inspiratio

PREVIOUSLY...

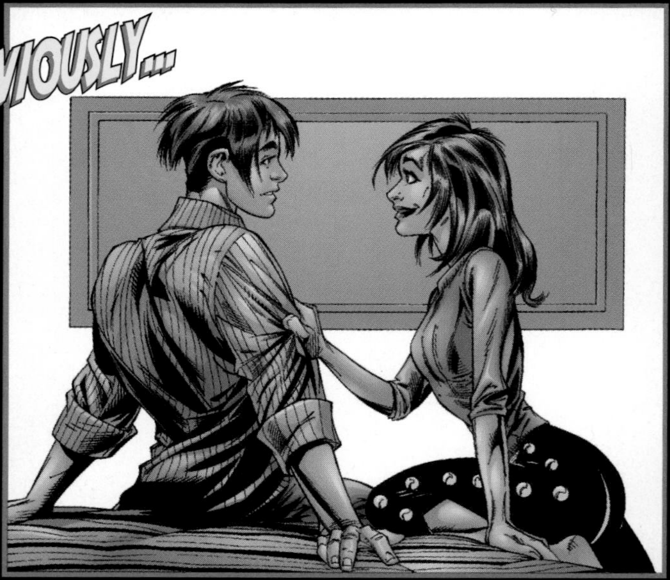

Accidentally bitten by a genetically altered spider, teenager Peter Parker now finds he has the proportionate abilities of a spider. This includes strength, agility, a spider-like sixth sense warning him of personal danger. And, most amazing of all — Peter can walk on walls.

When Peter learns through the recent tragedy of his Uncle Ben's death that with this great power then must come great responsibility, he fearlessly dons the costume of:

SPIDER-MAN

After two rousing trials by fire in the form of his first conflicts as a real life-superhero, Spider-Man came out victorious over the misshapen monstrosity of the Goblin and the underworld overboss; the Kingpin of Crime.

Peter has many unanswered questions about his powers and how he got them. One thing he does know is that by running around as Spider-Man, he has been hurting the feelings of the only true friend he has, the beautiful Mary Jane Watson. After defeating the Kingpin, the first thing he does is call Mary Jane over for a serious talk — where he reveals his secret identity to her.

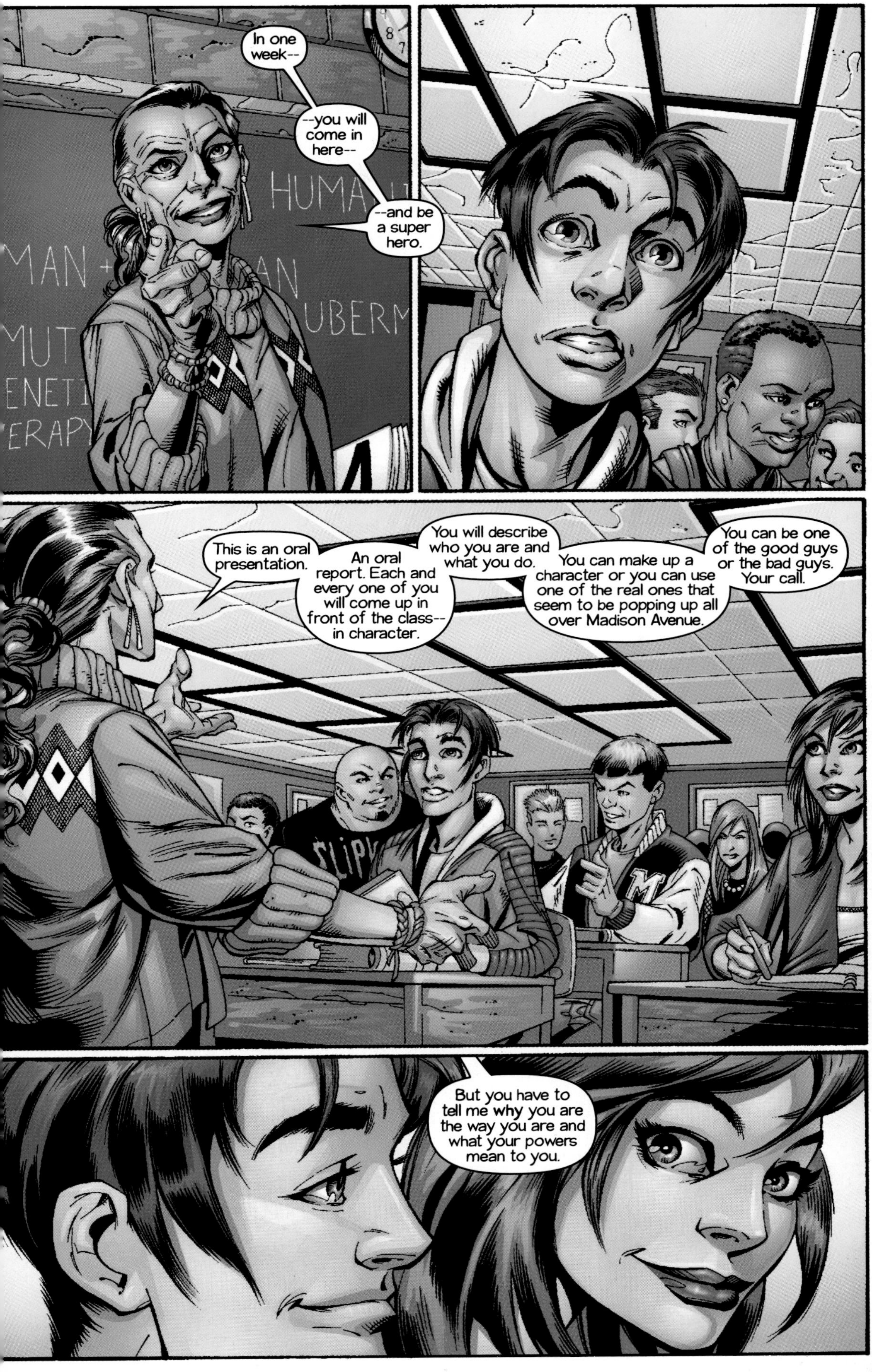

In one week--
--you will come in here--
HUMA
MAN +
UBERM
MUT
ENETI
ERAPY
--and be a super hero.
This is an oral presentation.
An oral report. Each and every one of you will come up in front of the class-- in character.
You will describe who you are and what you do.
You can make up a character or you can use one of the real ones that seem to be popping up all over Madison Avenue.
You can be one of the good guys or the bad guys. Your call.
But you have to tell me **why** you are the way you are and what your powers mean to you.

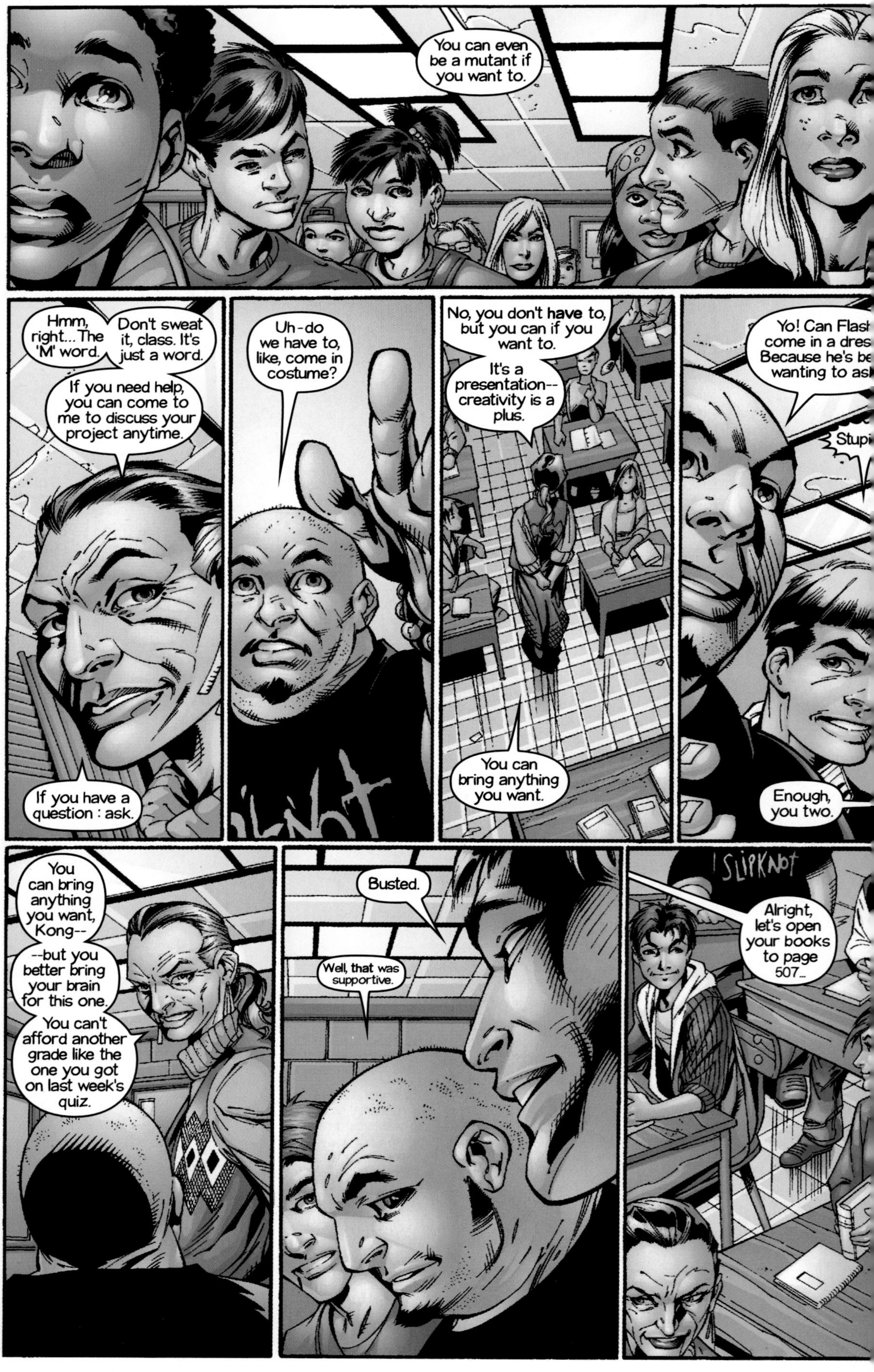

You can even be a mutant if you want to.
Hmm, right... The 'M' word.
Don't sweat it, class. It's just a word.
If you need help, you can come to me to discuss your project anytime.
If you have a question : ask.
Uh-do we have to, like, come in costume?
No, you don't **have** to, but you can if you want to.
It's a presentation-- creativity is a plus.
You can bring anything you want.
Enough, you two.
You can bring anything you want, Kong--
--but you better bring your brain for this one.
You can't afford another grade like the one you got on last week's quiz.
Busted.
Well, that was supportive.
SLIPKNOT
Alright, let's open your books to page 507...

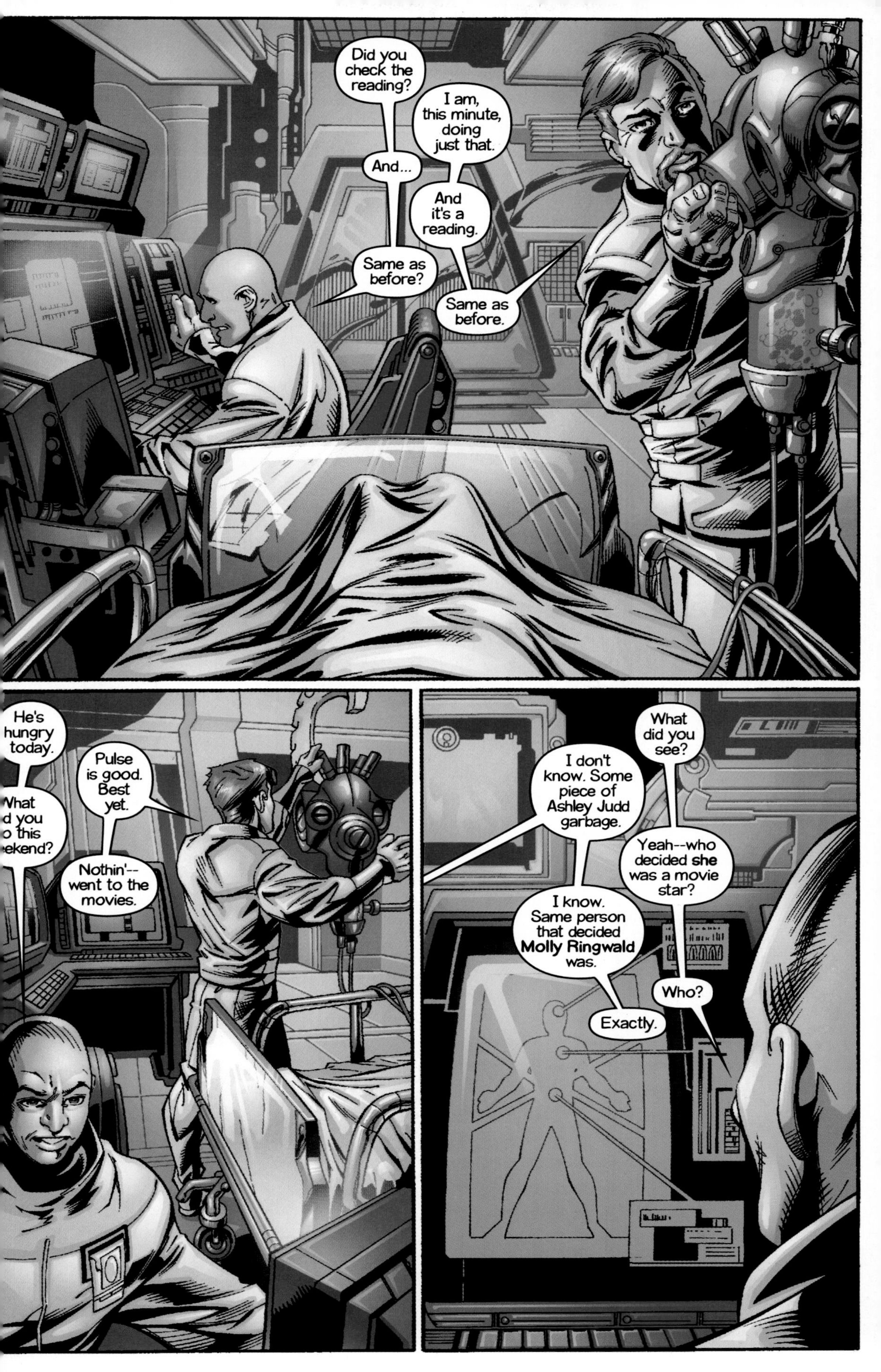

Did you check the reading?
I am, this minute, doing just that.
And...
And it's a reading.
Same as before?
Same as before.
He's hungry today.
Pulse is good. Best yet.
What d you o this eekend?
Nothin'-- went to the movies.
What did you see?
I don't know. Some piece of Ashley Judd garbage.
Yeah--who decided **she** was a movie star?
I know. Same person that decided **Molly Ringwald** was.
Who?
Exactly.

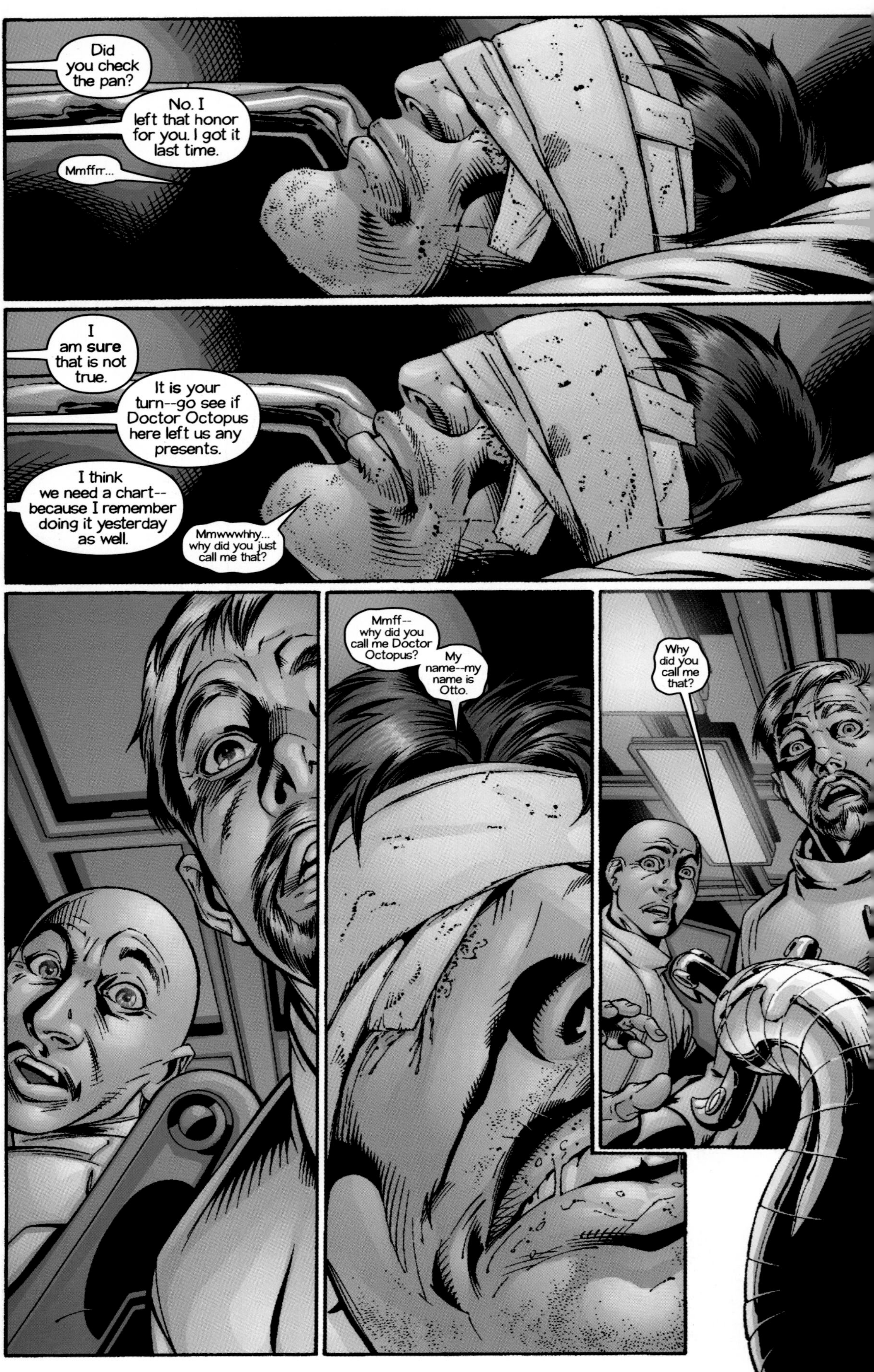
Did you check the pan?
No. I left that honor for you. I got it last time.
Mmffrr...
I am **sure** that is not true.
It **is** your turn--go see if Doctor Octopus here left us any presents.
I think we need a chart--because I remember doing it yesterday as well.
Mmwwwhhy... why did you just call me that?
Mmff-- why did you call me Doctor Octopus?
My name--my name is Otto.
Why did you call me that?

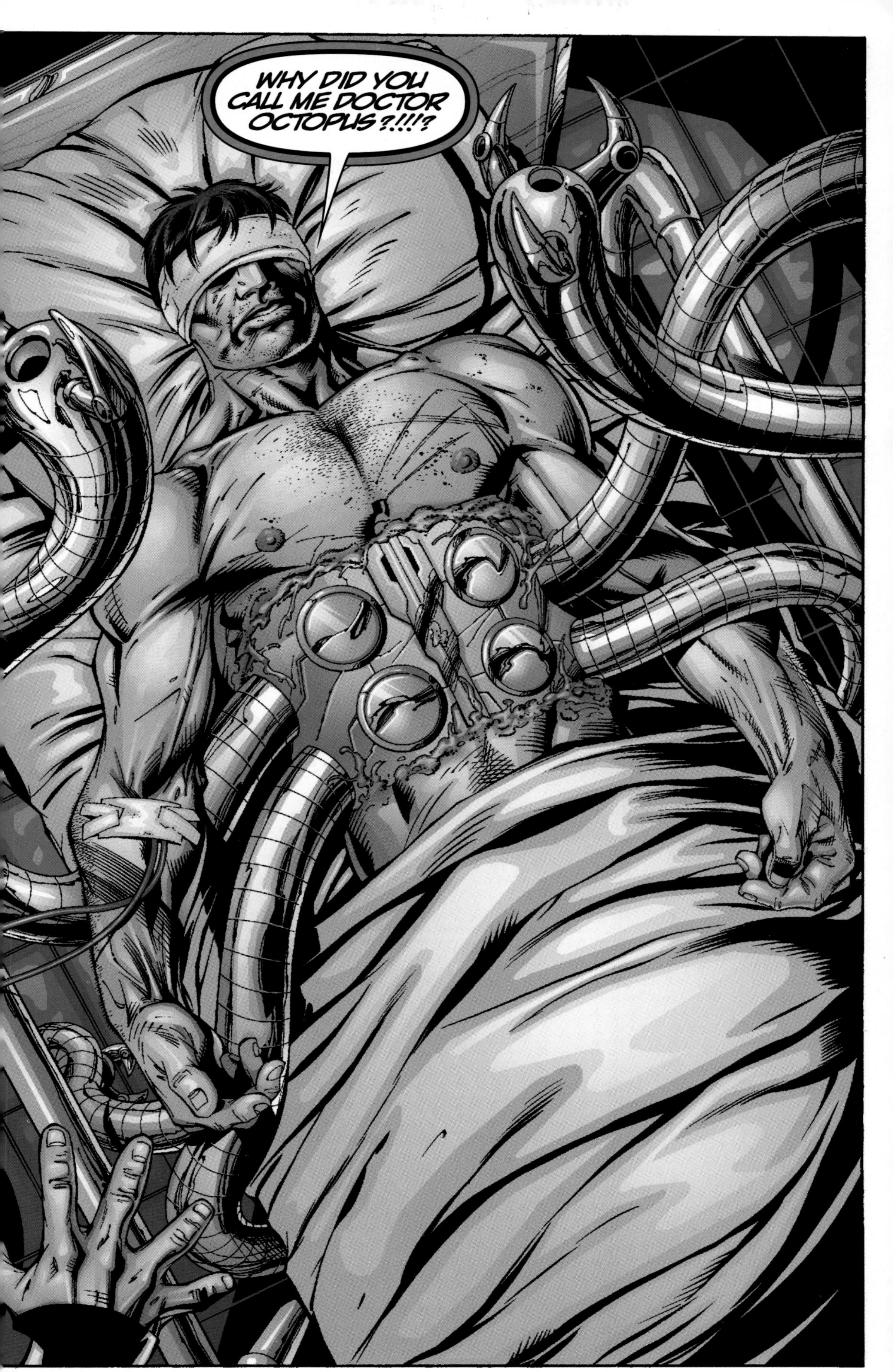
WHY DID YOU CALL ME DOCTOR OCTOPUS ?!!!?

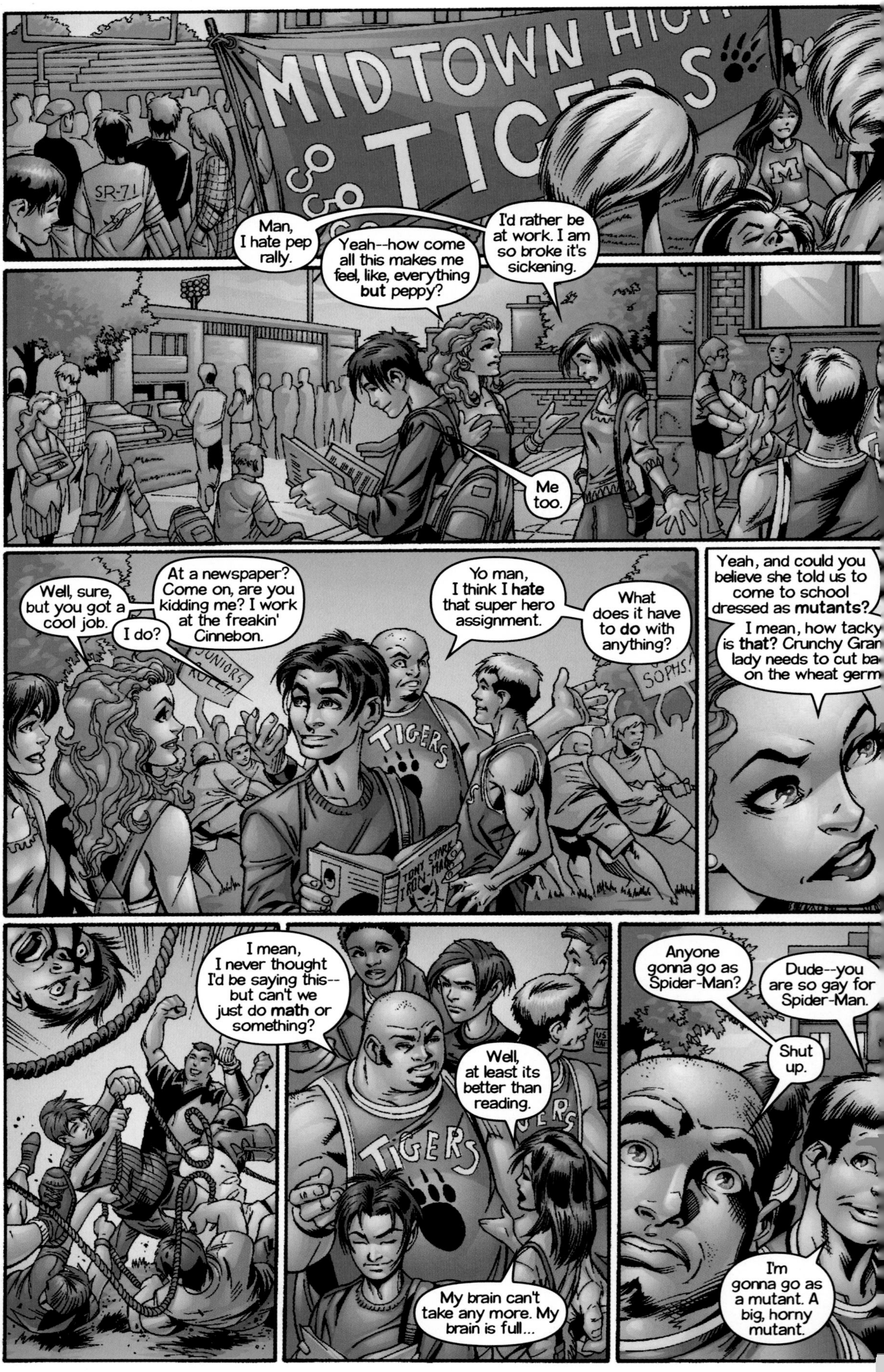
MIDTOWN HIGH
TIGERS
Man, I hate pep rally.
Yeah--how come all this makes me feel, like, everything but peppy?
I'd rather be at work. I am so broke it's sickening.
Me too.
Well, sure, but you got a cool job.
At a newspaper? Come on, are you kidding me? I work at the freakin' Cinnebon.
I do?
JUNIORS RULE!!
Yo man, I think I hate that super hero assignment.
What does it have to do with anything?
SOPHS!
TIGERS
TONY STARK IRON-MAN
Yeah, and could you believe she told us to come to school dressed as mutants?
I mean, how tacky is that? Crunchy Gran lady needs to cut ba on the wheat germ
I mean, I never thought I'd be saying this--but can't we just do math or something?
Well, at least its better than reading.
TIGERS
My brain can't take any more. My brain is full...
Anyone gonna go as Spider-Man?
Dude--you are so gay for Spider-Man.
Shut up.
I'm gonna go as a mutant. A big, horny mutant.

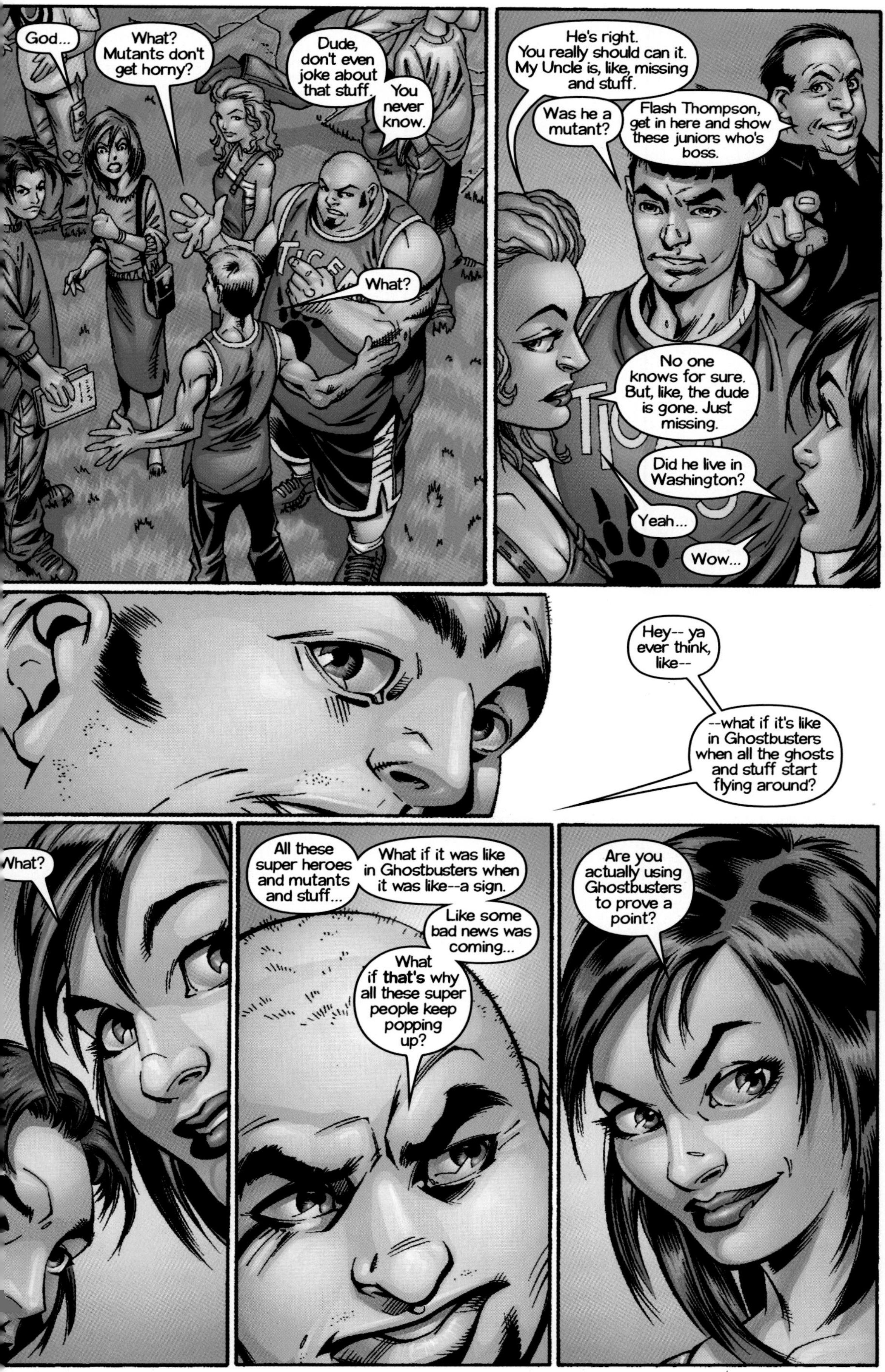
God...
What? Mutants don't get horny?
Dude, don't even joke about that stuff.
You never know.
What?
He's right. You really should can it. My Uncle is, like, missing and stuff.
Was he a mutant?
Flash Thompson, get in here and show these juniors who's boss.
No one knows for sure. But, like, the dude is gone. Just missing.
Did he live in Washington?
Yeah...
Wow...
Hey-- ya ever think, like--
--what if it's like in Ghostbusters when all the ghosts and stuff start flying around?
What?
All these super heroes and mutants and stuff...
What if it was like in Ghostbusters when it was like--a sign.
Like some bad news was coming...
What if that's why all these super people keep popping up?
Are you actually using Ghostbusters to prove a point?

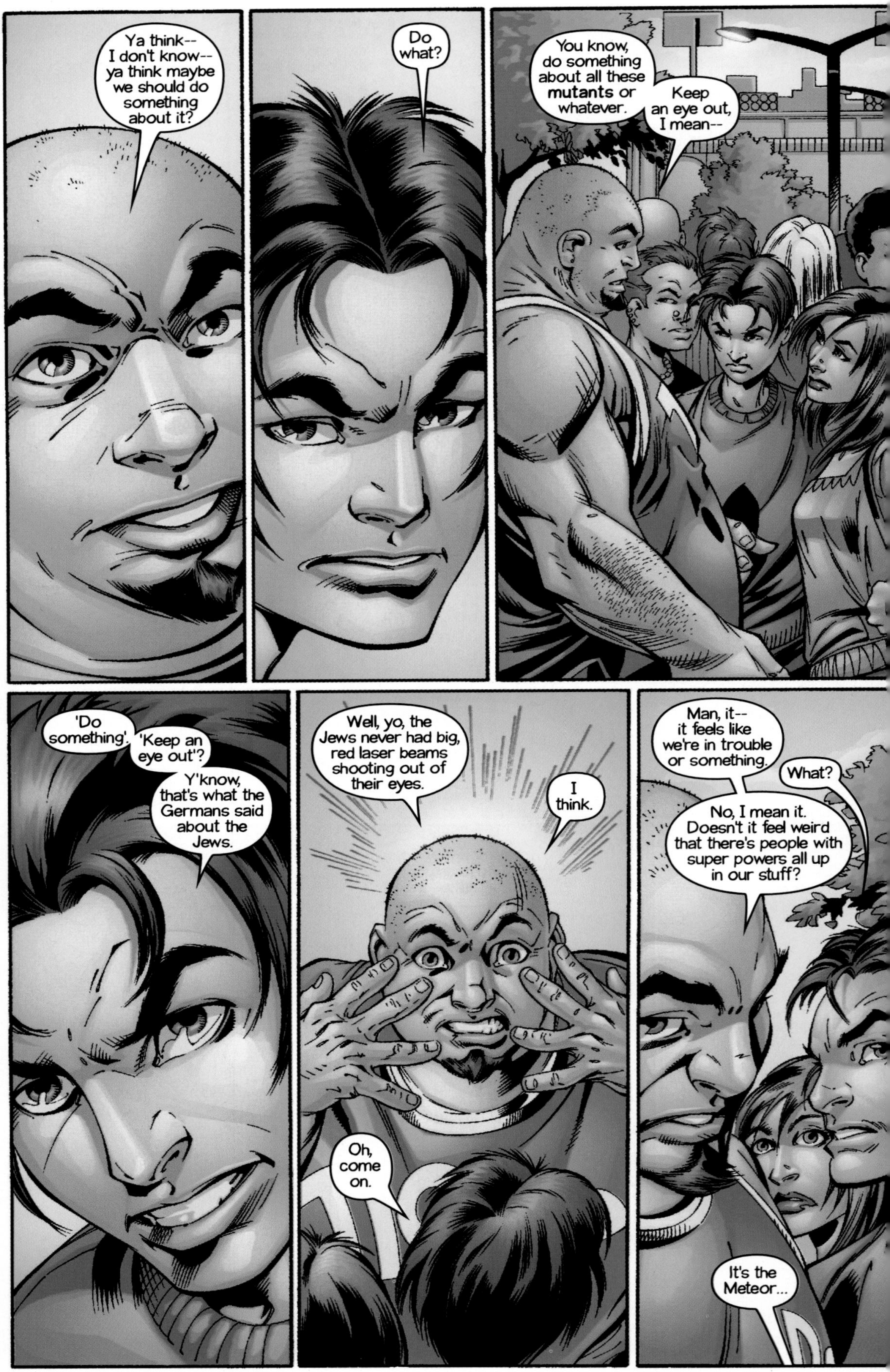
Ya think-- I don't know-- ya think maybe we should do something about it?
Do what?
You know, do something about all these **mutants** or whatever.
Keep an eye out, I mean--
'Do something'.
'Keep an eye out'?
Y'know, that's what the Germans said about the Jews.
Well, yo, the Jews never had big, red laser beams shooting out of their eyes.
I think.
Oh, come on.
Man, it-- it feels like we're in trouble or something.
What?
No, I mean it. Doesn't it feel weird that there's people with super powers all up in our stuff?
It's the Meteor...

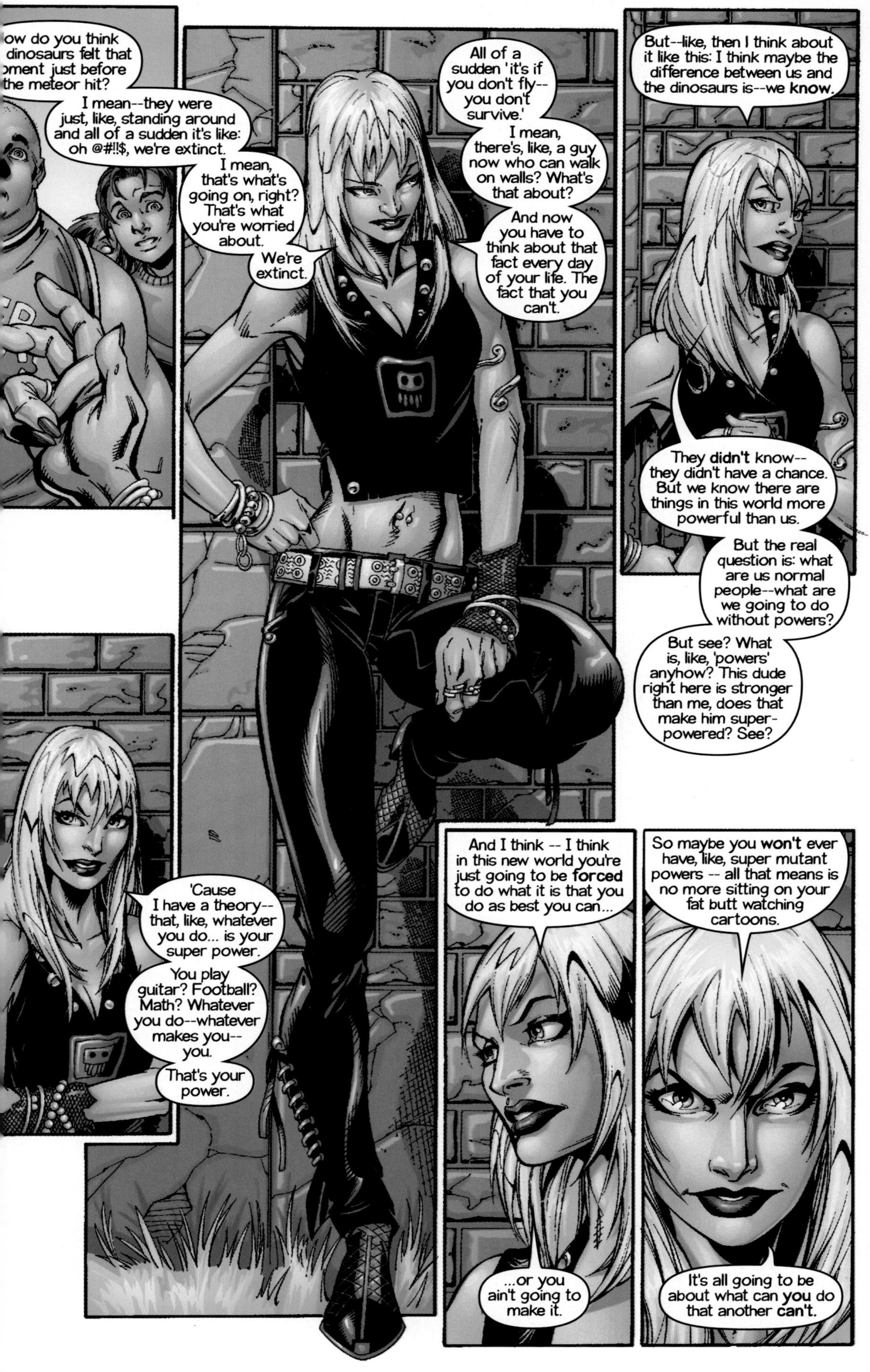
ow do you think dinosaurs felt that oment just before the meteor hit?
I mean--they were just, like, standing around and all of a sudden it's like: oh @#!!$, we're extinct.
I mean, that's what's going on, right? That's what you're worried about.
We're extinct.
All of a sudden 'it's if you don't fly--you don't survive.'
I mean, there's, like, a guy now who can walk on walls? What's that about?
And now you have to think about that fact every day of your life. The fact that you can't.
But--like, then I think about it like this: I think maybe the difference between us and the dinosaurs is--we **know**.
They **didn't** know--they didn't have a chance. But we know there are things in this world more powerful than us.
But the real question is: what are us normal people--what are we going to do without powers?
But see? What is, like, 'powers' anyhow? This dude right here is stronger than me, does that make him super-powered? See?
'Cause I have a theory--that, like, whatever you do... is your super power.
You play guitar? Football? Math? Whatever you do--whatever makes you--you.
That's your power.
And I think -- I think in this new world you're just going to be **forced** to do what it is that you do as best you can...
...or you ain't going to make it.
So maybe you **won't** ever have, like, super mutant powers -- all that means is no more sitting on your fat butt watching cartoons.
It's all going to be about what can **you** do that another **can't**.

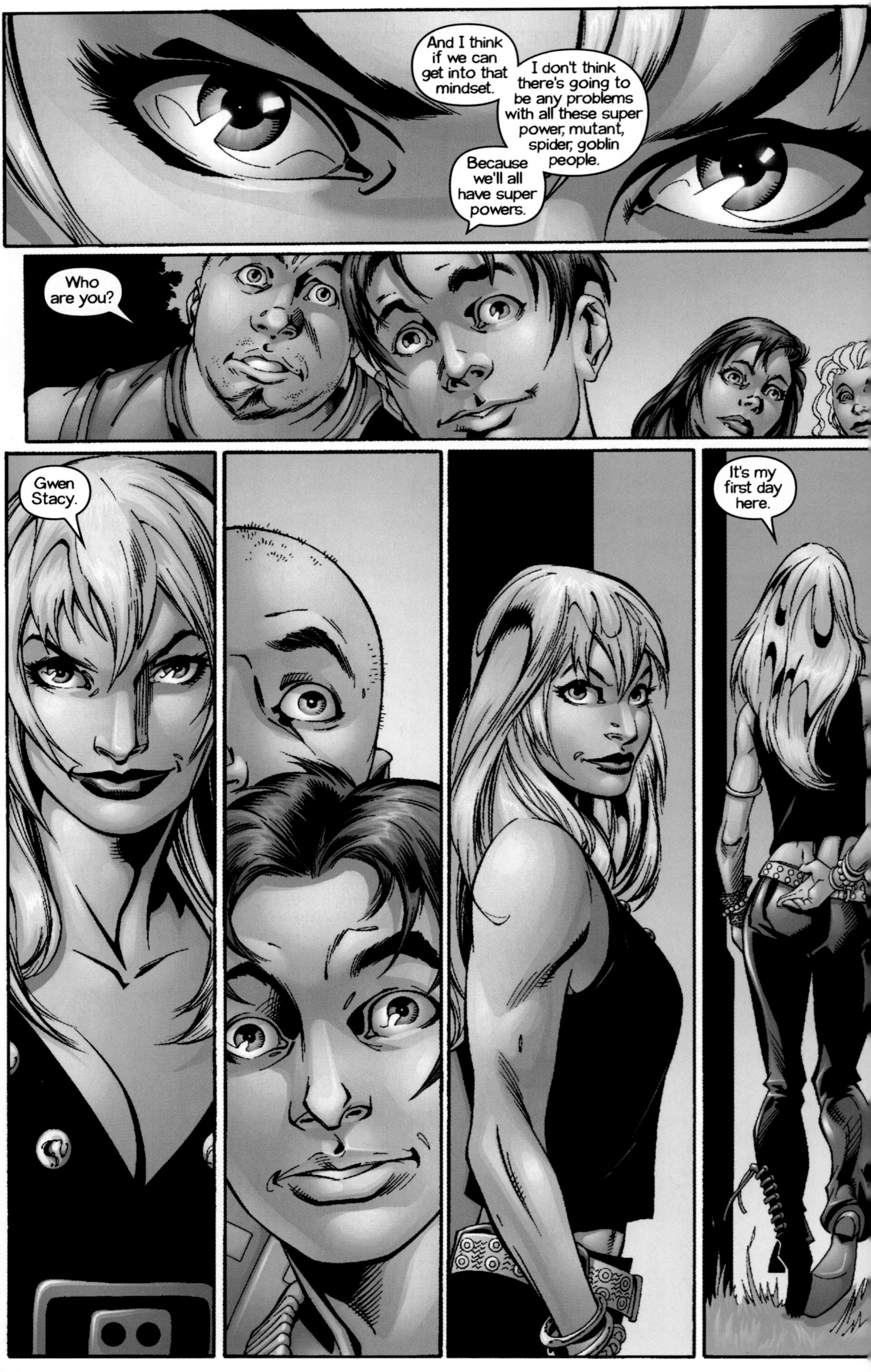
And I think if we can get into that mindset.
I don't think there's going to be any problems with all these super power, mutant, spider, goblin people.
Because we'll all have super powers.
Who are you?
Gwen Stacy.
It's my first day here.

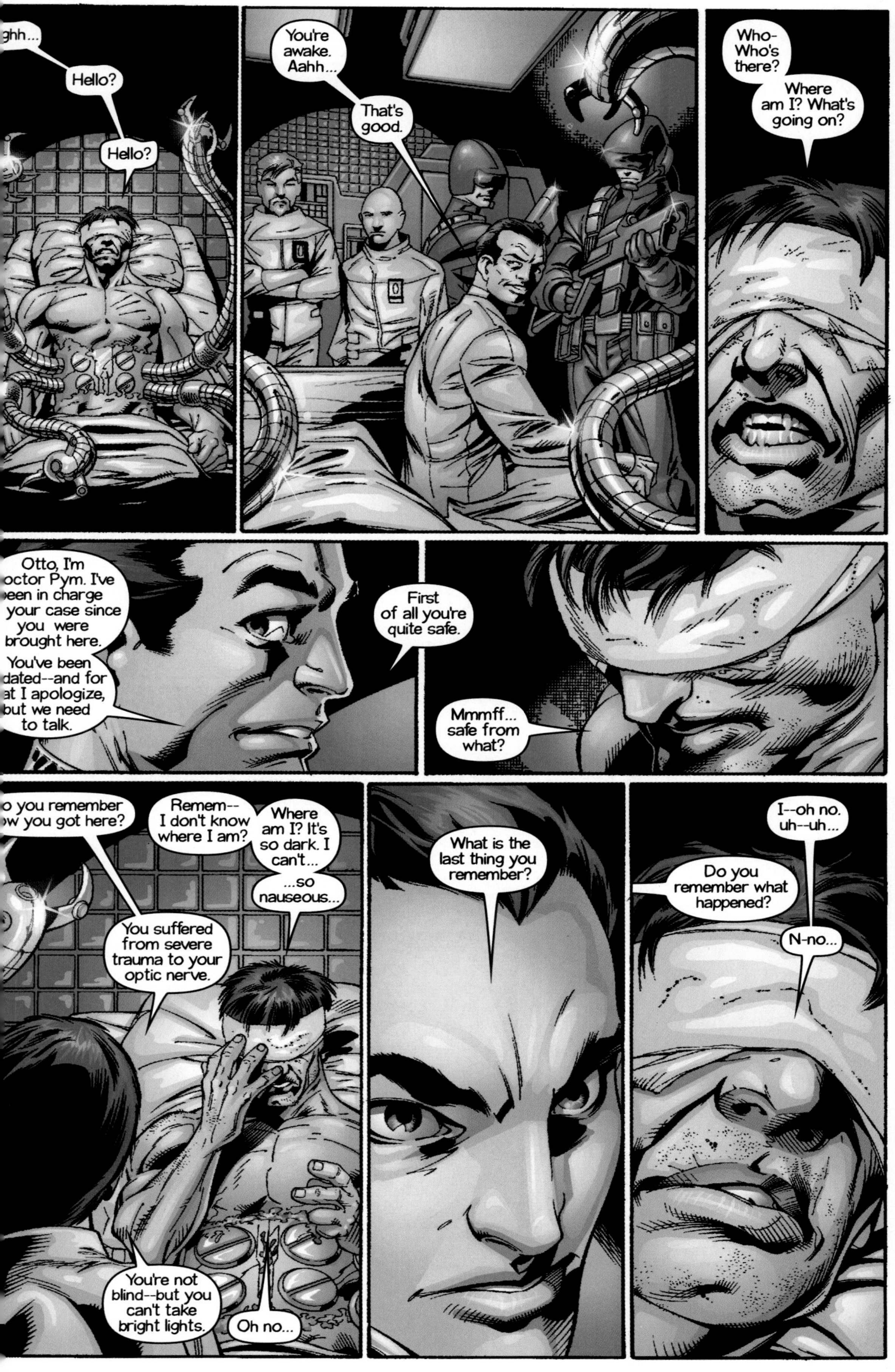
ghh...
Hello?
Hello?
You're awake. Aahh...
That's good.
Who- Who's there?
Where am I? What's going on?
Otto, I'm octor Pym. I've een in charge your case since you were brought here.
You've been dated--and for at I apologize, but we need to talk.
First of all you're quite safe.
Mmmff... safe from what?
o you remember w you got here?
Remem-- I don't know where I am?
Where am I? It's so dark. I can't...
...so nauseous...
You suffered from severe trauma to your optic nerve.
You're not blind--but you can't take bright lights.
Oh no...
What is the last thing you remember?
I--oh no. uh--uh...
Do you remember what happened?
N-no...

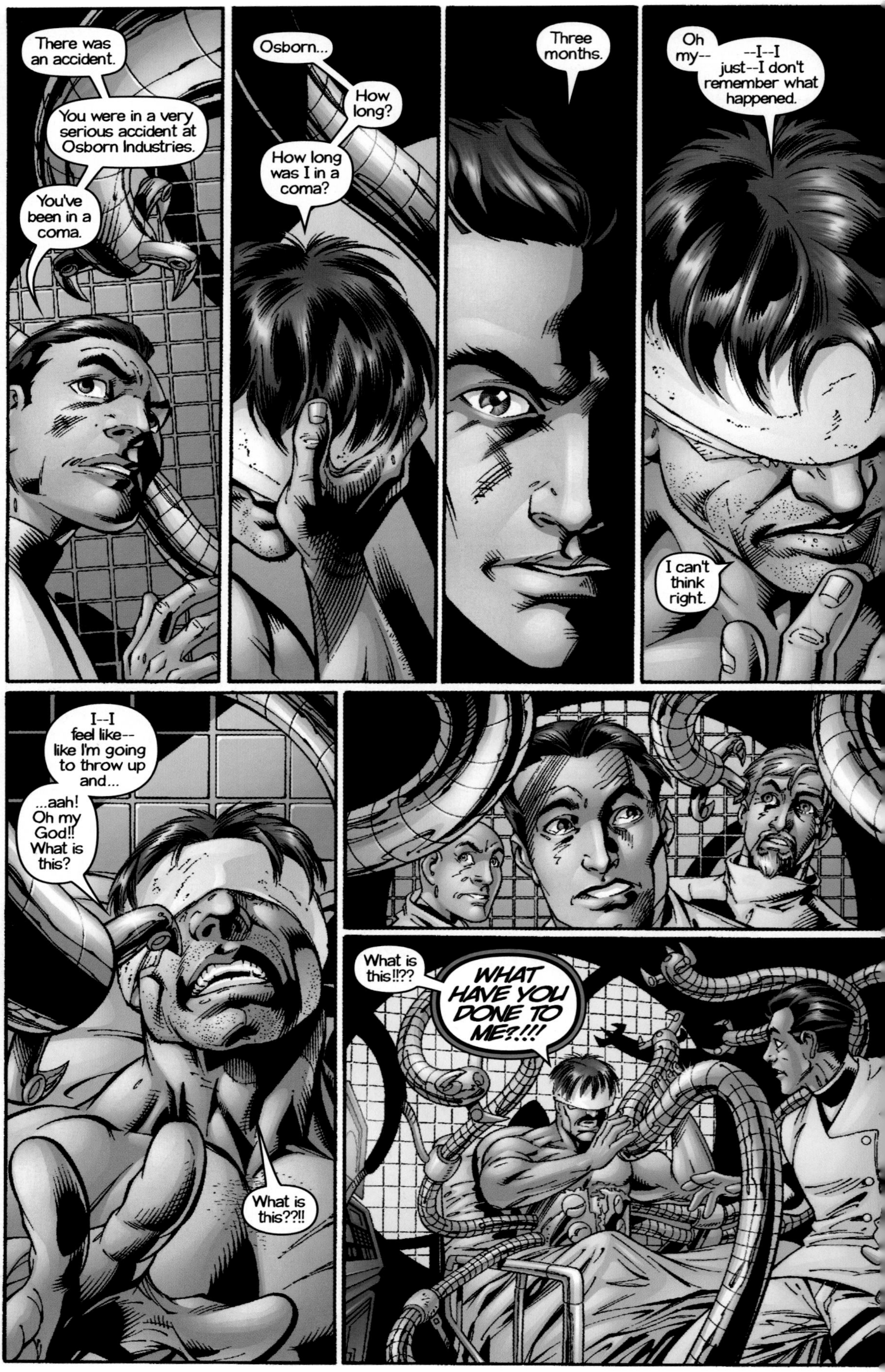

There was an accident.
You were in a very serious accident at Osborn Industries.
You've been in a coma.
Osborn...
How long?
How long was I in a coma?
Three months.
Oh my--
--I--I just--I don't remember what happened.
I can't think right.
I--I feel like-- like I'm going to throw up and...
...aah! Oh my God!! What is this?
What is this??!!
What is this!!??
WHAT HAVE YOU DONE TO ME?!!!

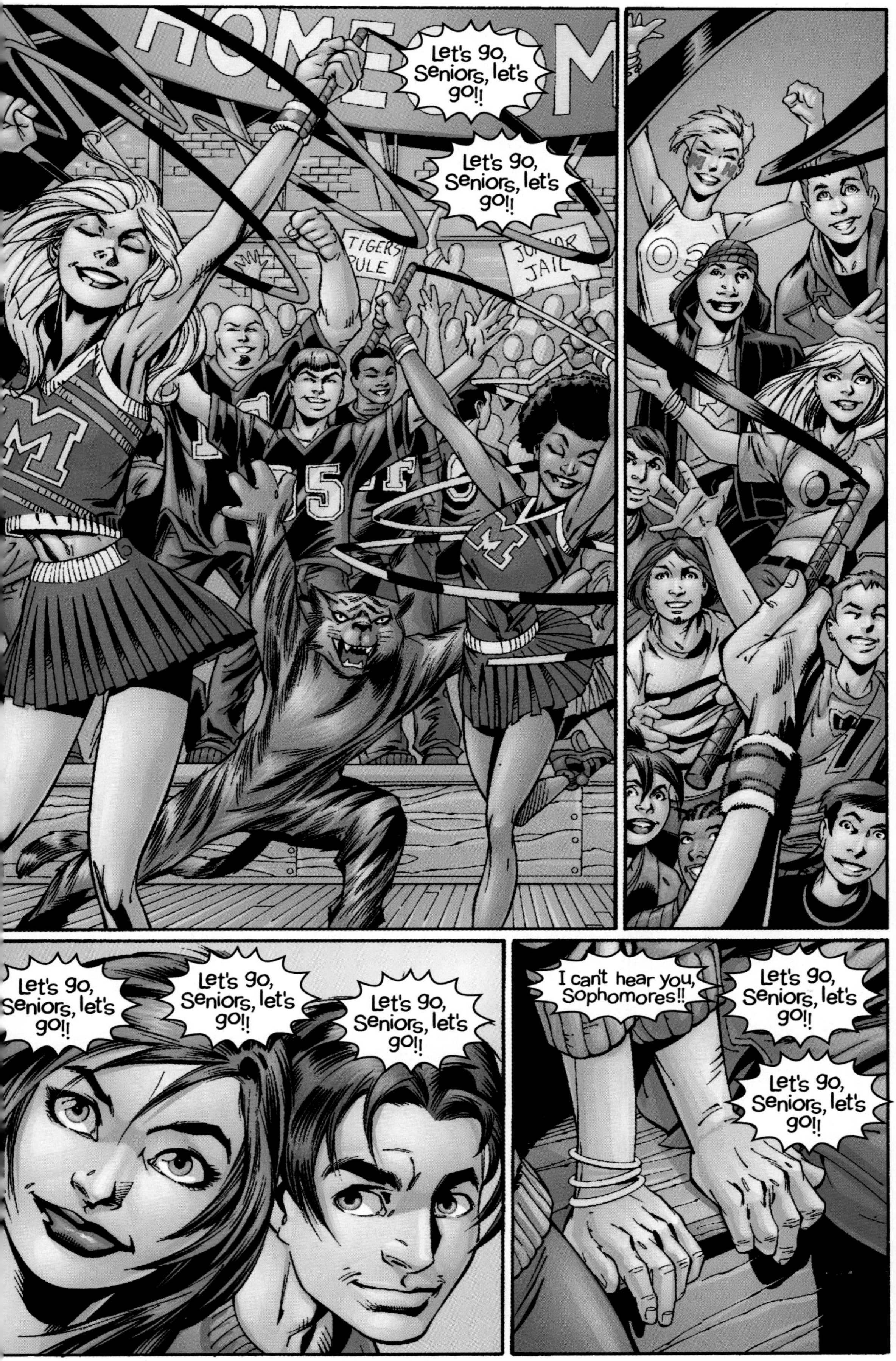
Let's go, seniors, let's go!!
Let's go, seniors, let's go!!
TIGERS RULE
Let's go, seniors, let's go!!
Let's go, seniors, let's go!!
Let's go, seniors, let's go!!
I can't hear you, Sophomores!!
Let's go, seniors, let's go!!
Let's go, seniors, let's go!!

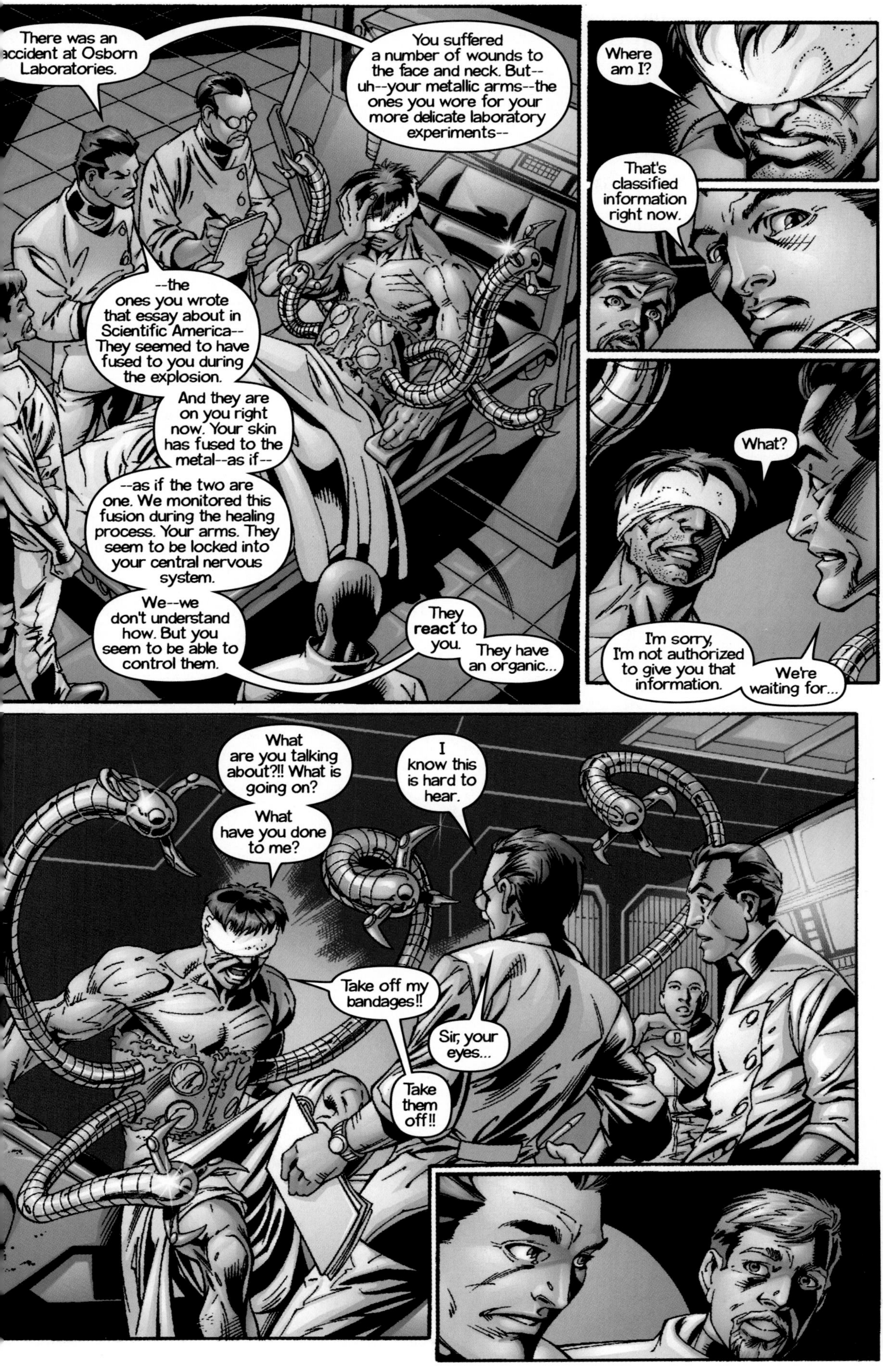
There was an accident at Osborn Laboratories.
You suffered a number of wounds to the face and neck. But--uh--your metallic arms--the ones you wore for your more delicate laboratory experiments--
--the ones you wrote that essay about in Scientific America--They seemed to have fused to you during the explosion.
And they are on you right now. Your skin has fused to the metal--as if--
--as if the two are one. We monitored this fusion during the healing process. Your arms. They seem to be locked into your central nervous system.
We--we don't understand how. But you seem to be able to control them.
They **react** to you.
They have an organic...
Where am I?
That's classified information right now.
What?
I'm sorry, I'm not authorized to give you that information.
We're waiting for...
What are you talking about?!! What is going on?
What have you done to me?
I know this is hard to hear.
Take off my bandages!!
Sir, your eyes...
Take them off!!

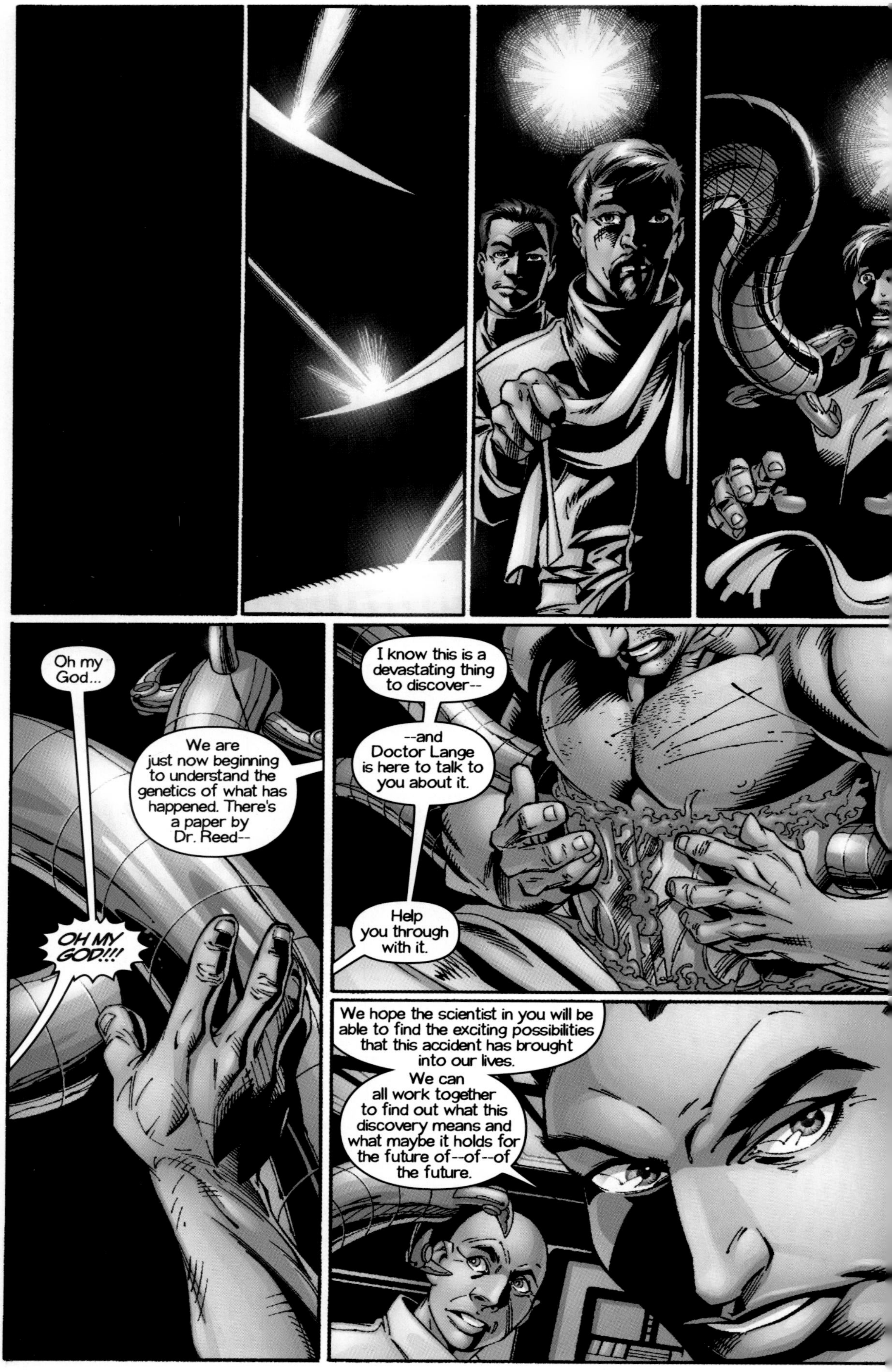
Oh my God...
We are just now beginning to understand the genetics of what has happened. There's a paper by Dr. Reed--
OH MY GOD!!!
I know this is a devastating thing to discover--
--and Doctor Lange is here to talk to you about it.
Help you through with it.
We hope the scientist in you will be able to find the exciting possibilities that this accident has brought into our lives.
We can all work together to find out what this discovery means and what maybe it holds for the future of--of--of the future.

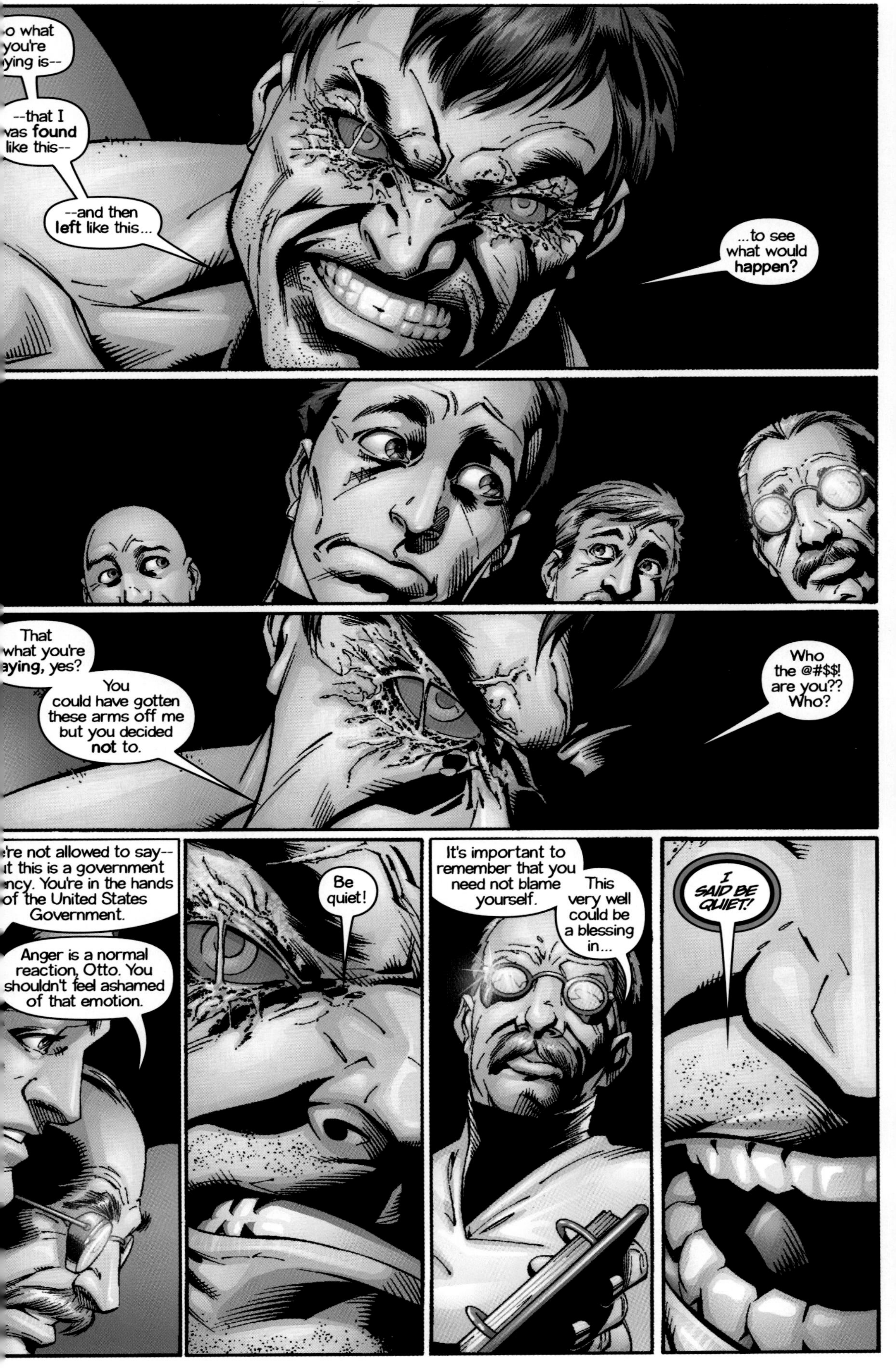
o what you're ying is--
--that I vas found like this--
--and then left like this...
...to see what would happen?
That what you're aying, yes?
You could have gotten these arms off me but you decided not to.
Who the @#$$! are you?? Who?
're not allowed to say-- t this is a government ncy. You're in the hands of the United States Government.
Anger is a normal reaction, Otto. You shouldn't feel ashamed of that emotion.
Be quiet!
It's important to remember that you need not blame yourself.
This very well could be a blessing in...
I SAID BE QUIET!

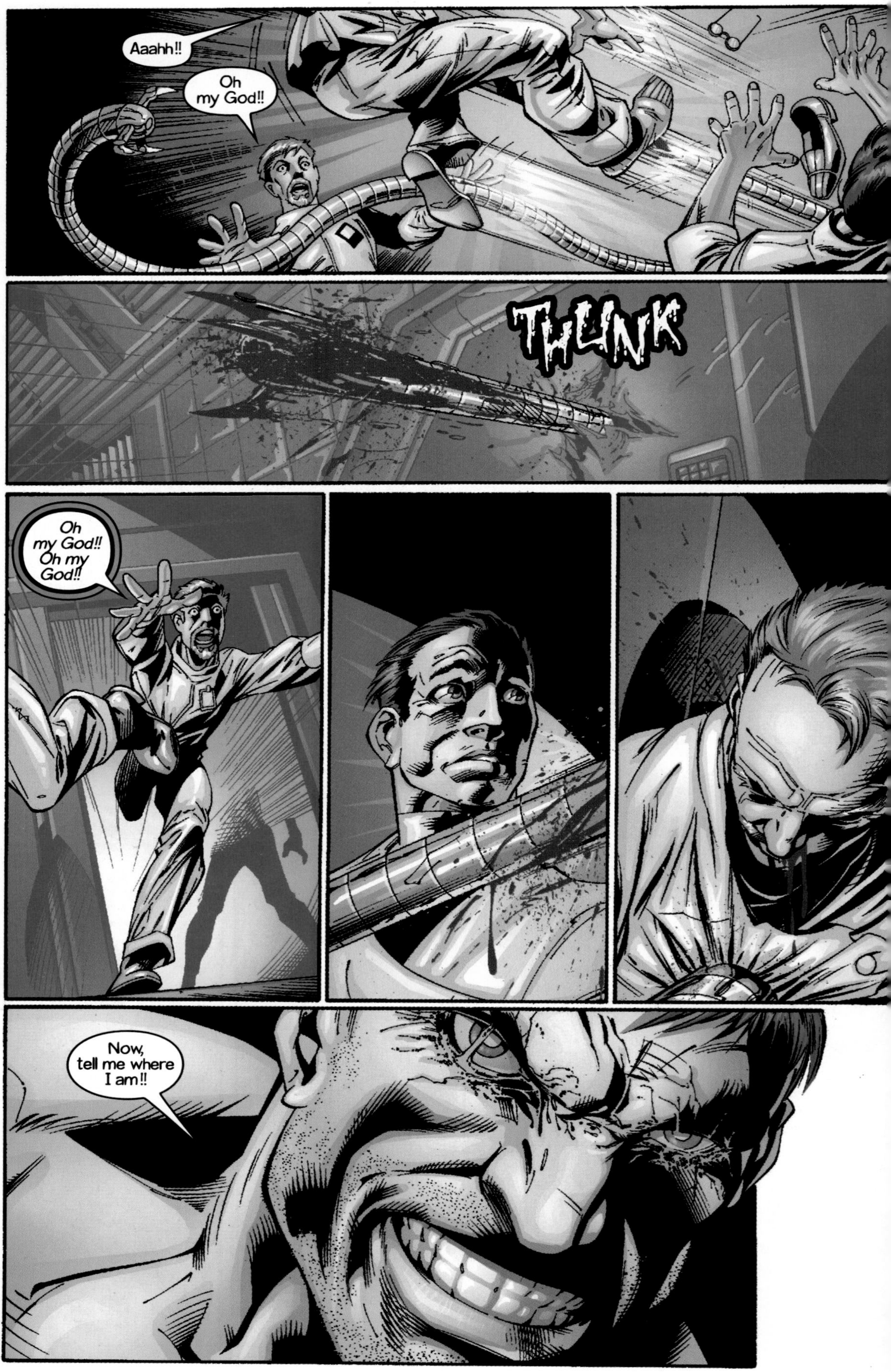
Aaahh!!
Oh my God!!
THUNK
Oh my God!! Oh my God!!
Now, tell me where I am!!

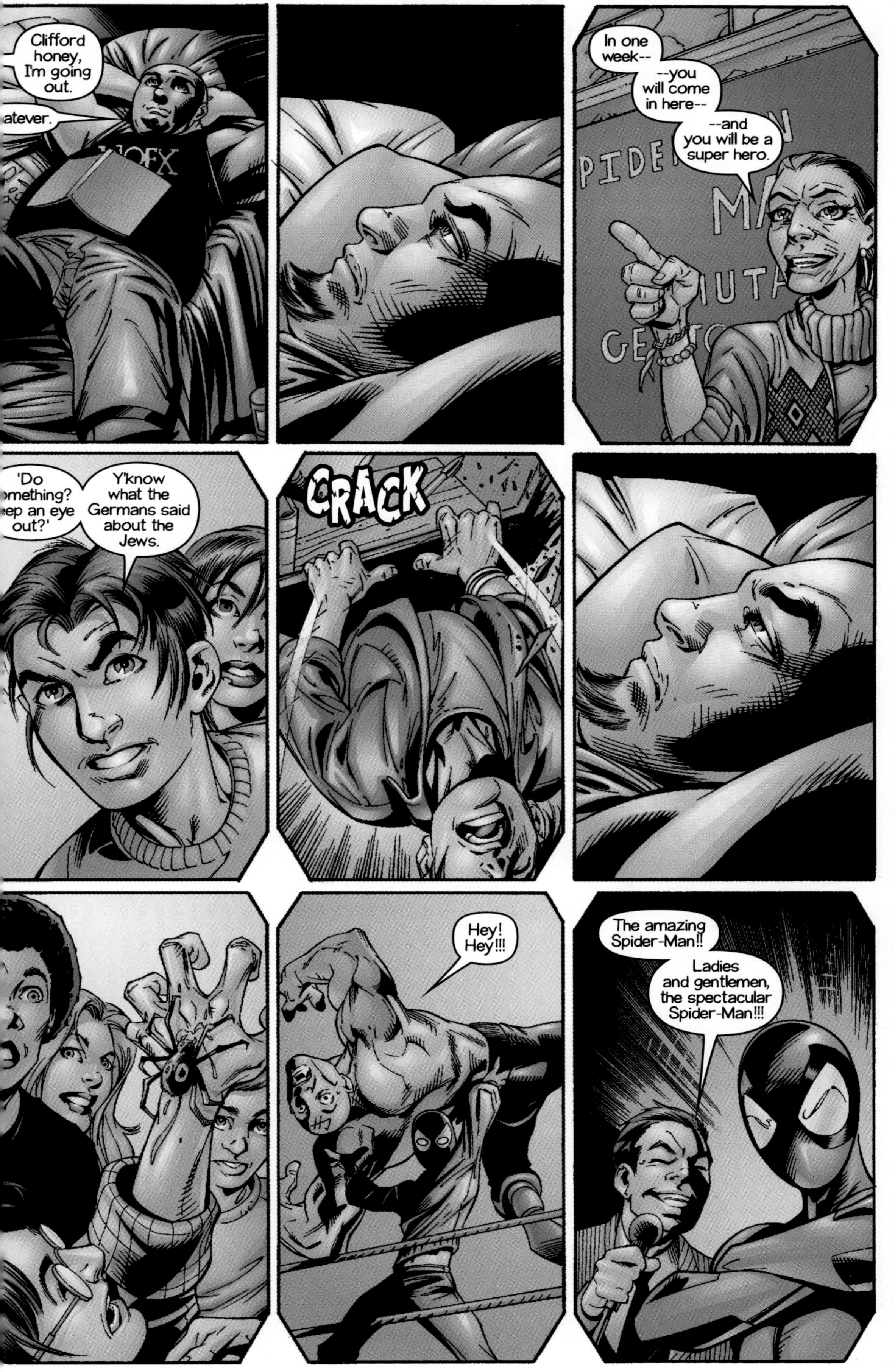
Clifford honey, I'm going out.
atever.
In one week--
--you will come in here--
--and you will be a super hero.
'Do omething? eep an eye out?'
Y'know what the Germans said about the Jews.
CRACK
Hey! Hey!!!
The amazing Spider-Man!!
Ladies and gentlemen, the spectacular Spider-Man!!!

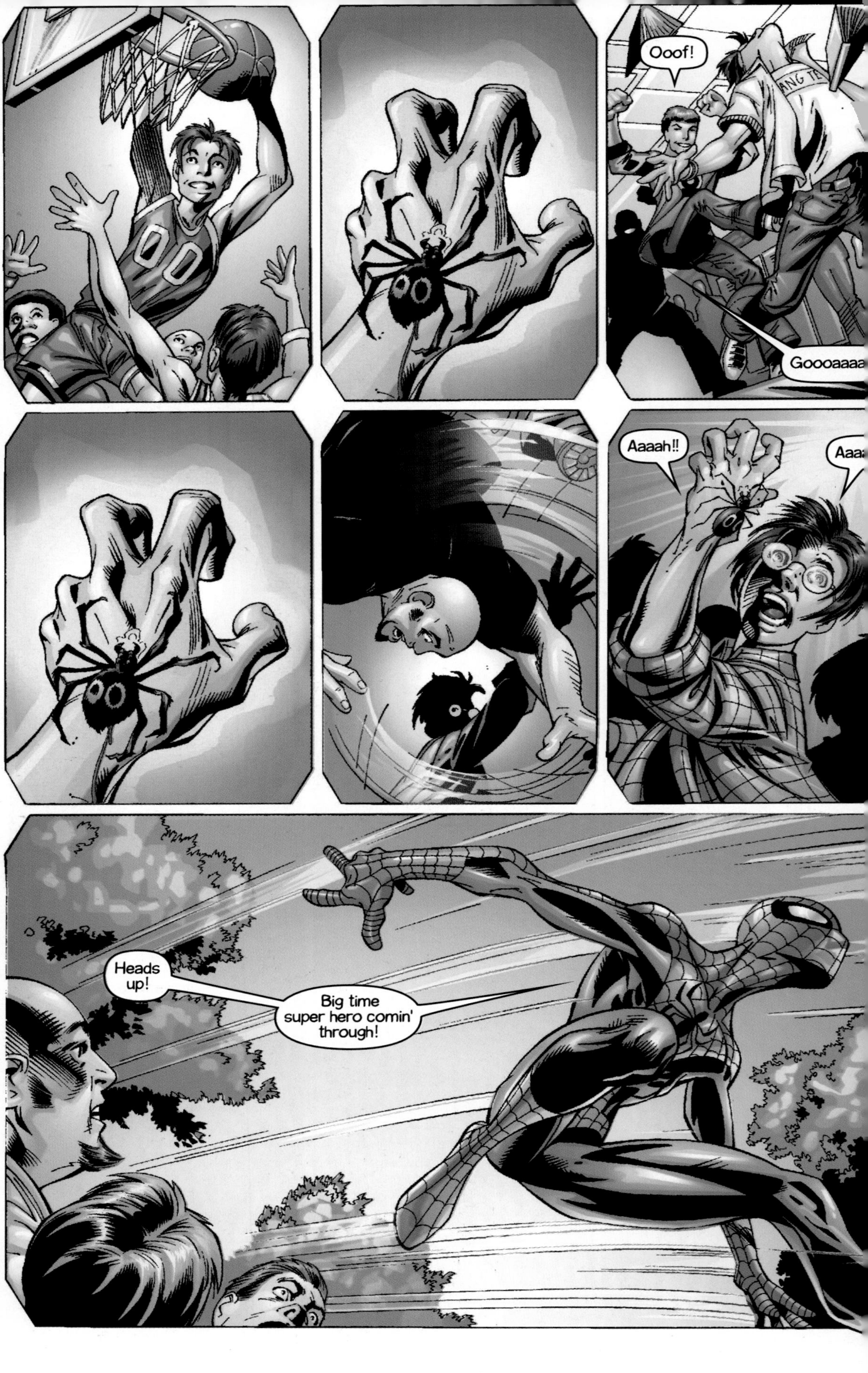
Ooof!
Goooaaaa
Aaaah!!
Aaa
Heads up!
Big time super hero comin' through!

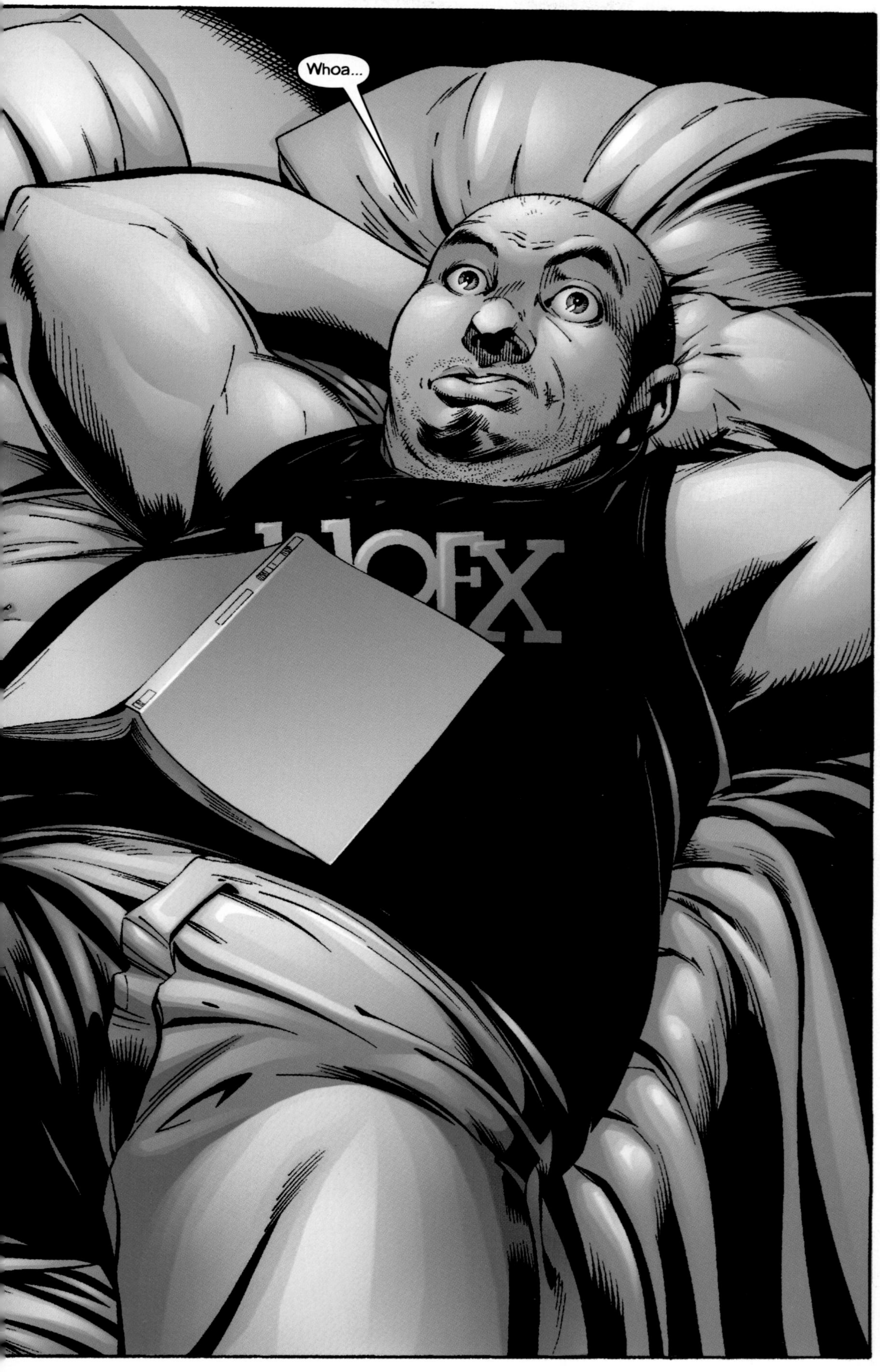
Whoa...

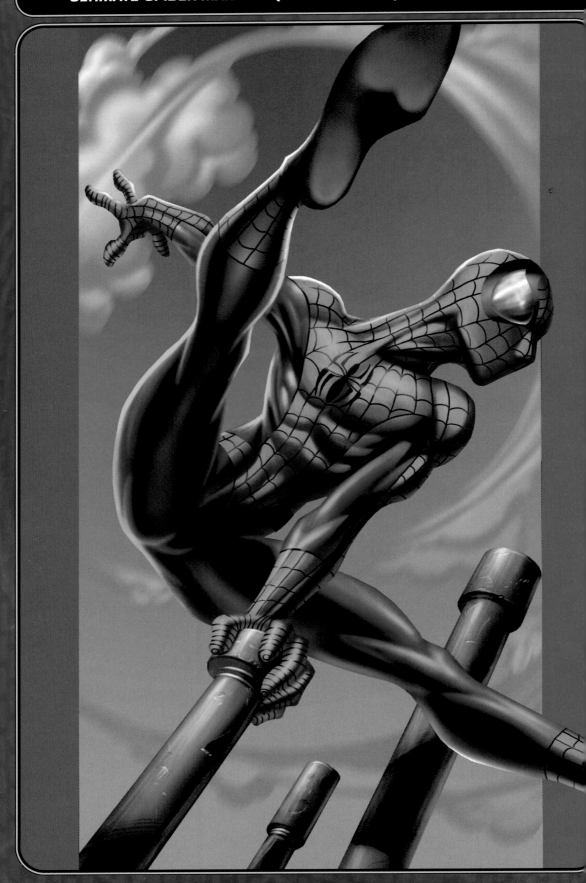

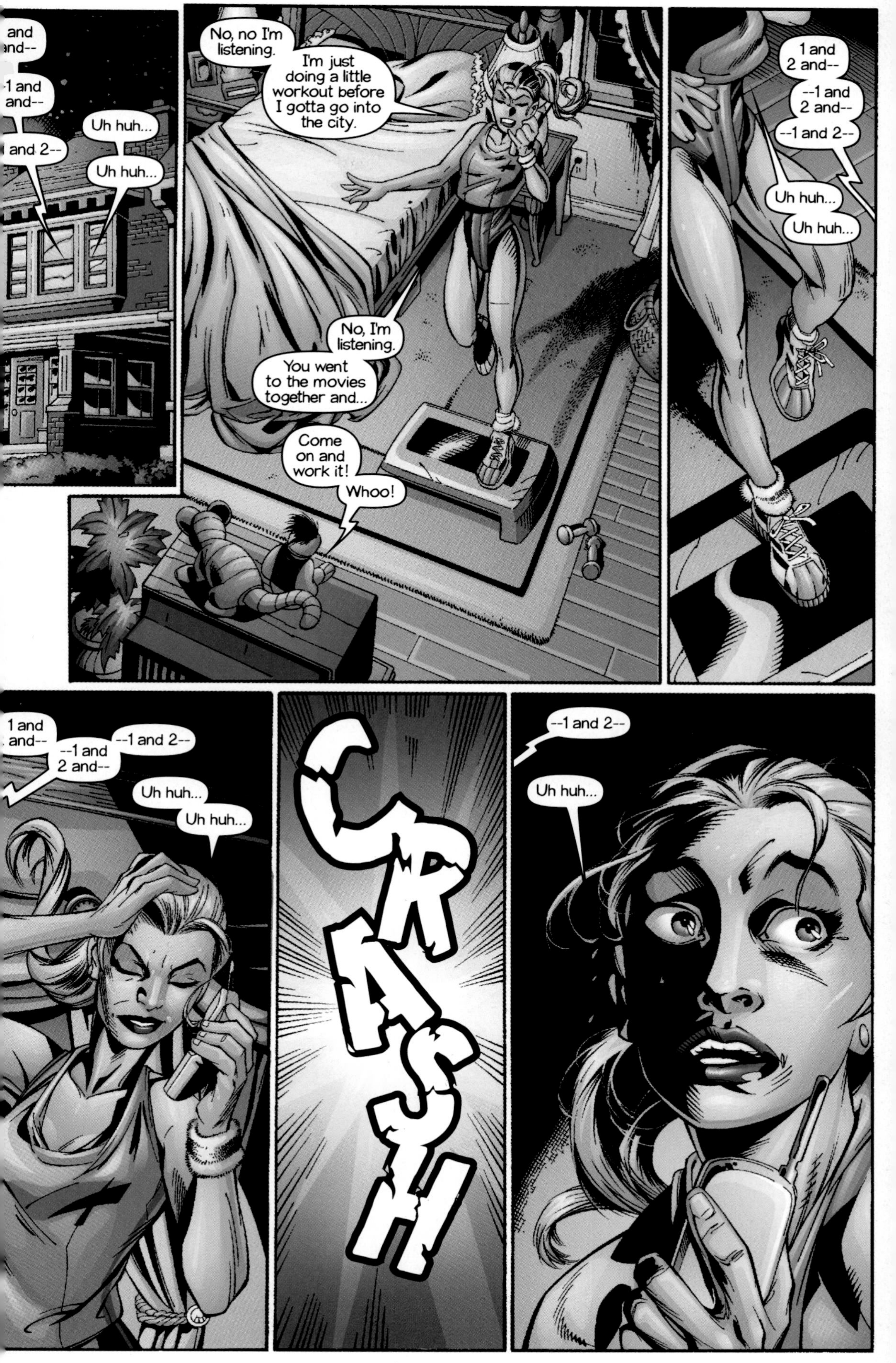

and
and--
-1 and
and--
Uh huh...
and 2--
Uh huh...
No, no I'm listening.
I'm just doing a little workout before I gotta go into the city.
No, I'm listening.
You went to the movies together and...
Come on and work it!
Whoo!
1 and
2 and--
--1 and
2 and--
--1 and 2--
Uh huh...
Uh huh...
1 and
and--
--1 and
2 and--
--1 and 2--
Uh huh...
Uh huh...
CRASH
--1 and 2--
Uh huh...

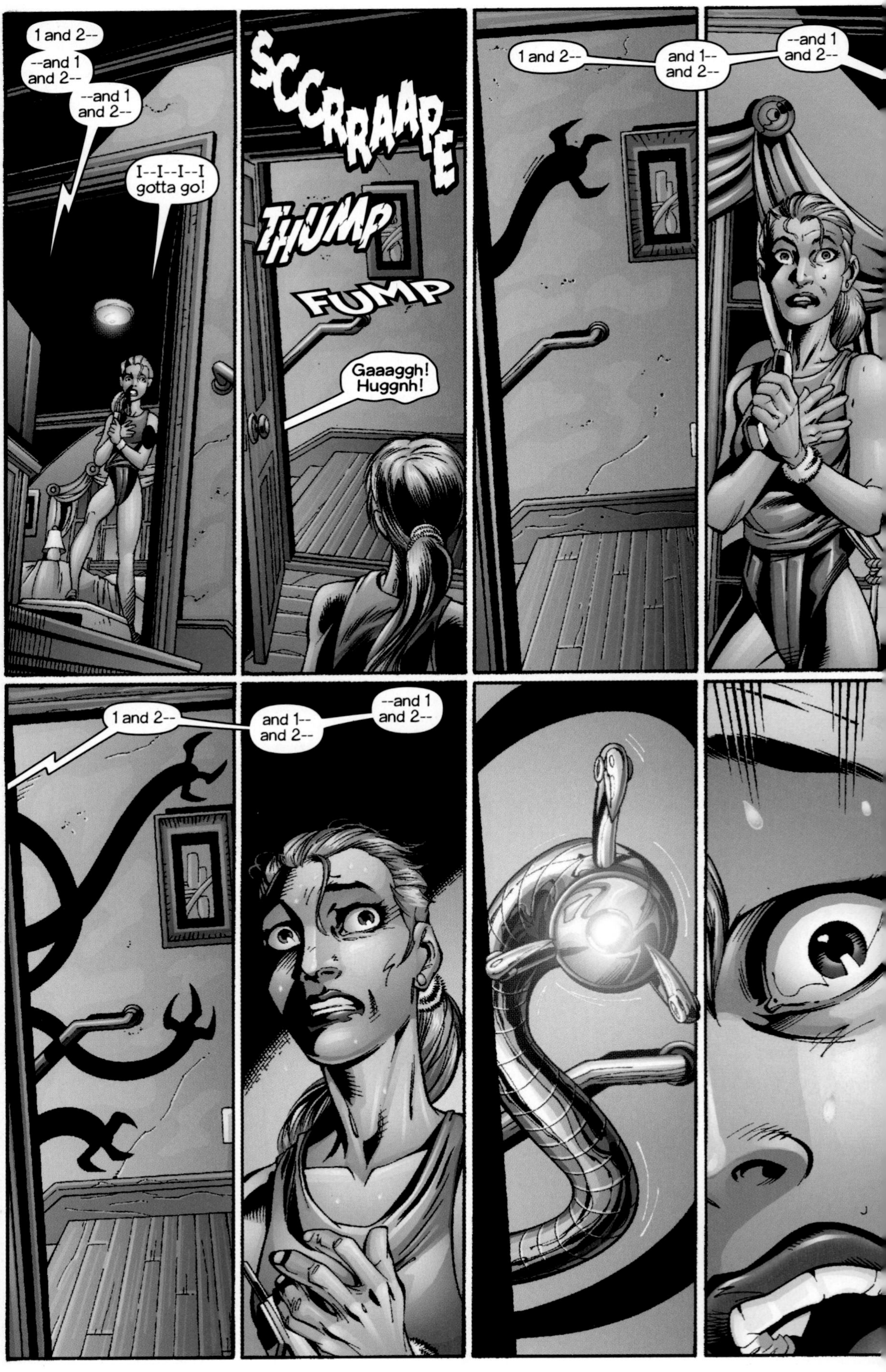
1 and 2--
--and 1 and 2--
--and 1 and 2--
I--I--I--I gotta go!
SCCRRAAPE
THUMP
FUMP
Gaaaggh! Huggnh!
1 and 2--
and 1-- and 2--
--and 1 and 2--
1 and 2--
and 1-- and 2--
--and 1 and 2--

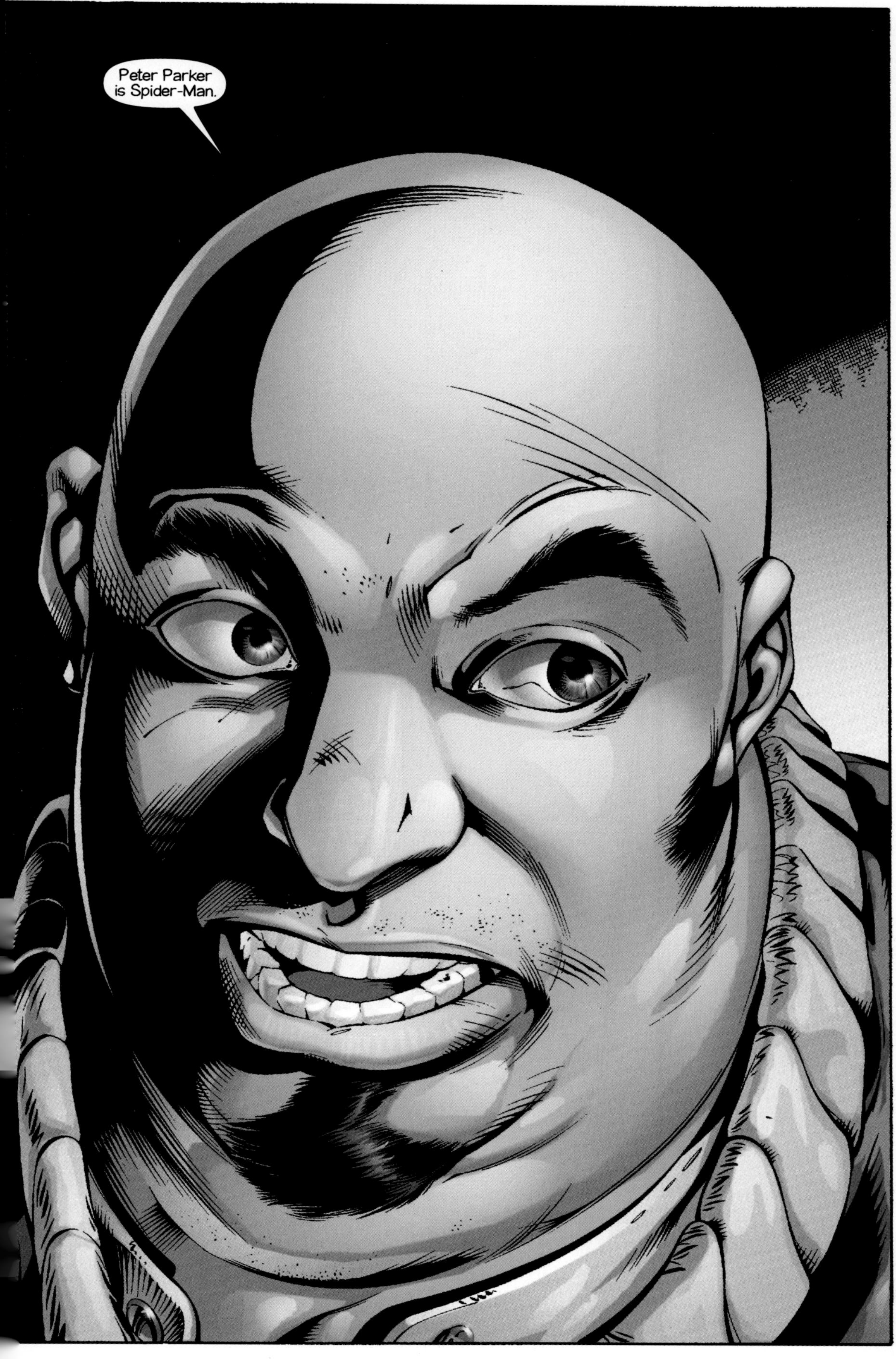
Peter Parker is Spider-Man.

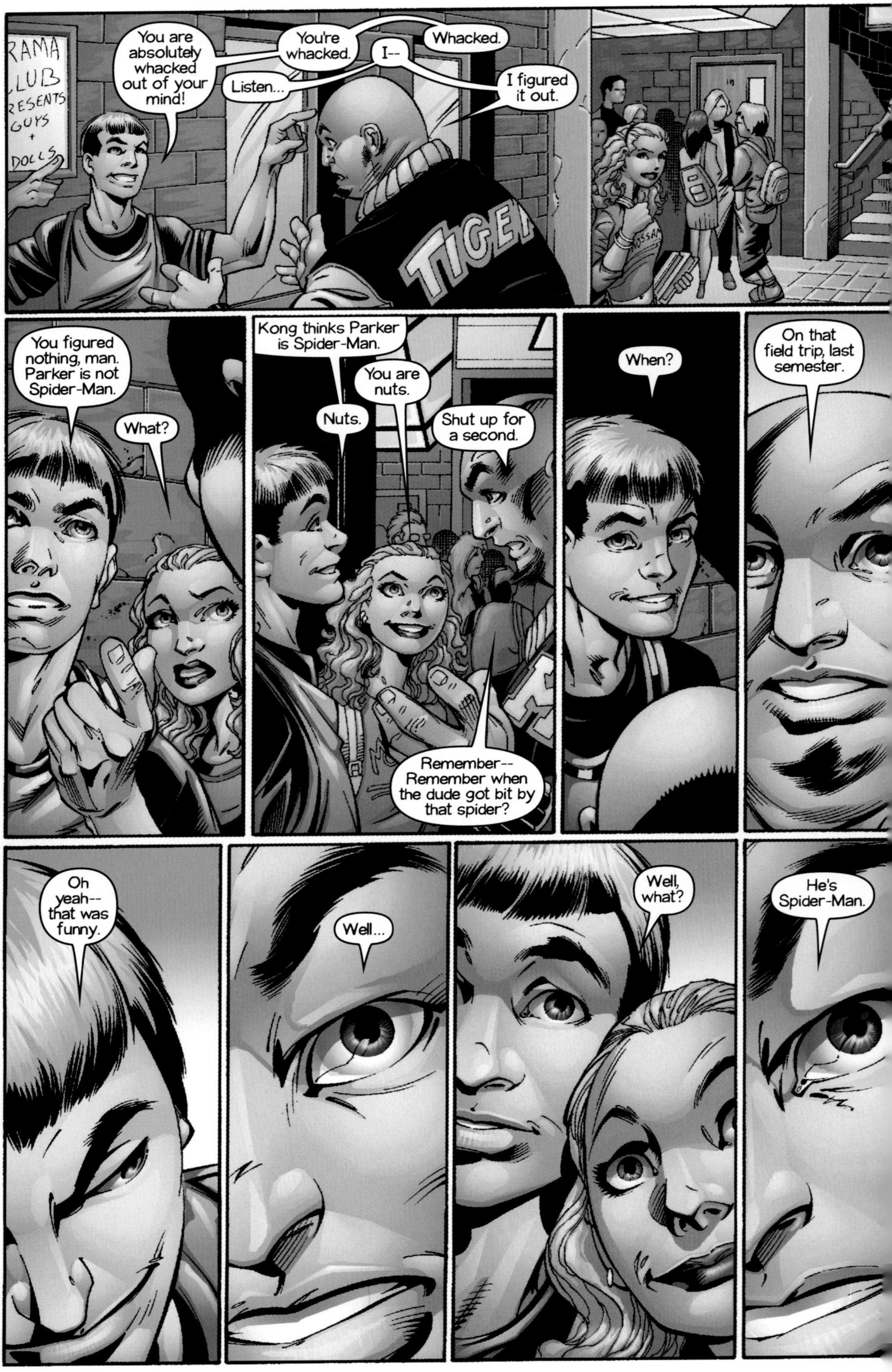

DRAMA CLUB PRESENTS GUYS + DOLLS
You are absolutely whacked out of your mind!
You're whacked.
Whacked.
Listen...
I--
I figured it out.
TIGE
You figured nothing, man. Parker is not Spider-Man.
What?
Kong thinks Parker is Spider-Man.
Nuts.
You are nuts.
Shut up for a second.
Remember-- Remember when the dude got bit by that spider?
When?
On that field trip, last semester.
Oh yeah-- that was funny.
Well...
Well, what?
He's Spider-Man.

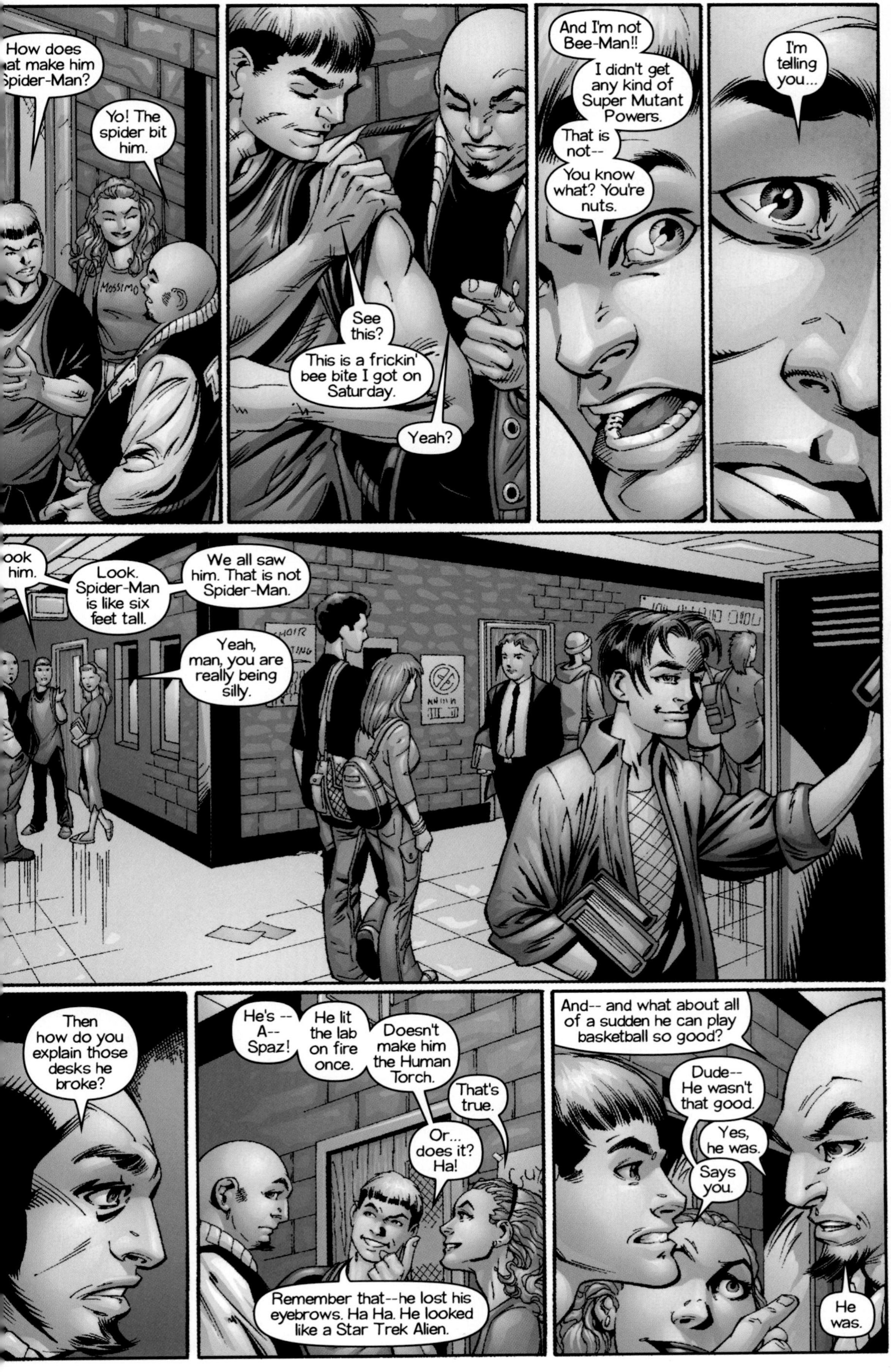
How does
at make him
Spider-Man?
Yo! The spider bit him.
MOSSIMO
See this?
This is a frickin' bee bite I got on Saturday.
Yeah?
And I'm not Bee-Man!!
I didn't get any kind of Super Mutant Powers.
That is not--
You know what? You're nuts.
I'm telling you...
ook
him.
Look. Spider-Man is like six feet tall.
We all saw him. That is not Spider-Man.
Yeah, man, you are really being silly.
Then how do you explain those desks he broke?
He's -- A-- Spaz!
He lit the lab on fire once.
Doesn't make him the Human Torch.
That's true.
Or... does it? Ha!
Remember that--he lost his eyebrows. Ha Ha. He looked like a Star Trek Alien.
And-- and what about all of a sudden he can play basketball so good?
Dude-- He wasn't that good.
Yes, he was.
Says you.
He was.

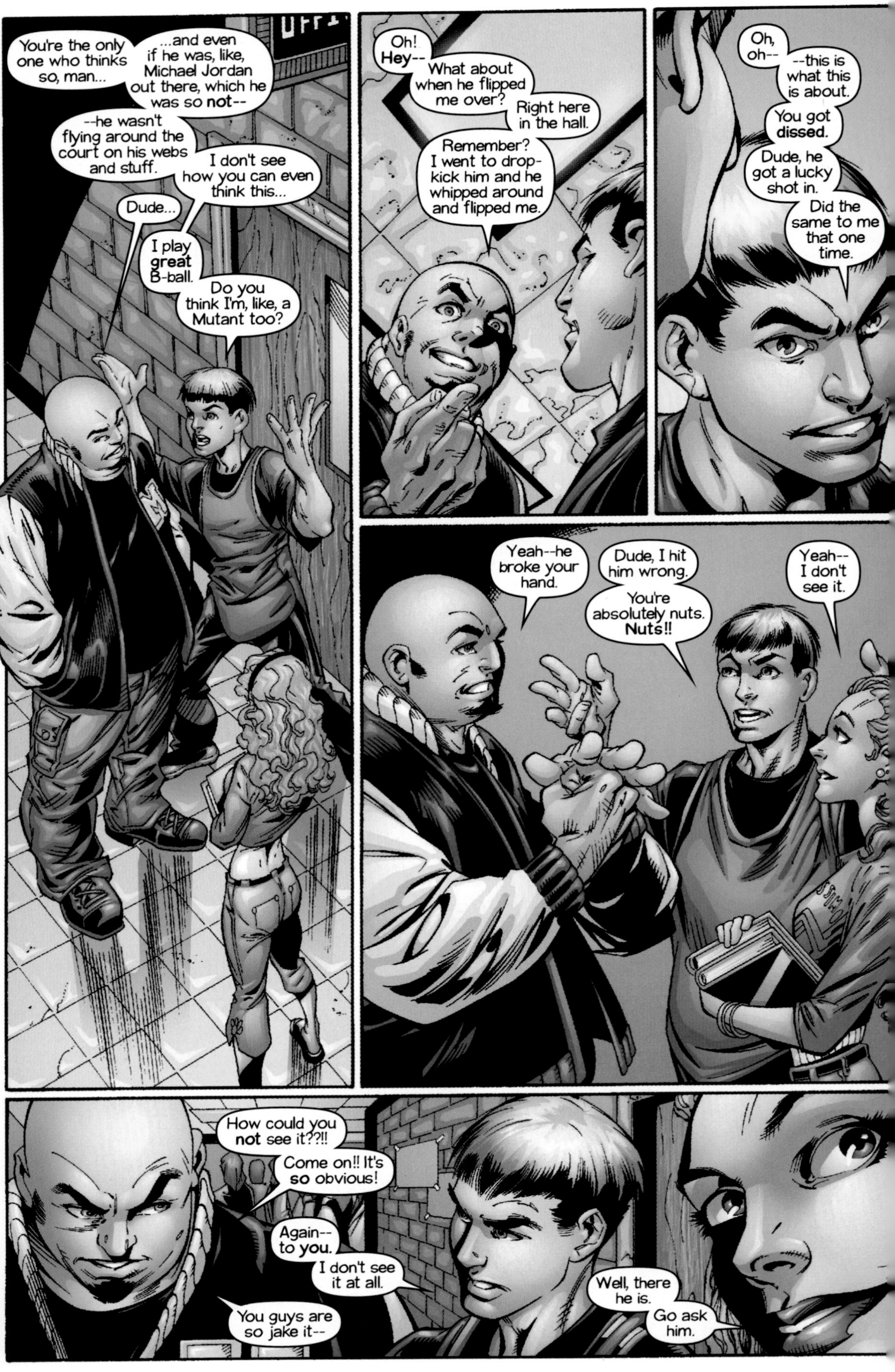
You're the only one who thinks so, man...
...and even if he was, like, Michael Jordan out there, which he was so **not**--
--he wasn't flying around the court on his webs and stuff.
I don't see how you can even think this...
Dude...
I play **great** B-ball.
Do you think I'm, like, a Mutant too?
Oh! **Hey**--
What about when he flipped me over?
Right here in the hall.
Remember? I went to drop-kick him and he whipped around and flipped me.
Oh, oh--
--this is what this is about.
You got **dissed.**
Dude, he got a lucky shot in.
Did the same to me that one time.
Yeah--he broke your hand.
Dude, I hit him wrong.
You're absolutely nuts. **Nuts!!**
Yeah-- I don't see it.
How could you **not** see it??!!
Come on!! It's **so** obvious!
Again-- to **you.**
I don't see it at all.
You guys are so jake it--
Well, there he is.
Go ask him.

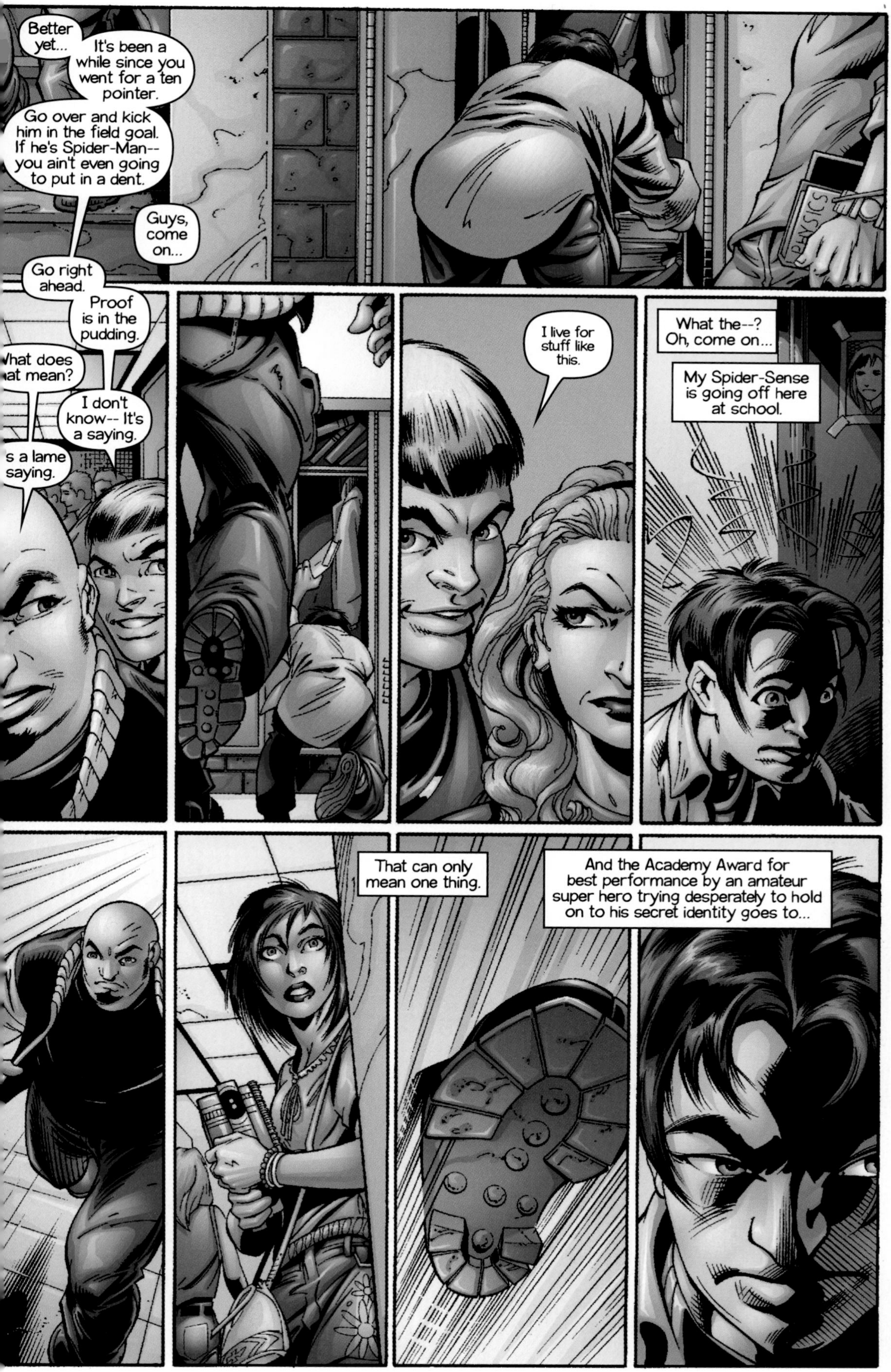

Better yet...
It's been a while since you went for a ten pointer.
Go over and kick him in the field goal. If he's Spider-Man-- you ain't even going to put in a dent.
Guys, come on...
Go right ahead.
Proof is in the pudding.
/hat does ıat mean?
I don't know-- It's a saying.
s a lame saying.
I live for stuff like this.
What the--? Oh, come on...
My Spider-Sense is going off here at school.
That can only mean one thing.
And the Academy Award for best performance by an amateur super hero trying desperately to hold on to his secret identity goes to...

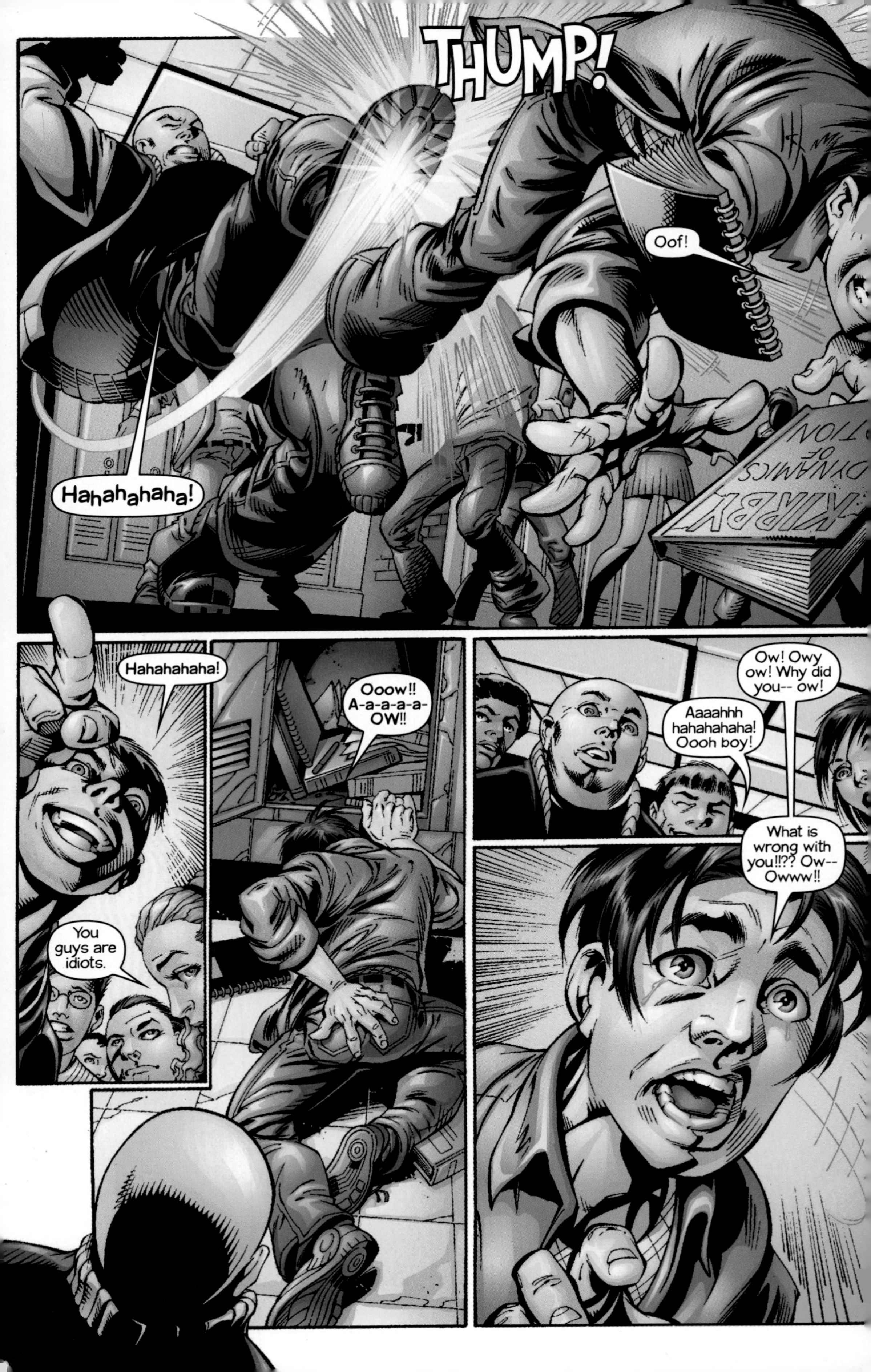
THUMP!
Oof!
Hahahahaha!
Hahahahaha!
You guys are idiots.
Ooow!! A-a-a-a-a-OW!!
Ow! Owy ow! Why did you-- ow!
Aaaahhh hahahahaha! Oooh boy!
What is wrong with you!!?? Ow-- Owww!!

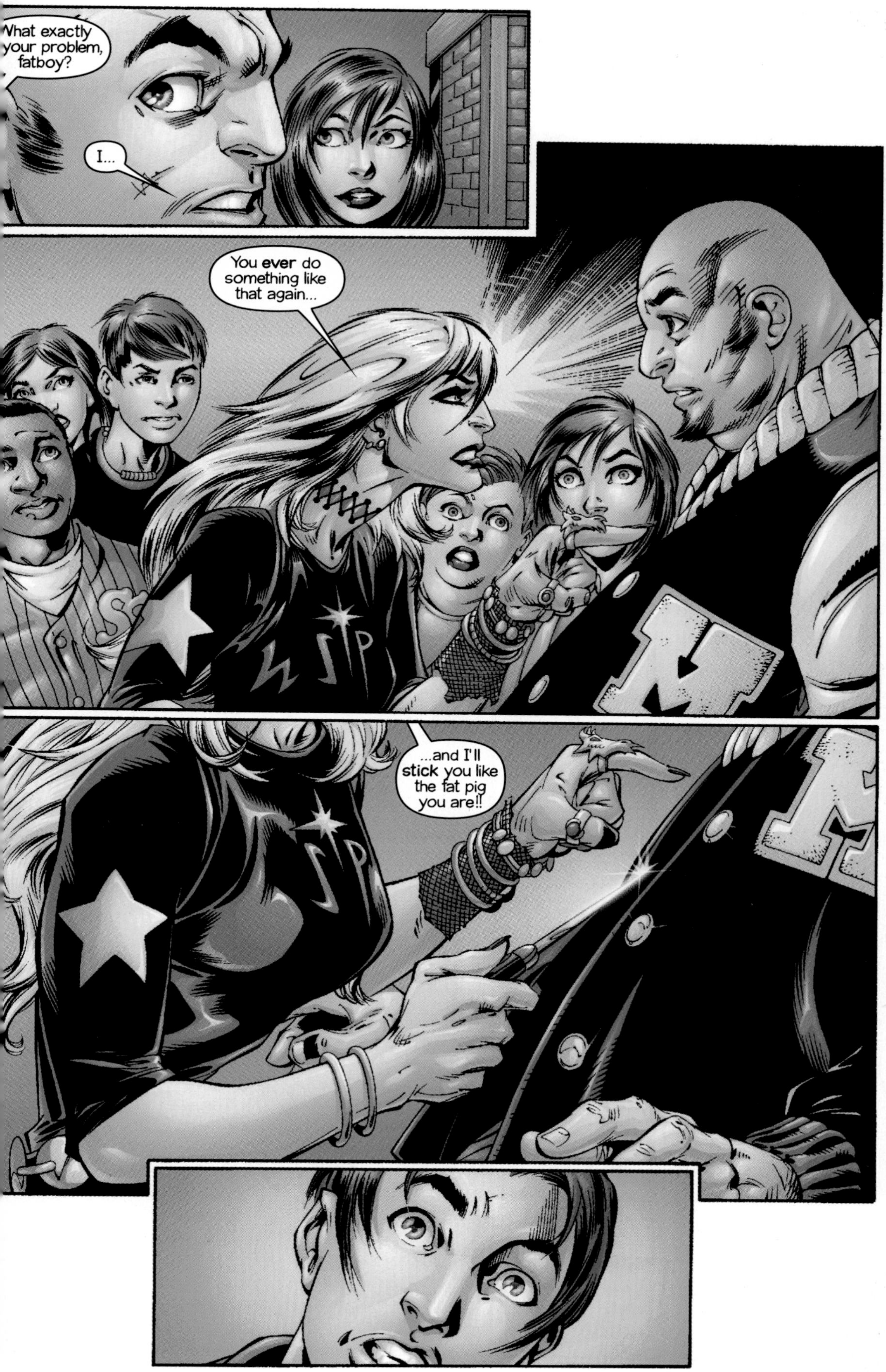

What exactly your problem, fatboy?
I...
You **ever** do something like that again...
...and I'll **stick** you like the fat pig you are!!

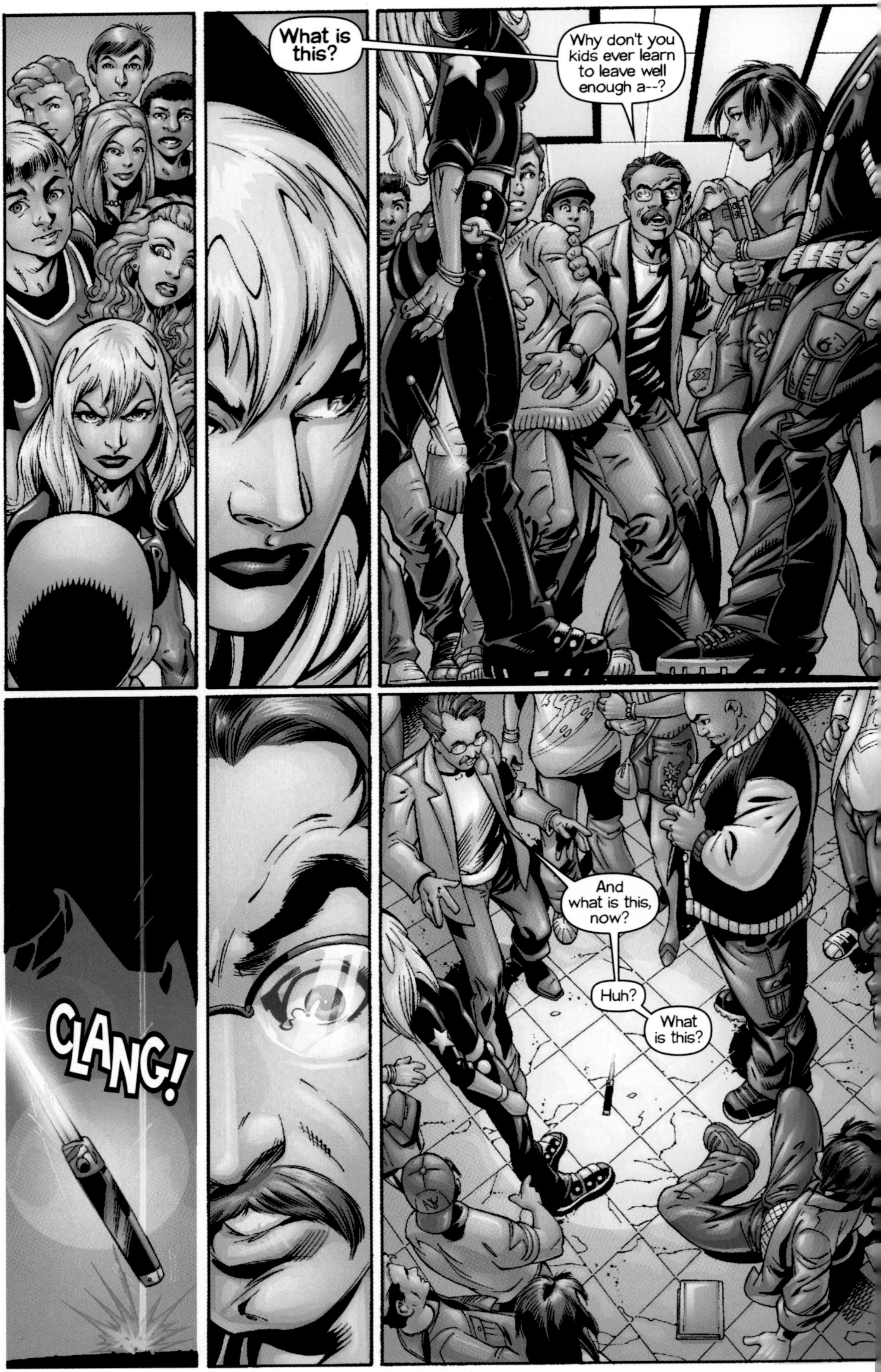
What is this?
Why don't you kids ever learn to leave well enough a--?
CLANG!
And what is this, now?
Huh?
What is this?

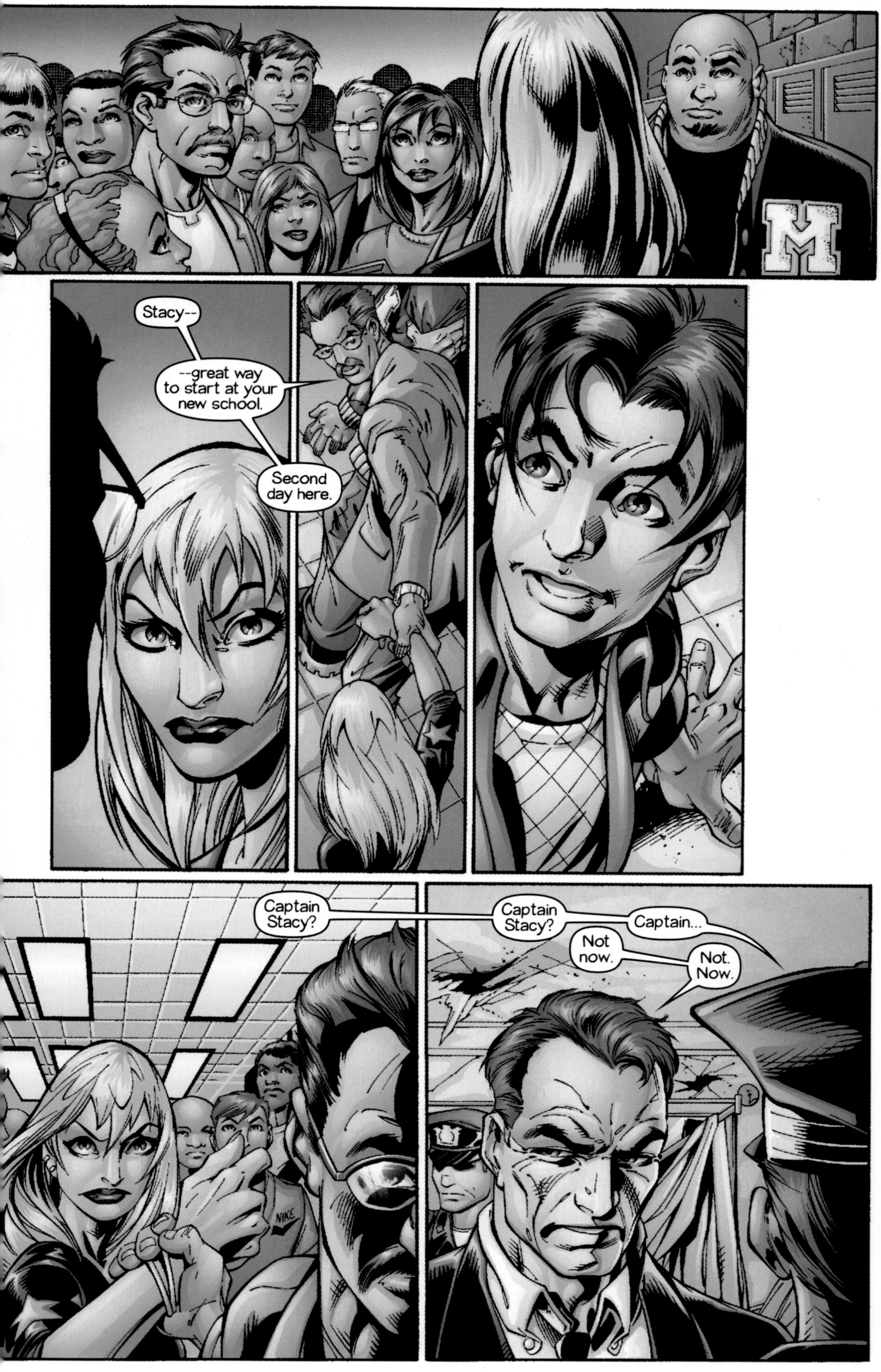
Stacy--
--great way to start at your new school.
Second day here.
Captain Stacy?
Captain Stacy?
Captain...
Not now.
Not. Now.

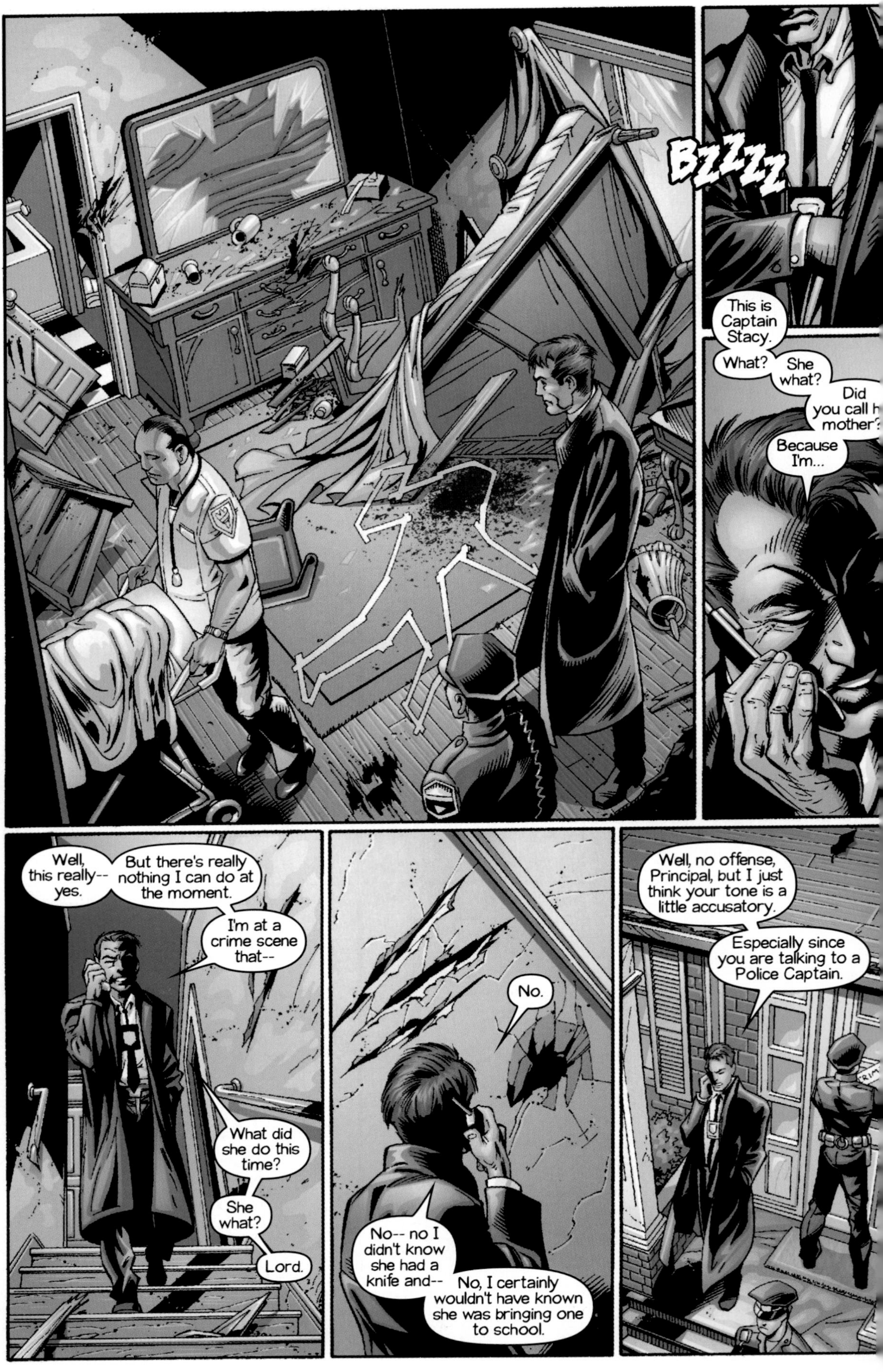
BZZZZZ
This is Captain Stacy.
What?
She what?
Did you call h mother?
Because I'm...
Well, this really-- yes.
But there's really nothing I can do at the moment.
I'm at a crime scene that--
What did she do this time?
She what?
Lord.
No.
No-- no I didn't know she had a knife and--
No, I certainly wouldn't have known she was bringing one to school.
Well, no offense, Principal, but I just think your tone is a little accusatory.
Especially since you are talking to a Police Captain.

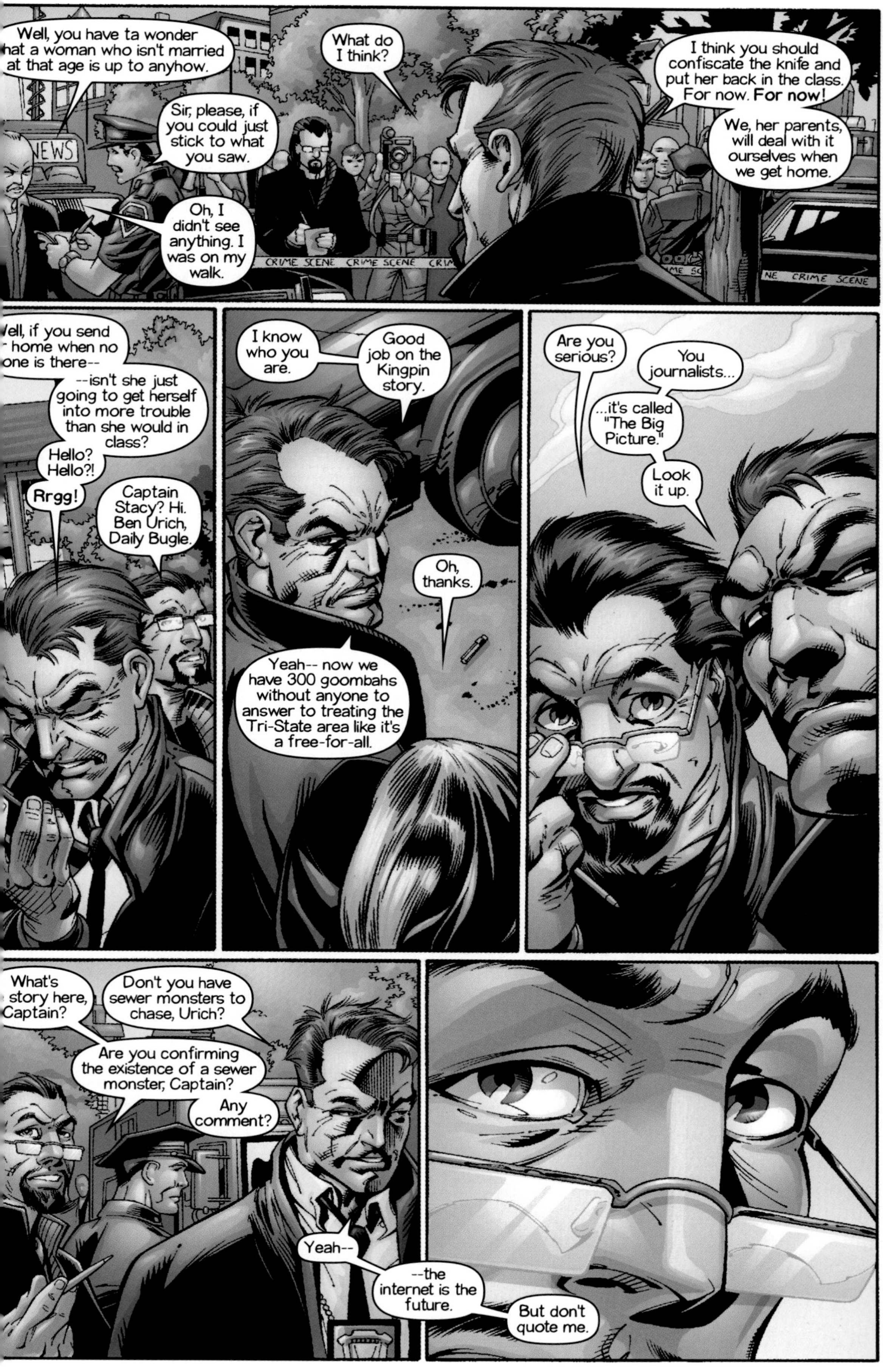
Well, you have ta wonder
hat a woman who isn't married at that age is up to anyhow.
Sir, please, if you could just stick to what you saw.
Oh, I didn't see anything. I was on my walk.
What do I think?
I think you should confiscate the knife and put her back in the class. For now. **For now!**
We, her parents, will deal with it ourselves when we get home.
NEWS
CRIME SCENE CRIME SCENE
Vell, if you send
home when no one is there--
--isn't she just going to get herself into more trouble than she would in class?
Hello? Hello?!
Rrgg!
Captain Stacy? Hi. Ben Urich, Daily Bugle.
I know who you are.
Good job on the Kingpin story.
Oh, thanks.
Yeah-- now we have 300 goombahs without anyone to answer to treating the Tri-State area like it's a free-for-all.
Are you serious?
You journalists...
...it's called "The Big Picture."
Look it up.
What's story here, Captain?
Don't you have sewer monsters to chase, Urich?
Are you confirming the existence of a sewer monster, Captain?
Any comment?
Yeah--
--the internet is the future.
But don't quote me.

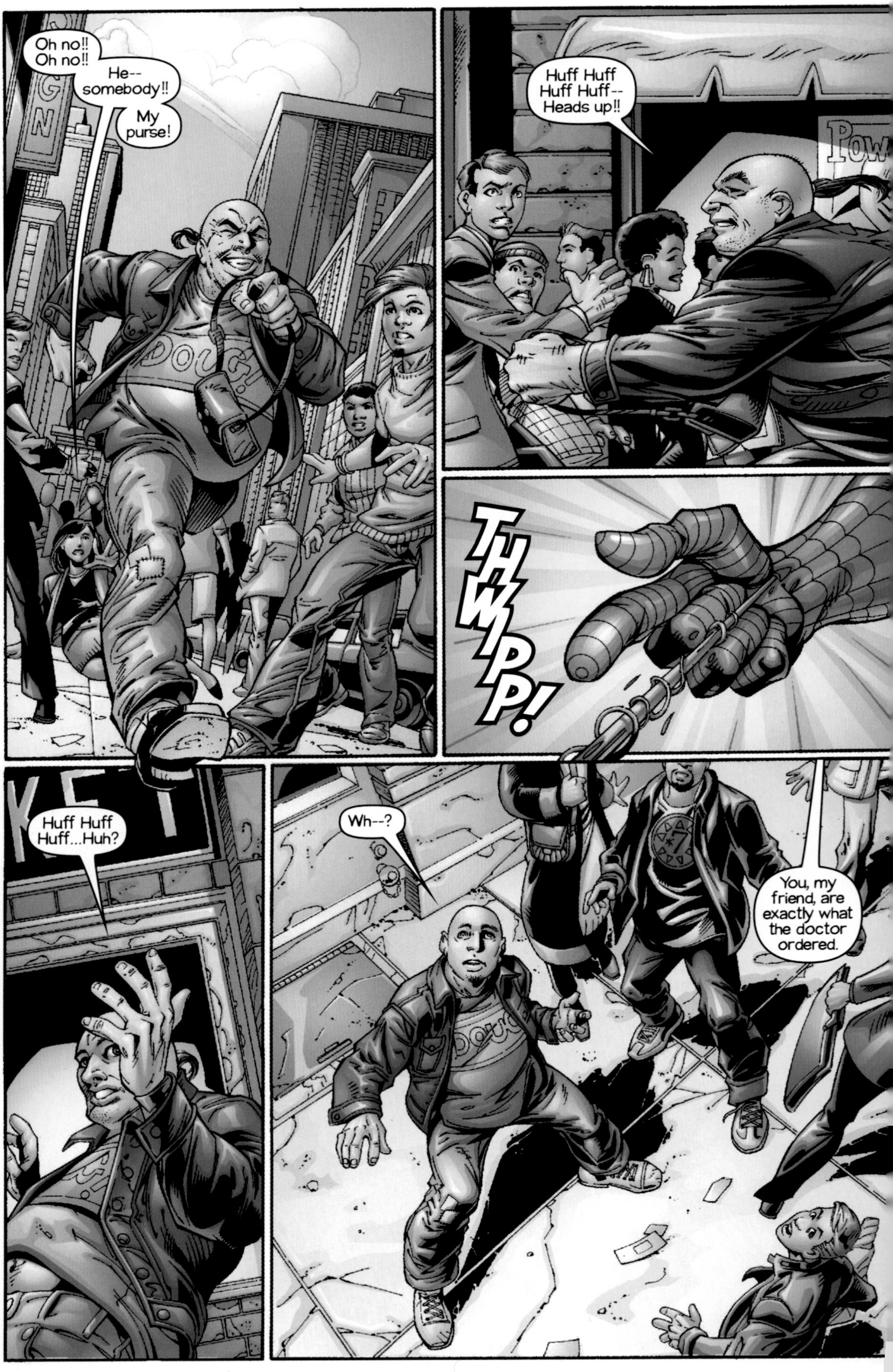
Oh no!! Oh no!!
He-- somebody!!
My purse!
Huff Huff Huff Huff-- Heads up!!
THWIPP!
Huff Huff Huff...Huh?
Wh--?
You, my friend, are exactly what the doctor ordered.

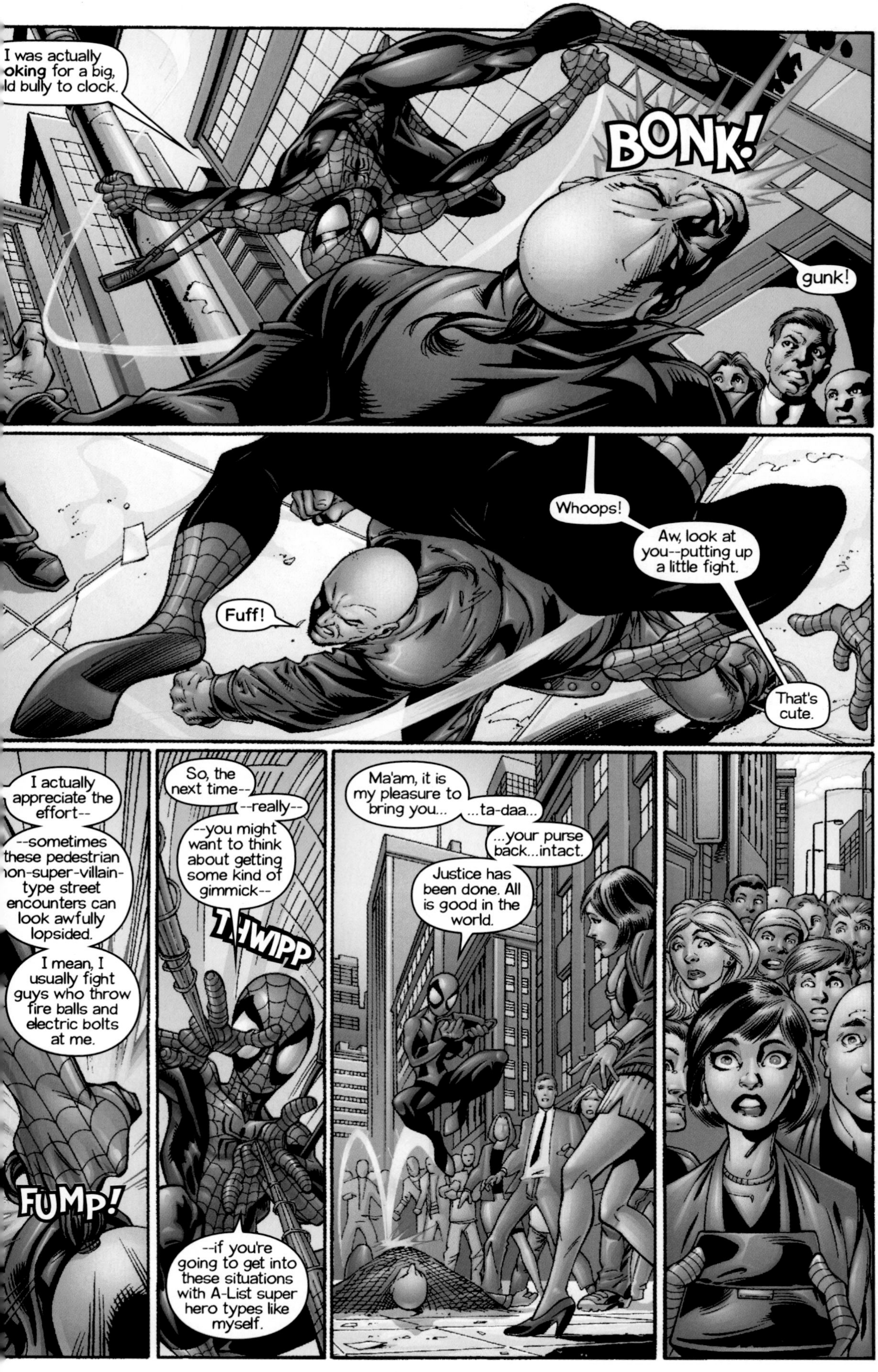

I was actually
oking for a big,
ld bully to clock.
BONK!
gunk!
Whoops!
Aw, look at you--putting up a little fight.
Fuff!
That's cute.
I actually appreciate the effort--
--sometimes these pedestrian non-super-villain-type street encounters can look awfully lopsided.
I mean, I usually fight guys who throw fire balls and electric bolts at me.
FUMP!
So, the next time--
--really--
--you might want to think about getting some kind of gimmick--
THWIPP
--if you're going to get into these situations with A-List super hero types like myself.
Ma'am, it is my pleasure to bring you...
...ta-daa...
...your purse back...intact.
Justice has been done. All is good in the world.

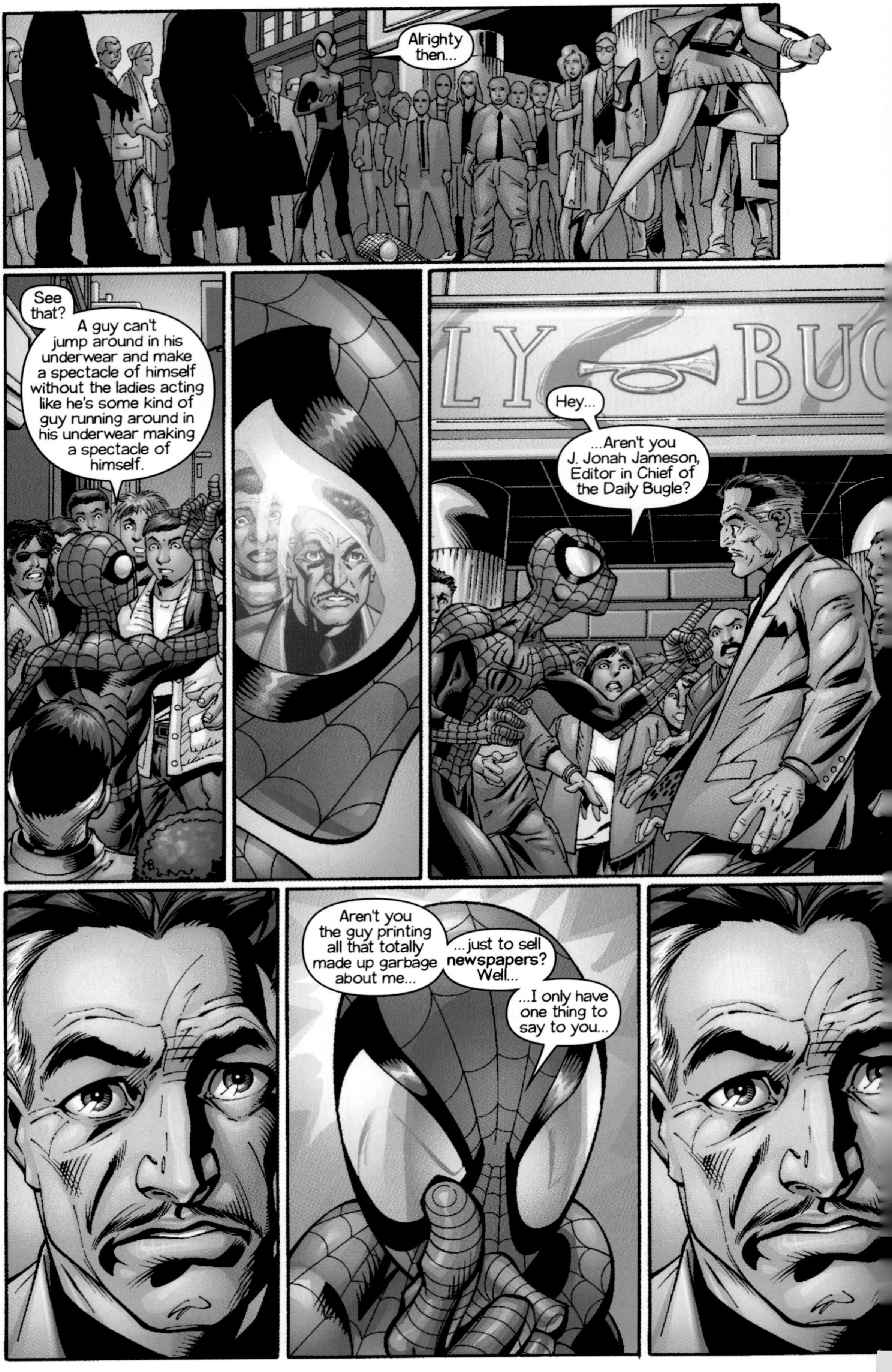
Alrighty then...
See that?
A guy can't jump around in his underwear and make a spectacle of himself without the ladies acting like he's some kind of guy running around in his underwear making a spectacle of himself.
Hey...
...Aren't you J. Jonah Jameson, Editor in Chief of the Daily Bugle?
Aren't you the guy printing all that totally made up garbage about me...
...just to sell **newspapers**? Well...
...I only have one thing to say to you...

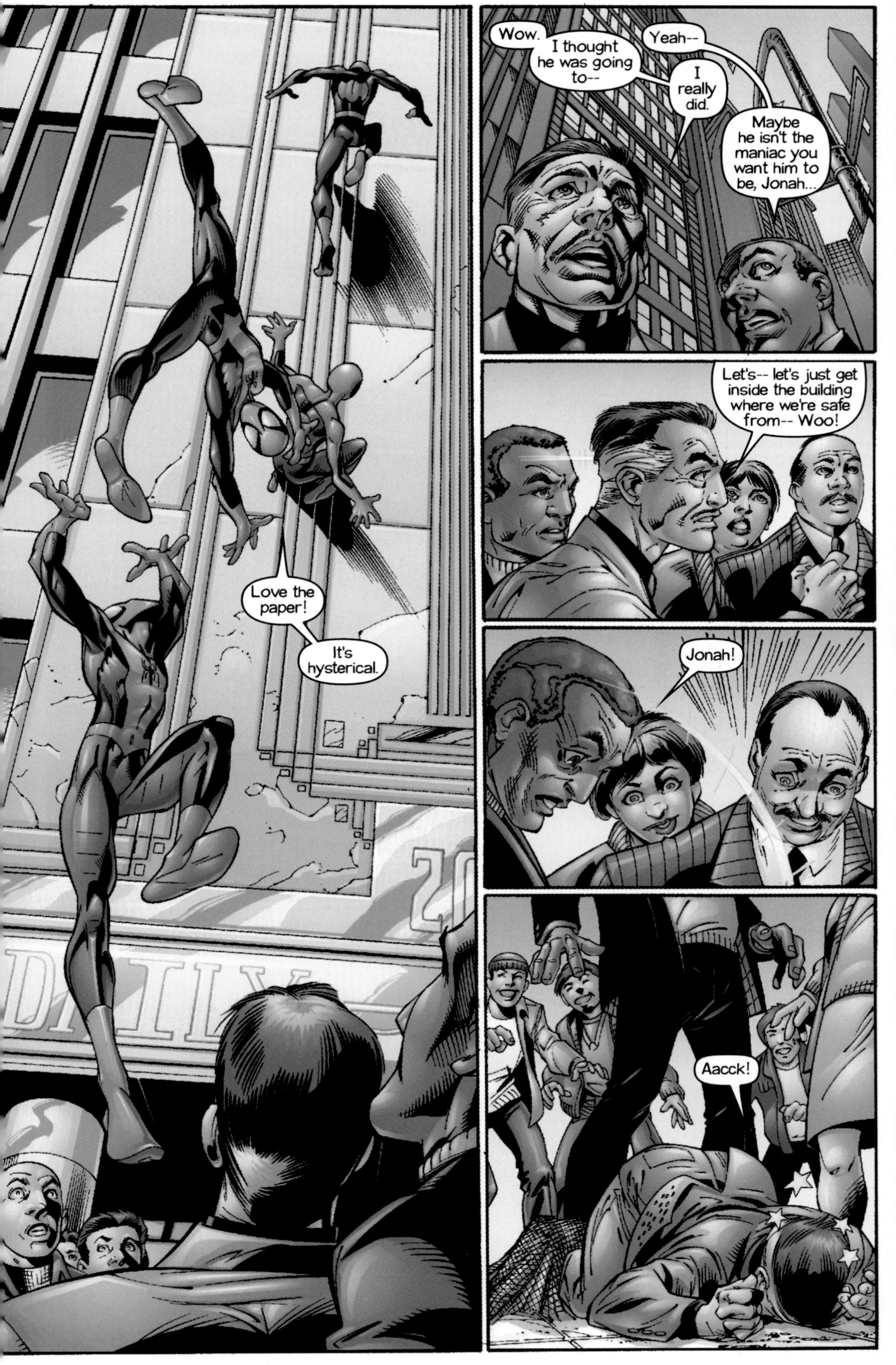
Love the paper!
It's hysterical.
Wow.
I thought he was going to--
Yeah--
I really did.
Maybe he isn't the maniac you want him to be, Jonah...
Let's-- let's just get inside the building where we're safe from-- Woo!
Jonah!
Aacck!

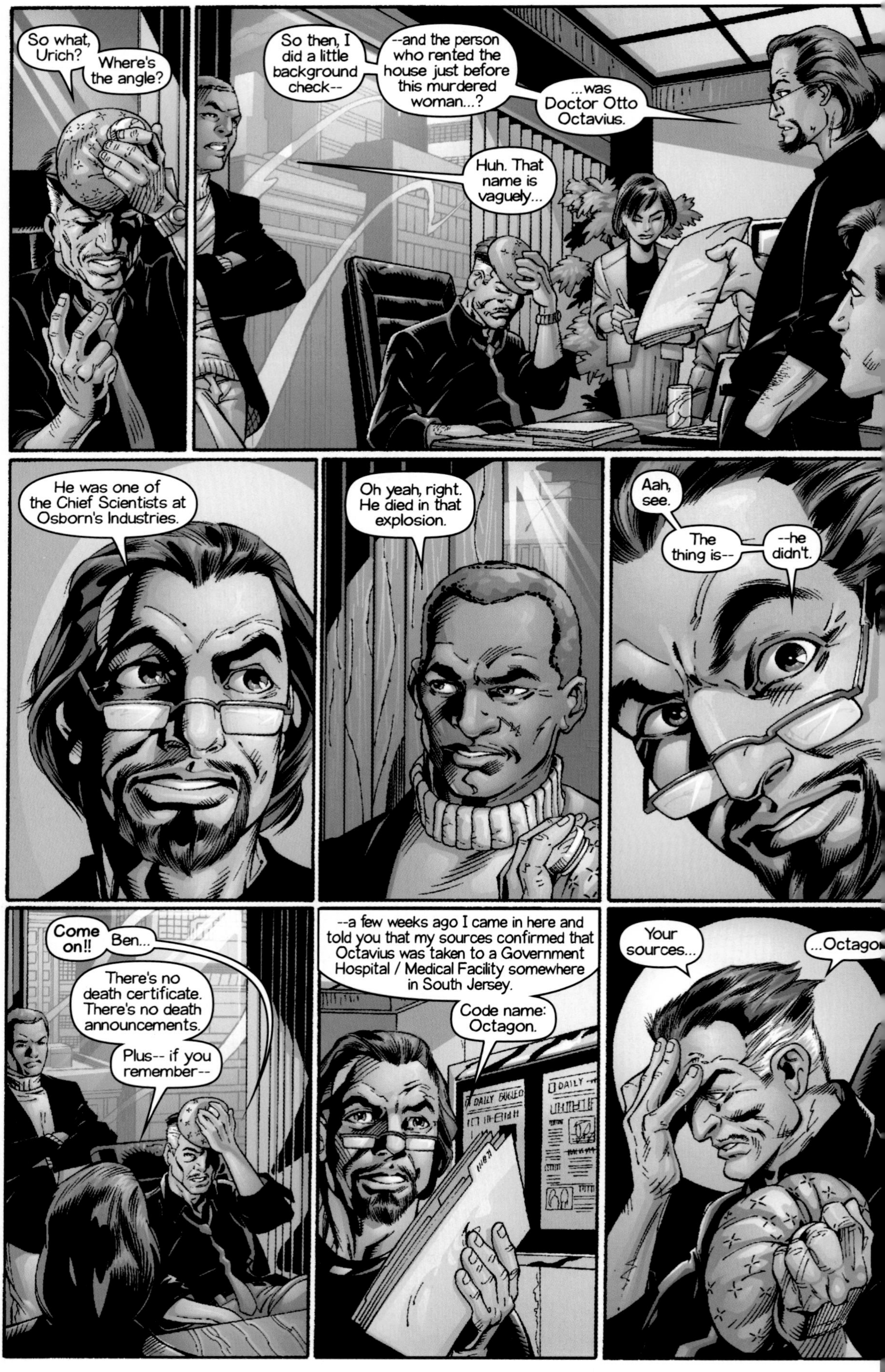
So what, Urich?
Where's the angle?
So then, I did a little background check--
--and the person who rented the house just before this murdered woman...?
...was Doctor Otto Octavius.
Huh. That name is vaguely...
He was one of the Chief Scientists at Osborn's Industries.
Oh yeah, right. He died in that explosion.
Aah, see.
The thing is--
--he didn't.
Come on!!
Ben...
There's no death certificate. There's no death announcements.
Plus-- if you remember--
--a few weeks ago I came in here and told you that my sources confirmed that Octavius was taken to a Government Hospital / Medical Facility somewhere in South Jersey.
Code name: Octagon.
DAILY BUGLE
DAILY
Your sources...
...Octagon

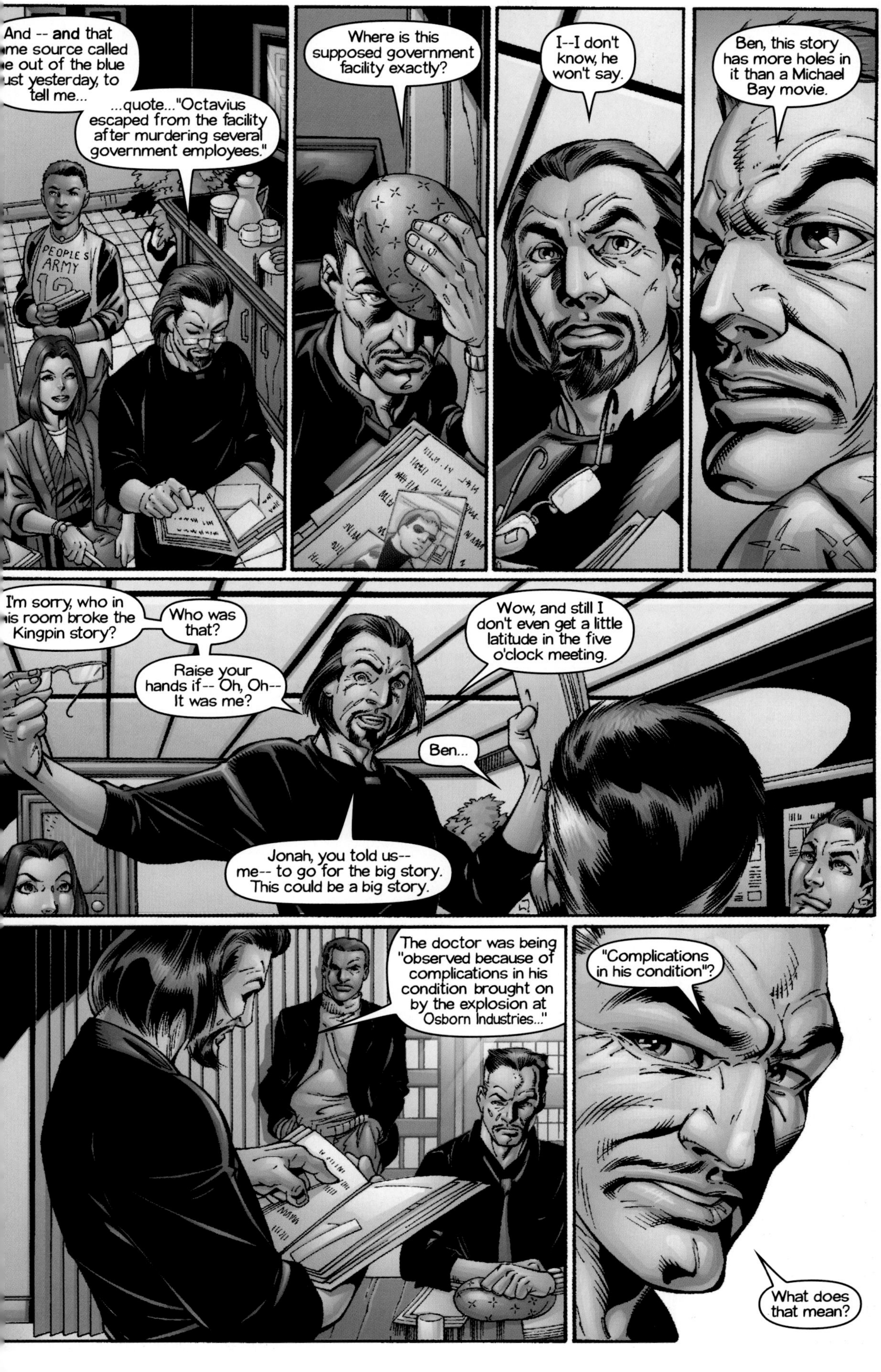

And -- and that
me source called
e out of the blue
ust yesterday, to
tell me...
...quote..."Octavius escaped from the facility after murdering several government employees."
PEOPLES ARMY 12
Where is this supposed government facility exactly?
I--I don't know, he won't say.
Ben, this story has more holes in it than a Michael Bay movie.
I'm sorry, who in is room broke the Kingpin story?
Who was that?
Raise your hands if-- Oh, Oh-- It was me?
Wow, and still I don't even get a little latitude in the five o'clock meeting.
Ben...
Jonah, you told us-- me-- to go for the big story. This could be a big story.
The doctor was being "observed because of complications in his condition brought on by the explosion at Osborn Industries..."
"Complications in his condition"?
What does that mean?

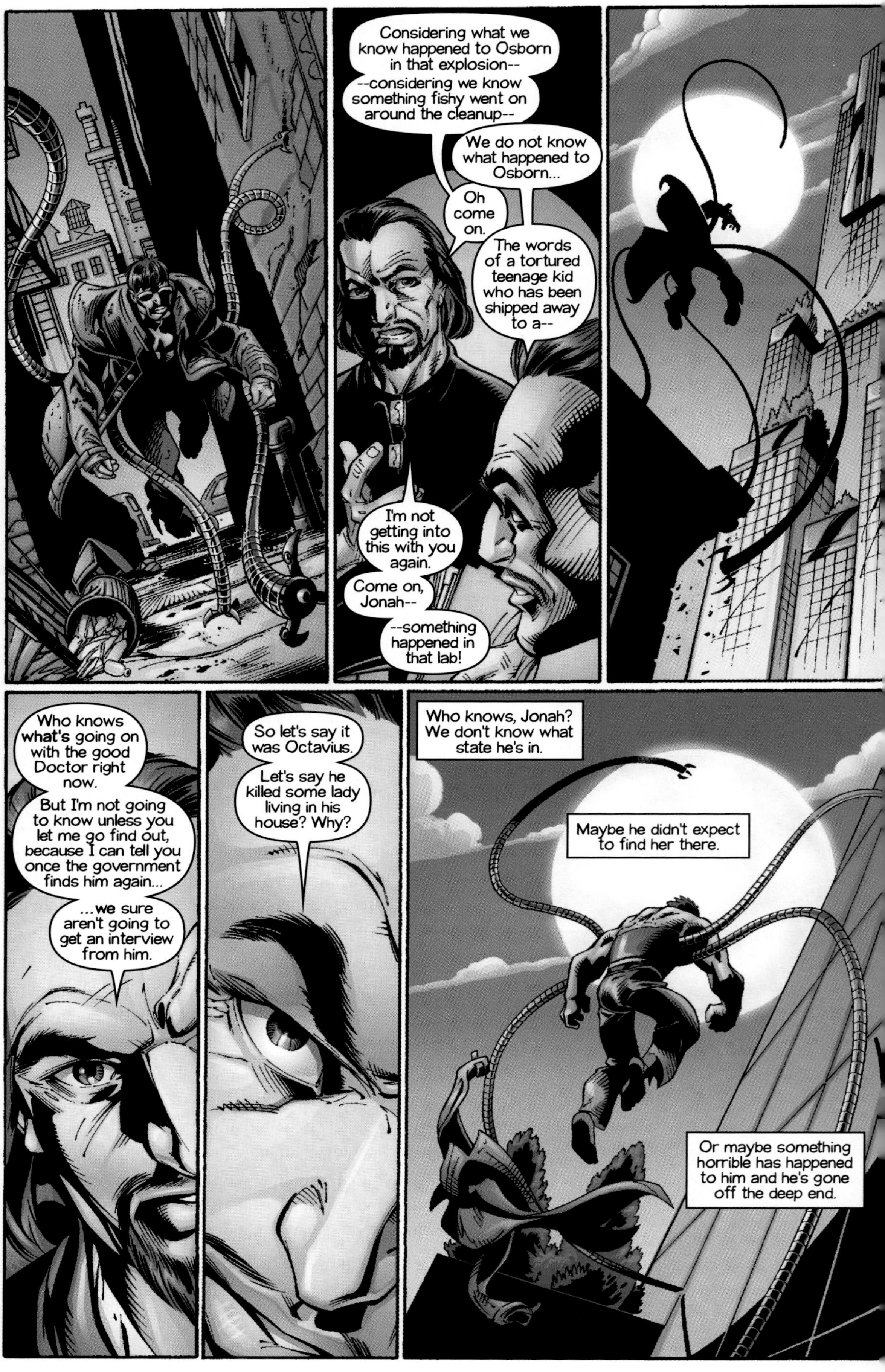
Considering what we know happened to Osborn in that explosion--
--considering we know something fishy went on around the cleanup--
We do not know what happened to Osborn...
Oh come on.
The words of a tortured teenage kid who has been shipped away to a--
I'm not getting into this with you again.
Come on, Jonah--
--something happened in that lab!
Who knows what's going on with the good Doctor right now.
But I'm not going to know unless you let me go find out, because I can tell you once the government finds him again...
...we sure aren't going to get an interview from him.
So let's say it was Octavius.
Let's say he killed some lady living in his house? Why?
Who knows, Jonah? We don't know what state he's in.
Maybe he didn't expect to find her there.
Or maybe something horrible has happened to him and he's gone off the deep end.

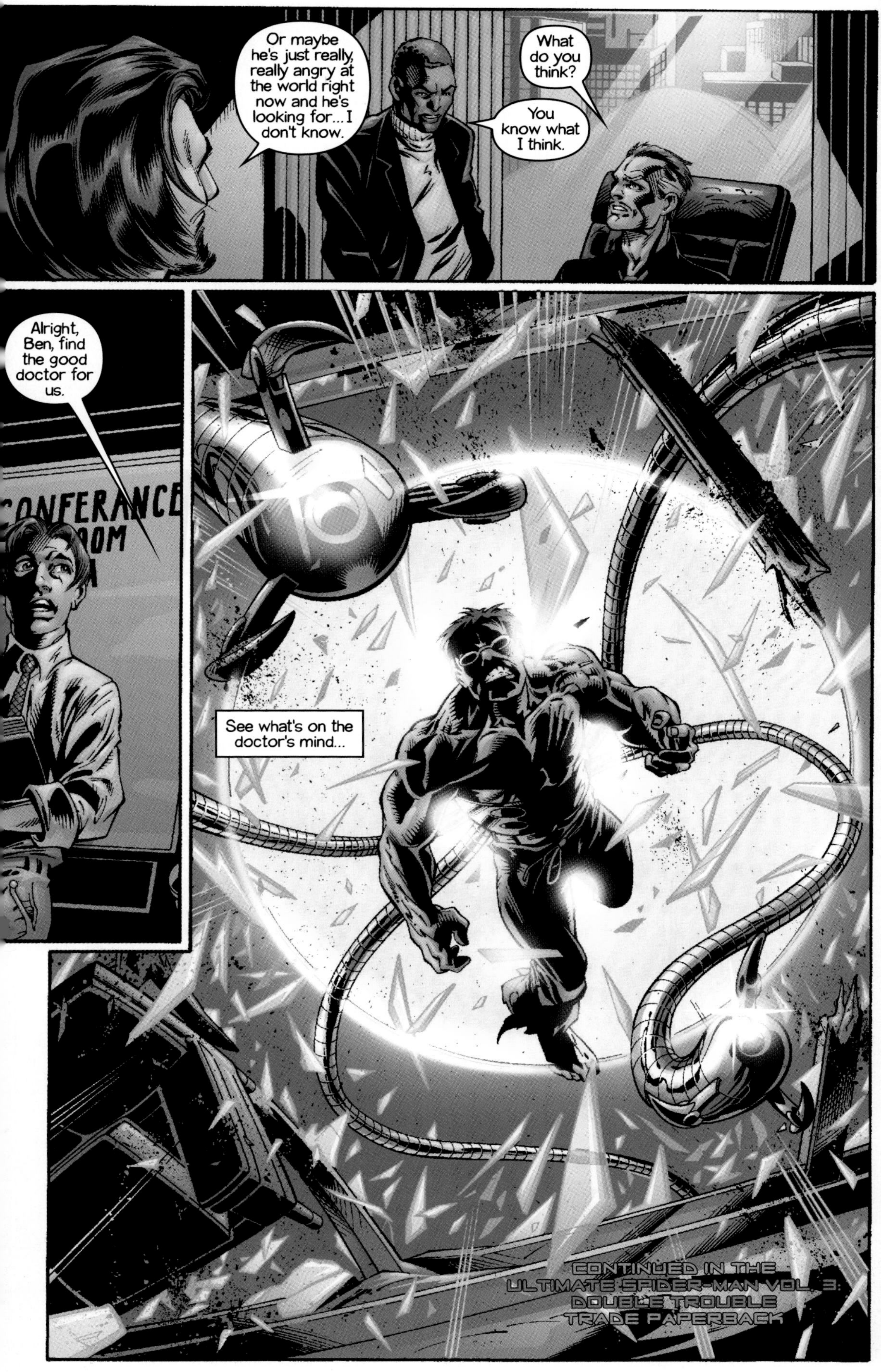
Or maybe he's just really, really angry at the world right now and he's looking for... I don't know.
What do you think?
You know what I think.
Alright, Ben, find the good doctor for us.
CONFERANCE ROOM
See what's on the doctor's mind...
CONTINUED IN THE ULTIMATE SPIDER-MAN VOL. 3: DOUBLE TROUBLE TRADE PAPERBACK

DOCTOR OCTOPUS

Real Name:
Otto Octavius

First Appearance:
Amazing Spider-Man #3 (1963)

Height:	5'9"
Weight:	245 lbs.
Eye Color:	Brown
Hair Color:	Brown

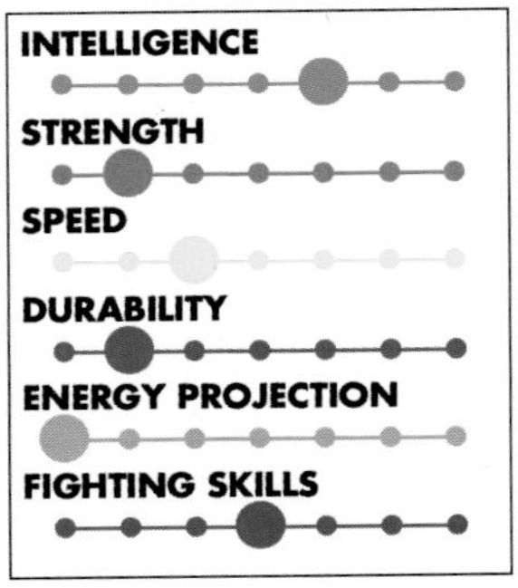

INTELLIGENCE
STRENGTH
SPEED
DURABILITY
ENERGY PROJECTION
FIGHTING SKILLS

POWERS/WEAPONS

- Four telepathically controlled, super-strong steel tentacles attached to a harness encircling his lower chest and waist
- Brilliant engineer and inventor
- Extraordinary intelligence and concentration, enabling him to perform multiple complex actions simultaneously with his tentacles

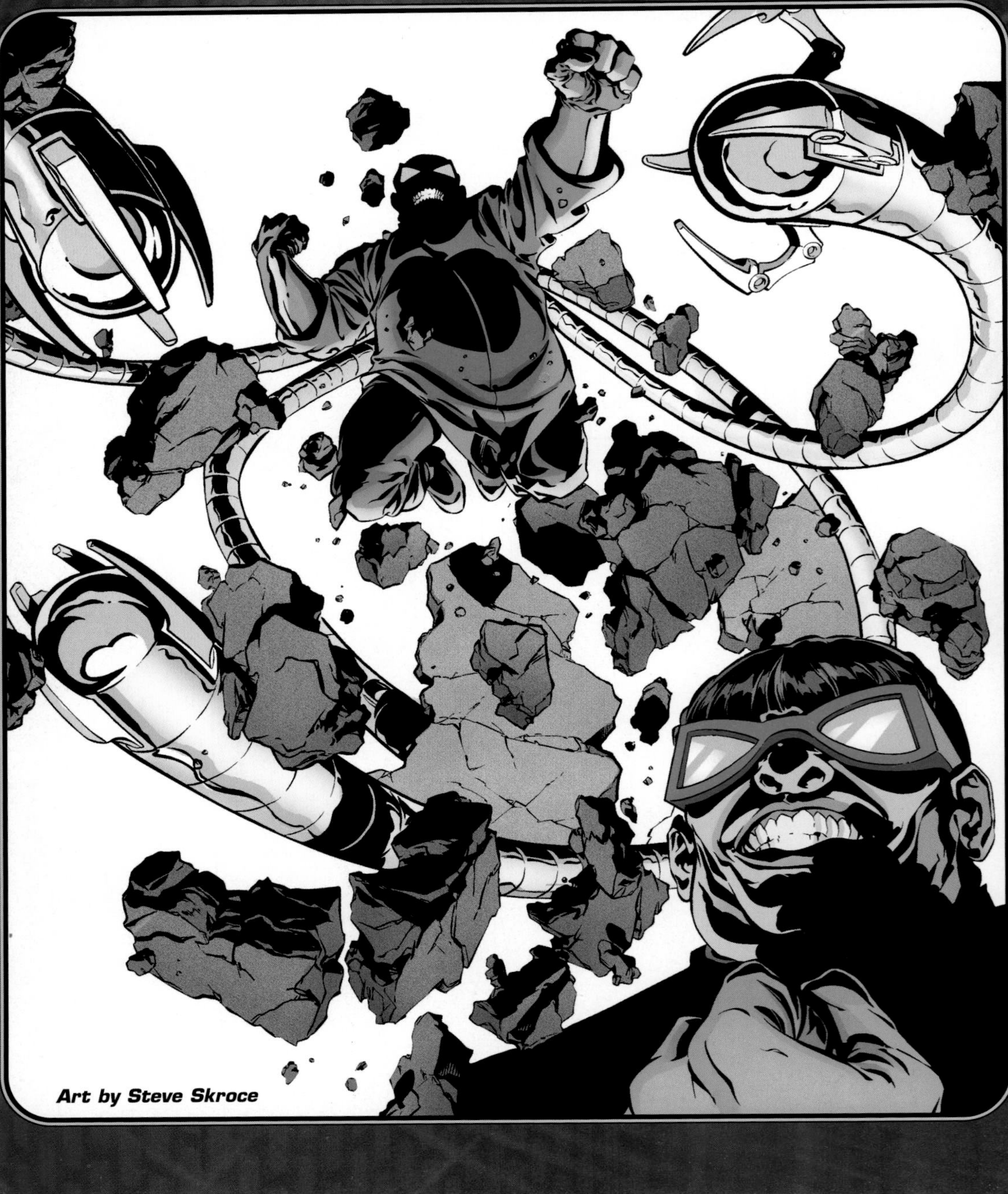

Art by Steve Skroce

The son of an overbearing mother and a bullying father, Otto Octavius grew up to become a reclusive but brilliant atomic researcher. To help manipulate radioactive substances from a safe distance, Otto constructed a chest harness controlling four mechanical, tentacle-like arms — earning himself the nickname Doctor Octopus. In a freak laboratory accident, volatile liquids exploded — bombarding the scientist with radiation. The substances left him capable of mentally controlling the arms, but the accident also caused irreversible brain damage — transforming the respected scientist into a megalomaniacal criminal. Waking in a hospital, Otto knew this newfound strength — combined with his awesome intellect — could render him supremely powerful. Holding the medical staff hostage, he easily defeated Spider-Man in their first meeting. Doc Ock then took control of a leading nuclear research facility and again squared off with the wall-crawler, who this time defeated him with one punch to the jaw.

After serving time, Doc Ock attempted to raise funds by springing gangster Blackie Gaxton from prison — assisted by Gaxton's lawyer, Bennett Brant. Spider-Man foiled the scheme, but could not save Bennett from being shot in front of his sister, Betty Brant. Octopus then assembled the first Sinister Six to combat Spider-Man. He plotted to take Betty hostage, knowing Spider-Man had previously rescued her and would likely do so again. May Parker, visiting Betty at the time, was also captured. Otto treated May kindly, and she remained blissfully unaware she had been kidnapped by the charming villain.

Following Spider-Man's defeat of the Sinister Six, Ock assembled another group of criminal underlings and established an undersea base. Calling himself the Master Planner, he embarked on a series of thefts of experimental substances — seeking to further expand his mastery of the atomic sciences. His goal: to develop a radiation ray with which he could rule the world. But his path was fated to entwine with Spider-Man's: When May fell sick, Peter provided her with a blood transfusion — not realizing the radioactivity in his plasma would kill her. The only substance capable of saving her was the experimental ISO-36. Peter managed to obtain enough money to fund the operation, but the Master Planner's forces hijacked the shipment for their own deadly research. Spider-Man tracked the Master Planner to his underwater hideout and confronted his foe, revealed to be Doc Ock. After the base was destroyed, Doctor Octopus escaped once more. Spider-Man recovered the ISO-36 and saved Aunt May's life with the aid of Dr. Curt Connors (Lizard).

Doctor Octopus' next scheme involved the theft of a projector that could disable any device. After two failed attempts, Otto finally succeeded on his third. Turning the Nullifier against Spider-Man, he caused the wall-crawler to lose his memory and persuaded him they were allies. He then enlisted Spider-Man's help to steal the remaining components for the device. Though the hero had not regained his memory, his instinctive spider-sense persuaded him not to trust Doc Ock, and he defeated him once more. Now imprisoned, with his arms confiscated, Otto demonstrated that the range of his psionic control over the limbs had increased to a far greater distance than previously believed. The arms freed him from captivity; in the ensuing battle between Doc Ock and Spider-Man, George Stacy was killed while protecting an innocent child.

Free again, Doctor Octopus seized upon the Kingpin's absence to gather his forces and launch an all-out gang war against Hammerhead's thugs. But Spider-Man's involvement quickly resulted in Otto's return to prison. While incarcerated, Doctor Octopus learned May Parker had inherited a small Canadian island containing a commercial nuclear reactor. On his release, he set out to woo and marry May. But Hammerhead interrupted the wedding, and the ensuing chase and brawl led to the destruction of the reactor.

When Doc Ock went to war with the Owl, Spider-Man and the Black Cat attempted to intervene. Devastated that the confrontation had left the Black Cat near death, a cold-hearted Peter said farewell to his friends before entering what he believed to be his final showdown with Doctor Octopus. Spider-Man's victory was remorseless, and Doc Ock developed a morbid fear of his arachnid foe. Imprisoned in a mental institution, Otto struggled with his overwhelming phobia of Spider-Man. Knowing he could not face his foe directly, Ock's next plan involved the use of biological weapons to kill the entire population of New York. Spider-Man was forced to fake a humiliating defeat lest the city be destroyed, restoring Otto's self-confidence.

Still, Otto had clearly changed. As a young scientist, he had fallen in love with a fellow researcher, Mary Alice Burke — but his demanding mother jealously sabotaged the relationship. Learning Mary Alice was dying from AIDS, Otto began a desperate search for a cure — stealing research materials to do so. His attempts failed, Mary Alice died, and the villain meekly surrendered to Spider-Man. A world-weary Otto nonetheless escaped from prison. At the time, Spider-Man was dying from a chemical virus. Hoping to one day kill the hero himself, Doc Ock captured and unmasked his foe. Analyzing the virus, Otto offered him a cure. Daring to trust his enemy, Peter accepted the mixture and was healed.

But having found his own salvation in this act, Doctor Octopus did not live to enjoy it. Intending to protect Peter by killing his enemies, Kaine murdered Doc Ock by snapping his neck. But Dr. Carolyn Trainer, Otto's young assistant, had been working with him in the area of solid holographic projection and mind-to-computer communication. Prior to Peter's unmasking, she had created a backup brain-imprint of Doc Ock. With Otto's passing, the backup of his mind became a software projection known as the Master Programmer, and Carolyn used his tentacles to become the second Doctor Octopus. Meanwhile, the Rose (Jacob Conover) employed a cult, the True Believers, to magically resurrect Doctor Octopus as an empty-minded servant. Aas soon as he was raised, Carolyn uploaded the Master Programmer persona into Octavius' brain. She returned his tentacles to him, and they fled.

With his memories restored from a past snapshot, Otto has forgotten he once knew Spider-Man's true identity. He remains very much the deadly and manipulative criminal genius he was in his heyday.

Art by John Romita Jr.